The Journals
of
Constant Waterman

The Journals of
Constant Waterman

PADDLING, POLING, AND SAILING
FOR THE LOVE OF IT

Matthew Goldman

BREAKAWAY BOOKS
HALCOTTSVILLE, NEW YORK
2007

The Journals of Constant Waterman: Paddling, Poling, and Sailing for the Love of It
Text and illustrations copyright 2007 Matthew Goldman

ISBN: 978-1-91369-73-5
Library of Congress Catalog Number: 2007925653

Published by Breakaway Books
P.O. Box 24
Halcottsville, NY 12438
www.breakawaybooks.com

The following originally appeared in these publications:

Messing About in Boats (July 1, 2005 through September 15, 2007)
Little Narragansett Bay; A View from the Masthead; White River Junction; C&D Canal; Whalebone Cove; February Thaw; The East River; Rudy; Cod Fishing; Winter Amusements; Chapman Pond; Annapolis; The Peapod; Rigging the Canoe; Giraffe; The Wood River; Dreamtime; The Old Haying Grounds; Petite Chose; A Proposition; San Juan; A Boatwright; A True Story; An Inland Voyage; A Waterwoman; In Need of a Breeze; Grantchester; Everglades City; Mysteries of the Deep; Sans Souci; The Cape Dory Typhoon; Another Spring Freshet; Late Launching; Hamburg Cove; Block Island; The Sea Serpent; The Marina; A Murmur from the Brook; A Three-Day Paddle; Falling in Love; The One That Got Away; Sanibel Island; Boating Season; Sippican Harbor; Selden's Island; Little Beach; An Afternoon With the Goldfinch; Cape Ann; The Wily Flounder; The Flood.

Good Old Boat

In Need of a Boat (January/February 2006); The Jet (July/August 2006); Learning the Ropes (April/May 2007).

WindCheck

The Petrel (October 2006)

FIRST EDITION

Contents

The Petrel

A WORD FROM THE WATERFRONT

Hadlyme and Thereabouts

Mystic and Noank

Farther Shores

For Paula, who makes it possible.

WUNG OUT

INTRODUCTION

Everyone wants to categorize my writing. "Are these journals, memoirs or essays?" they ask. "Is there a point? Is there a focus? A thread that ties them all together?" All I can answer is, "Yes." They all deal with the water—from the puddle to the sea. They are reflective as a sandy-bottomed brook. They are wistful as an idle boat in summer. They are jubilant as broaching porpoises.

Listen carefully. Read these aloud. I used to be a poet and still write as though I were. But don't tell anyone. Everyone knows what poets are like.

Nowadays, I work in a boat shop, making boats sound and beautiful. But not before half past ten. This is what I do while I'm having my coffee: I reminisce, I reflect. Sometimes it hasn't to do with boats, at all. Sometimes I think about other writers. Sometimes I think about people I've loved. Sometimes, I just think. But always it has to, someway, do with water.

Some people say it's because I'm a Pisces. I don't much hold with astrology. I don't much hold with much of anything. But I love the water. Not like, but love. *Love* is a word you're supposed to save for God. *Love* is a word you're supposed to save for family. That's what I've done. The Lord is in the river and the Lord is in the sea. And all of the creatures, humans included, who inhabit the water are my family.

I don't spout religion. That's something each of us has to work out on our own. I don't tell you how to sail a boat, where to stay on your travels, or when to don your life vest. I haven't come to tell you about my problems. I'm here to express my love and respect for a world that is mostly water. If you find me amusing, don't let it spoil your day.

I haven't done nearly the boating that some people have. I haven't spent weeks aboard a boat. I haven't been far. I haven't been in storms that threatened my life. I'm just someone who can't leave water alone. It's hard for me to pass a puddle. It's hard for me to leave the sea. I like to varnish but I'd rather sail. I like to swim but I'd rather canoe. I've built an octagonal studio on an island. I've owned a few boats and may own one or two more. Sailing, for me, gives Heaven some close competition.

If we have decent weather this weekend, I'll be out on the water. If not, I'll stay home and tell you about the time the Naiad got caught in my breast hook. Just put up your feet and listen . . .

Paddling,
Poling,
and
Rowing

HITHER AND YON

THE PAWCATUCK

HORSESHOE FALLS ~ PAWCATUCK RIVER ~ SHANNOCK , RHODE ISLAND

For several years, I lived near the Pawcatuck. This shallow river runs less than fifty miles, interspersed with dams and some harmless riffles. Near the University of Rhode Island, it scarcely qualifies as a creek, called the Chipuxet. From the local state landing to the sea is twenty miles by rail. The river rambles forty-four miles to get there. I've paddled perhaps twenty-five of them.

Taylors Landing, near the university, has a little, sandy stepping-in place where you needn't get too wet unless you want to. The river ascends a few miles above this place but I don't believe it worthwhile navigating. Even the first few hundred feet below this landing are so narrow, you'll have trouble plying a double paddle. Eventually it widens, and the brush has been cleared back. Sometimes the trees have also been cut back and difficult limbs removed from fallen trees. But not always. You may have to climb on a fallen tree and drag your kayak over it.

But the rest of this river isn't that confining. The worst problem we encountered, while passing through a clearing where the stream wends slenderly amid the waving reeds, took the form of an angry swan whose low nest lay nearby. One rampant swan, as Horatius did, can ward a narrow way. Wanting neither to hurt him nor be hurt, we turned around and ascended the sluggish stream. We had our double kayak that day. It maneuvers with all the agility of an old tobacco barn. As only two kayak lengths separated the banks, we managed to turn our craft around in something less than an hour.

The Chipuxet's descent is quiet and pristine. Much of this water-course passes through conserved or managed areas. An abandoned spur of the railroad that used to service the mills in the town adjacent crosses the river on a derelict steel trestle. We used to walk the railbed, from which the ties had been removed, and pick wildflowers and visit a tiny burial site consisting of half a dozen shards of unmarked shale half hidden beneath the laurel in a long-deserted field. A mile beyond, the railroad ran through a marshy pond graced by a beaver lodge.

These gentle creatures at times drop trees only to eat the tender twigs and buds. Their dams impact the local ecosystems. They often block drainage conduits on purpose. Compared with Man, the change they wreak is totally insignificant. Besides—they were here first. On one excursion on the Chipuxet, we watched a beaver loll beneath our boat, unconcernedly swimming on his back.

No buildings or clearings profane this stretch, and the many marshes overflow with birds. After three miles, the river empties into Wordens Pond. A mile and a half across, this has an isle at its center, on which stands a diminutive red cottage. On the southern shore, an adequate landing sprawls. When the wind blows out of the southwest, it takes considerable effort to paddle to the opposite shore where the river, now called the Pawcatuck, resumes its rural course.

Nine dams obstruct the stream between here and the ocean, but most of the mills are ruined, abandoned, gone. A couple of dams have fallen apart and scarcely impede one's passage. The Pawcatuck likes to meander and has a few switchbacks. With no high banks or hills to restrict it, the spate in spring may readily spread a quarter mile, intrude among the wading trees, skirt a drowning dam.

One spring, I navigated a swollen switchback. As it passed amid an ancient farm, the flood formed a sylvan pool. It flowed around a new-formed isle, encroached on the pastures, crept among the red maples. A grazing carthorse, bored with his reminiscences, leisurely sloshed fetlock-deep to commune with a fellow spirit. I found I had more in common with him than with many people I know.

Farther on, the river spread to inundate a broad marsh. A dismantled railroad trestle halted halfway across it. I strained to recollect how close the twenty-first century lurked. Scarcely a breeze-blown mile away, cars and trains and factory whistles dominated Mankind. Here the cattails thrust their shoots toward the sun. Here the osprey wheeled above the water.

A mile away, imperative lights and bells and buzzers dictated a frenetic pace of life. I rested my paddle across the gunwales and drifted slowly downstream. Above my head, a chickadee presumed to disturb the silence. A mile away, overwrought people fought the galling harness of their strident civilization.

Whatever could have possessed them to give up this for that?

THE WOOD RIVER

The crocuses, both purple and white, spread to the buttery sun. This Sunday the temperature finally attains the fifties; the first of the male goldfinches dons his brilliant array of courtship plumage.

I drag my goldfinch-colored kayak from its hibernation above the woodshed, dump out the spiders, and put it into my truck. Down the road a short piece lies a public landing just above the weir across the Wood River.

A couple of men lean across a pickup truck and jaw. Their amphibious canoes lean on the bank, their tails still in the water. They've had a swim in the millpond and now can't see much reason to leave the water. If left to themselves, they'll wriggle back down the bank and venture off.

In moments, I am afloat. The recent torrential rains have swollen this normally docile river. The gravid millpond approaches parturition; the water drops noisily over the concrete dam.

I work upstream for most of a mile to where the pond spreads out and becomes a marsh. The freshet has swallowed whatever dry spits existed—the underbrush stands up to its waist in water; the river runs into the weathered wood duck boxes.

It takes me awhile to locate the actual river—I haven't been up this way in a couple of years, and the copious water flows and spreads with abandon. There—that sandy slope with the stout white pine mark where the river bends.

Suddenly a red-tailed hawk, a-roost in a tall red maple, takes flight overhead in silent, awesome, graceful, astounding beauty. She wheels once and disappears among the budding trees. My dripping paddles poised, my gaze aloft, I drift back into the cattails and get a well-deserved scolding from some redwings.

I traverse more marsh, and a pair of mallards takes off with loud alarm. I approach two swans who haven't yet nested, else I might have to excuse myself to the cob. They paddle away, demurely, and I paddle away and promptly take the wrong turning. So much water flows that I mistake a cul-de-sac for the real river.

After a dozen double strokes I realize my mistake but continue forward. The water slows and spreads out. On a weathered snag, a painted turtle raises his little head. I drift within a few yards before he tumbles into deep water and disappears. Ahead, I can see the river through the alders.

I find a gap and pull my way through and again ascend the stream. Now the current strengthens and I have to exert myself. A mile or so upstream stands another dam—it will take me an hour to work my way so far. On a tiny spit of land, connected in drier times to a grassy road, rests an old, old bench—up to its arthritic knees in water. Really two Adirondack chairs that share a common frame, their barn-red paint all but weathered away. They've stood here for years—without a house in sight.

But soon I come to a cottage, a field, another house, and then the Woodville Road. Piled froth rides the water—a heady beverage for any who would partake. Ahead, I can hear the thundering of the falls. Eight feet high and eighty broad, they grace the front yard of a trim colonial house. The mill has long since gone. The driven water spills yellow-white; the pool below the falls swirls, alive and loud and violent.

I reach the bridge just below the pool and grab hold of a girder. I haven't headroom, the river in spate, to use a double paddle. I bounce in place for a minute or two as I watch the water: foreordained to fall downstream—foreknowably and forever. Then I let go, to enjoy a free ride home.

At least as far as the millpond. There I find the wind blows in my face. The water spreads out, the current offers little help, and I have to work the last mile back to the landing. A dozen Canada geese announce my passage and, swim warily off, indignant and vociferous as only geese can be.

Ahead stands the big brick mill. The road across the roaring dam resounds with scurrying traffic. Half a mile more, and I get to stretch my legs, and surprise my old but contented truck—dreaming beneath the maples.

AN AFTERNOON
WITH THE GOLDFINCH

Another warm day and a fair one and a Saturday, no less. Unloaded firewood from the truck and re-covered the woodpile as it threatens to cloud over and reward us with raindrops later on for having been so good. Put the Goldfinch—my bright yellow kayak—into the truck and tootled off through the village and out the river road.

Just upstream from the interstate lies a little public landing where one can park a dozen cars and launch innumerable boats. I saw half a dozen vehicles but not a single boat. They probably went down stream toward the ocean and Mystic Seaport and the ice cream shop by the bridge. I went up the river. I didn't see much except for houses, a cemetery, a small flock of buffleheads, some mallards, and a solitary swan.

Except upriver lay a little sloop, perhaps twenty-three feet long, aground on the shore, heeled well over and napping quite peacefully. She didn't seem disconcerted by her berth, and the shore, there, is gradual and gravelly with considerable pampas grass for soft reposing. She was tethered to a sturdy tree to prevent her wandering off. Sailboats are subject to such whims.

I saw a fellow aboard her just last week. I thought at first he'd careened her to fix her bottom. But I saw no evidence. Her mast lay lashed on her cabin top; her drop boards had been removed. She had a spade rudder but that had been unshipped. I'm sure her owner can easily kedge her off when the tide is full.

Were I the ambitious (i.e., stupid) type, I'd try to find out who belongs to her and maybe buy her cheap. But I'm not, and I already have a sailboat to care for. I used to think I would make a living by fixing up old boats. I've been disabused of that conceit. And a very good thing, too. For three or four thousand dollars I can buy an old sailboat in better shape than this one—one with a boom, a rudder, and a motor. If I worked my whatsis off an entire season to make her lovely, I couldn't sell her for more than six or eight thousand. By the time I paid for materials and hardware, rebuilt the motor, and bought new running rigging, I'd earn four dollars and nineteen cents per hour. I've done the math. In this part of the country, you can earn twice that by mating buns with burgers.

So all I did was look and keep on paddling. The Mystic River spreads a quarter mile wide about the Seaport. It alternately narrows and spreads until it approaches Old Mystic. Then it suddenly narrows to a fifteen-yard-wide brook. Then it becomes a stony creek just deep enough for a trout. A smallish trout. One without ambitions. I made it up to the redbrick mill in Old Mystic where the river makes a bend and becomes the brook. Another hundred yards, I encountered a riffle too rapid to ascend.

Turning, I sped beside the retaining wall beneath the mill, paddled a quarter mile of mild water, then entered the expansive stretch with a rising breeze in my face. Up on a knoll, by a modern house, a formidable set of tubular chimes hurled from side to side—ringing out a convocation for worship. The wind busily baptized me with spray from its worldwide font, and I came away blessed, as usual. As usual, I hadn't drowned and had found the day inspiring.

Amazingly, the sailboat was still stranded when I returned. Whether she came there by chance or design I'll never know. We have a few gusty afternoons when the wind tears through the harbors at fifty knots. A boat anchored out, unsheltered, can quickly go adrift. Some people still don't know about anchoring scope and many have never heard about chafing gear.

The photographs I've seen from the aftermath of Hurricane Katrina depressed me. Many boats have never been found. They may bask on the beach in Belize or keep company with starfish. A few recline on porches or up in trees.

I'd hate to see *MoonWind* perching in a tree. She hasn't the nesting instinct. Even leaning on poppets seems wearisome and highly overrated. A boat belongs on the water, embracing a breeze. Or messing about an estuary, as I was this afternoon. As any boater will gladly affirm, avidly and at great length, life is too short to spend much time ashore.

Be patient with your boaters and let them rant. Most of them will get over it come December.

GRANTCHESTER

Cambridge, England, a quiet town whose university dates from the thirteenth century, takes its famous name from the River Cam. With the help of my sister, who worked for Cambridge University Press, I wangled a job in a boatyard there one summer. The backs of several stately colleges—acres of manicured lawns and gardens—slope gradually down to the Cam. One can hire a punt, canoe, or rowboat and meander along "the Backs." The opposite shore, seldom thirty yards off, remains mostly a bosky park, and the mile ride past the colleges is tantamount to drifting through some late-medieval dreamland. One passes Queens College, Kings College, Clare, Trinity, and St. John's; one lingers to admire the Bridge of Sighs.

At the upstream end of the university, just above the landing where you rent your boat, a modest dam surmounted by a small bridge separates the upper reach, the Granta, from the Cam. Just upstream from the bridge stands a second boatyard. They busily rent the same small craft to ascend the placid Granta. Here I worked for several weeks, cleaning out boats and helping people to get aboard and cast off. Sometimes I collected fares. The currency, then, was pounds and shillings and pence, and it took quick thinking to make proper change from the vast assortment of coins. My pay was five shillings per hour—five "bob"—the equivalent of seventy cents.

Both reaches of the river run slowly and shallowly. This makes them ideal for punting. Our darkly varnished punts gleamed, as did our canoes and rowboats. A punt is slender: a yard wide and twenty-four feet in length; lightly built, flat-bottomed, square ended, and decked across the stern for several feet.

This deck was the punter's platform. Stage, if you will. We provided performers a long, light pole and a minimum of instruction. Amateurs supplied us a constant source of amusement. They shoved too hard and the punt jumped from beneath them. They overbalanced and fell into the river, often to loud applause from other punters. It took some practice to harmonize the steerage and propulsion. Most amateurs wove over and back across the Granta trying to maintain a course. Competent punters, graceful and efficient, drove their boats straight upstream with little effort.

One afternoon, I exercised my prerogative and borrowed a punt. Cambridge, although a small city of eighty thousand, scarcely knew the affliction of urban sprawl. Half a mile upstream, in meadows, placid cows munched wildflowers or dozed beneath the willows. They kindly overlooked my artless efforts. A couple of miles above the town a mossy weir spanned the river. Just below it, a rusticated pier joined the footpath that led to Grantchester—as pretty a hamlet as sixty years earlier when the glamorous poet Rupert Brooke immortalized it in his lament "The Old Vicarage, Grantchester."

Enormous elm trees shaded the quiet streets. The public house displayed numerous poems penned by Brooke before his untimely death during World War I. Within the pub I found shadow and repose. By the window, an old man tilted his book to the dappled light. Without, historic England drowsed in the sun.

After my pint, I strolled back to my punt accompanied by swooping and swerving swallows. I pushed off gently; turned slowly to align myself with the stream. Now I felt the energy flow from planted pole, through arms and legs, to my boat upon the water. The center of my effort became the helm. I leaned against the long spruce pole just so and drove my slim and responsive craft swiftly, true, and gracefully down the Granta.

AN INLAND VOYAGE

I've just completed Robert Louis Stevenson's *An Inland Voyage,* in which he and a companion paddled and sailed their two canoes from Antwerp nearly to Paris in September 1876. The first portion of this adventure they traversed canals with numerous locks; the second they descended the River Oise. The total comprised a seventeen-day journey, during which they sheltered at night in local inns. Not knowing their way or having reservations, they sometimes found themselves stumbling around strange villages in the dark and the rain, looking for kindly souls to take them in.

Weak and consumptive, Stevenson pushed himself to overcome the drawbacks of his body, and spent a good part of his life in traipsing this Earth.

"I travel not to go anywhere," he relates, "but to go."

And go he did, the better part of his sickly forty-four years; much of his latter travel in the hope of finding a most salubrious climate. For nearly three years he sailed the South Pacific, visiting the Hawaiian Islands, the Gilberts, Tahiti, Samoa.

At Samoa he settled with his devoted wife; cleared the land and built his house; conferred with the natives—to whom he was always advocate and friend—and, as always, wrote. He exhausted himself his entire life, but managed to produce during such an exiguous existence the masterpieces that keep him in our hearts: *Treasure Island, Kidnapped, David Balfour, Jekyll and Hyde, The Black Arrow, The Master of Ballentrae,* and *A Child's Garden of Verses.*

As a man, we should remember him best as a friend to the world— companionable to all without regard to race or attainment—someone so very much in love with life as enabled him to rise above the burden of his body.

During his trip through Belgium into France it rained nearly every day. Wet through much of the time, he never complained, but laughed at life and sought for the good, the amusing, at every turn. He was always happier out of doors; the years aboard his chartered yacht, visiting South Sea islands, were perhaps his happiest. Everywhere he went he made new friends.

"God knows I don't care who I chum with; perhaps I like sailors best," he wrote. On Belgium's Willebroek Canal he became enamored of canal boats and bargees.

Of all the creatures of commercial enterprise, a canal barge is by far the most pleasing to consider. It may spread its sails, and then you see it sailing high above the treetops and the wind-mill, sailing on the aqueduct, sailing through the green corn-lands: the most picturesque of all things amphibious. Or the horse plods along at a foot-pace as if there were no such thing as business in the world; and the man dreaming at the tiller sees the same spire on the horizon all day long . . . There should be many contented spirits on board, for such a life is both to travel and to stay at home . . . I am sure I would rather be a bargee than occupy any position under Heaven that required attendance at an office. There are few callings, I should say, where a man gives up less of his liberty in return for regular meals . . . and so far as I can make out, time stands as nearly still with him as is compatible with the return of bedtime or the dinner hour. It is not easy to see why a bargee should ever die.

Eventually, Stevenson bought a barge and christened her *The Eleven Thousand Virgins of Cologne.* He spent much money having her refurbished—then sold her without ever taking her on the water. With this I can sympathize. Someday I'll tell you about the venerable wooden sloop who moved into my old red barn and took up lodgings there . . .

ANNAPOLIS

Perhaps you think the Water Rat doesn't mess about in boats anymore. I stayed with some friends outside of Annapolis one spring a few years back. Well, maybe more than a *few* years—about 1973. That's the year I fell in love twice and almost . . . anyway, you don't really want to hear about my love life. You wanted to hear a story about the muskrat.

I wandered that year. I had an old VW Beetle with a thirteen-foot Grumman canoe strapped on the roof racks, a box of woodworking tools, another box of books, and ten pounds of granola. That and a sleeping bag ought to be enough for anyone. I stopped to visit a friend of mine who shared an old Victorian house a mile from Chesapeake

Bay, way down an atrocious dirt driveway and out in the middle of a hay field. From the widow's walk you could easily see the water.

I found work doing carpentry around Annapolis and my visit became prolonged. Come April, and fair weather, we decided to take the canoe for a little swim. She gets kind of grumpy just sleeping on top of the car. We dumped her into one of the many estuaries, grabbed our fishing poles, and paddled off. After a bit, we tied up alongside a grassy bank about head-high and settled down to do some serious fishing.

But we hadn't consulted the water rat. Here he came, scurrying down to the bank in his frivolous way.

"Five o'clock!" he muttered. "Time for tea!"

Then he launched himself, as usual, into the creek. A small furry body hurtled by my ear. Our canoe was definitely not a part of his schedule. His "messing about" consisted of dashing from end to end of the boat and snapping at our unprotected toes. I slid my paddle under him and familiarized him with our man-overboard drill—without boring him overmuch with the subsequent rescue routine.

Consequently, he made it home to his cozy hole in the riverbank, where he promptly seated himself in front of a cheery fire and proceeded to bring his journal up to date. This is what water rats do. I read it in a book.

Cats, however, are notoriously poor journalists. You never know what *they* think. When we first went out to our island, we took our cat, the Fabulous Fuzz McGee: Miss Petite, Miss Fluff, Miss Staunchly Independent. She wasn't thrilled about the canoe trip but, after all, she trusted us. She seemed to enjoy the island that summer—a hundred acres without another dwelling—and we left her there to hunt those days we went upriver.

After a while, though, she disappeared. No Fuzz McGee could we find for a month or more. Until—lo! We surprised her up at the landing outside the store. And she turned her back on us and stalked away.

Another unusual passenger—not counting Giraffe—was a squirrel. (I think I'll save Giraffe for another story.) Returning to the island one day, I observed his little gray head poking up from the water. He swam strongly *away* from shore. He'd come perhaps a hundred feet and had at least a quarter of a mile to go. He'd be lucky to make the farther bank by Tuesday.

"Having an affair in Chester," I mused. "Or forced to flee the minions of the law." Reading Mr. Grahame provokes such sentiments.

I slipped my paddle under him, and he crawled his weary way up its length and toppled into my boat. He lay there, his little chest heaving, as I paddled him back to shore. I put the gangway out and off he went—rather tentatively—rehearsing those plausible explanations I had helpfully suggested. I rather doubt that his wife believed a word of them.

But I've given up corrupting little animals: I haven't had a snapping turtle in my canoe for nearly twenty years . . .

EVERGLADES CITY

We spent the first couple of weeks of February in Everglades City, Florida. This began as a busy and prosperous town back in the twenties, when Barron Collier built that portion of the Tamiami Trail, the road from Tampa to Miami, which runs through Collier County. Today ECity remains a sleepy backwater but would-be tourist attraction. Its greatest assets consist of the innumerable waterways of Everglades National Park and the shallow lagoon offshore among the Ten Thousand Islands National Wildlife Refuge.

Everglades City is bordered by Barron River to the north and Halfway Creek to the south. The Turner River, farther south, is connected to Halfway Creek by a smaller estuary. All three rivers empty into the Gulf of Mexico. These waterways are ideal for paddling. A couple of local outfitters rent every color kayak and canoe.

"Oh, but you mustn't rent a canoe from a commercial place," said my sister. "You must visit with the Cat Lady and borrow *her* canoe."

The Cat Lady lives on a little canal just off Halfway Creek. A high, cat-proof fence surrounds her yard. Within are two or three dozen strays, for whom she attempts to find homes. My son and I spent a cheerful half hour with her and several cats on her screened-in porch, drinking limeade—made fresh from her lime tree, thank you—and being instructed on the navigation of the various creeks and passages. I gave her a contribution for cat food and we slid her old canoe into the canal.

For the first half mile, we paddled by pretty cottages surrounded by palms and citrus and banana trees; by hyacinths and orchids and bougainvilleas. Soon the cottages on Halfway Creek grew farther apart. Suddenly there was nothing save a narrowing, shady slot amid the mangroves. These were small and serried and grew to the muddy banks of the stream. We couldn't step ashore. We looked in vain for alligators; we looked in vain for birds. We reached an intersection and took the estuary.

This creek finally opened into a little pond. We drifted and shared our crackers and cheese and dates. We checked our chart (courtesy of the Cat Lady). A couple of miles more and we would enter a good-sized pond; the creek beyond that would spread to admit the sky. We resumed our paddle up the shady slot. The mosquitoes, having devoured the alligators, resorted to us.

The second pond had islands in it, on one of which an osprey had her nest. The male alighted nearby and assured us we weren't to come ashore. Soon after, we startled a great blue heron who, in the inimitable way of herons, always alighted just far enough ahead of us to be continually startled for most of a mile. But herons and ospreys we see most days in Connecticut. We wanted alligators and plenty of them. They should have been chasing our canoe and trying to have us for supper. All of this paddling just to see a blue heron? Yep. We went as far as the Turner River and made our equally uneventful return. So much for the Everglades. At least the mosquitoes were friendly.

The Cat Lady had departed. We cleaned her canoe and hosed the mud from its bottom. The cats were not amused. The following day, we drove east along the Tamiami Trail to Big Cypress National Preserve. A "borrow canal"—from which the road fill had been borrowed—runs parallel to the road. Several yards broad and several feet deep, it's backed by miles of marshes. Every couple of hundred yards, an alligator basked on its muddy banks. Some of them would fill a small canoe. We might have paddled this canal the length of Collier County in the company of herons, egrets, cormorants, and countless little birds. I supposed we might deprive the cats of their boat a second time and traverse the borrow canal. One of the largest alligators yawned. He had the most impressive set of dentures.

"It wouldn't be fair to interrupt their nap," remarked my son.

GIVING A SNAPPER THE SACK

The largest turtle I ever saw was while paddling in the Adirondacks—probably in Schroon Lake. I belonged to the outing club at college, and the Adirondacks were our playground. We climbed Mount Marcy, hiked the woods, and paddled on Lake George and the numerous brooks and lakes around northeastern New York. The only boats we had were seventeen-foot aluminum canoes. They can be noisy if you allow the paddle to strike the gunwale, and they certainly transmit the cold, but they weigh only seventy-five pounds.

Two of us could easily carry the boat as well as light packs. We took only overnight or weekend trips, so we didn't carry much gear.

Our tent was the bulkiest item by far. Sleeping bags, life vests, clothes, food, and a bow saw made up the remainder. Most of our jaunts we traversed still water. By the time spring freshets arrived, everyone needed to prepare for final exams. Still, we managed to have a good time.

This turtle basked on a muddy bank, perhaps a yard from the water. I wish I could remember more details, but the decades have a way of clouding the brightest beams. I'm sure she had a smooth shell. This would make her an eastern softshell. The females grow to be as large as snappers, although their heads are much different, being long and narrow, rather than globular. Both books I've consulted give the maximum size of eastern softshells as seventeen inches. This is the length of the carapace—the upper shell. Snappers attain eighteen inches. This turtle seemed huge. As I recollect, her carapace looked nearly two feet long. I wish I'd had a tape measure with me that day.

My partner and I stopped paddling and glided alongside the bank. As soon as we drew alongside, I shoved my paddle beneath her, thinking to flip her over. I might just as well have tried to flip over my truck. The next moment she lunged for the water and disappeared. She obviously had no intentions of setting any new records.

The snapper I found in my mother's garden had a carapace of fifteen or sixteen inches. She (not my mother) intended to make her slow way down to our pond. Where she came from I can only surmise. Our little brook connects to the river by way of a larger stream, but I've never seen any turtles in it. The river wends a mile away and our house is one hundred fifty feet above sea level.

Why should a turtle leave the river, which houses numerous snappers, to spend days dragging herself uphill in the hope of finding a pond? A pond too small to support a brood of large turtles.

My father most certainly did not want this beast in his pond, killing the fish and ducks and endangering his grandchildren. He called me up at my machine shop in the barn next door. I had a client with me. He brightened at the prospect of something different to start his day. I rummaged in the barn and found a large canvas sack.

"I have to cross the bridge on my way to work," he said. "I'll drive down to the tour boat landing and dump her in the river."

The turtle napped peacefully amid the daffodils. Perhaps she dreamed of laying a clutch of eggs. She didn't appear the least alarmed when we interrupted her nap. Not to begin with.

"You hold the sack," I directed my friend. "I'll insert the turtle."

Try it sometime. Hoist a twenty-five pound snapper, preferably by the back edge of her shell, and see what happens. Remember to keep her away from your body. Not only can a snapper bite, but her formidable claws can make you the envy of every zebra in town.

For some reason, this turtle had little interest in exploring our lovely sack. She spread her legs, extended her neck, and fought with perseverance. Isn't that always the way of it? Whenever you try to liberate anyone, they fight you, beak and claws. Just as I thought my arm would give out, we managed to convince her. Off she went to the river—where turtles belong—and the world was safe for democracy once again.

THE SEA SERPENT

Once upon a river there was a fellow with a canoe. It happened to be myself. I was young once, although you may find that difficult to believe, and dated this young lady from up the river. It hadn't taken me long to discover that she was a waterwoman.

I used to drive up on weekends with my little canoe strapped tightly to my orange VW Bug with the black paisley design on the hood. I crammed it with paddles and sleeping bags and homemade granola and life preservers and books about the care and feeding of mermaids. I wooed this gal with granola and followed that up with the river for a chaser.

It worked, by golly. She went canoeing with me. Our very first trip, we put in by the concrete bridge. Just downriver, there's a dam so tall that you've time for the whole Lord's Prayer from when you go over until you bounce off the rocks. We chose to go up the River.

We went for a very sedate and delightful paddle until the twilight filled with bats and moonglow. Then we made camp on a slim, convenient island. I hauled the canoe up the beach a bit and then just walked away.

"Aren't you going to tie it?" she asked.

"This is the river," I answered. "It hasn't a tide this far from the sea.

Why should I tie my canoe?"

"Aren't you going to haul it farther up the shore?" she asked.

"We are miles and miles away from the sea," I replied. "There is no tide. And the last sea serpent seen around here died of remorse from bolting a kayak thirty years ago."

"I wasn't even born then," she objected. "How was I to know?"

We built a small fire of sticks and toasted some granola.

"What do sea serpents look like?" she inquired. Of course, I had to tell her. That took most of the evening. Then the moon started to set and we climbed into our sleeping bags and held hands until the sun demanded attention.

When I returned from stumbling about in the bushes, she was staring at the shore. I followed her gaze and, sure enough, there was nothing there to look at. The little canoe had snuck off during the night. The river had risen nearly three feet and had just begun to recede.

"Another sea serpent," I ventured. "You can see where he's dragged his tail up the shore."

"That's the mark of the keel," she said. "You don't fool me one bit."

That's the trouble with women—they're so pragmatic.

"They opened the floodgates up at the dam," she continued. "They do that when they expect a heavy rain."

"That wasn't fair," I accused her. "You had local knowledge and purposely withheld it."

"It is fun fooling strangers," she agreed.

"I'm not strange at all," I averred. "Not after I've had my coffee."

We rolled up our sleeping bags and toasted some more granola. We kept our eyes on each other in the hope of rescue.

"We could just swim to shore," she suggested. "It's only a hundred yards. Let's take off our clothes and hold them above our heads."

"But the fish," I exclaimed. "We don't want to be responsible for shocking the poor little fish. What would their mothers say? Wouldn't you rather languish here for thirty years—hoping for some wandering bark to take us home to England?"

"I don't know about you," she said, "but I have to get home today to feed my cat." She actually commenced removing her clothes.

Fortunately, a calamity was averted.

"Look!" I exclaimed. "Canoes!"

The Boy Scouts were out—earning their merit badges for search and rescue. After they left us at the landing, we sought for my canoe. I whistled and called. I even made paddling noises.

"It's probably over the dam by now," she sighed. "There won't be much of it left."

"The little canoe isn't fond of dams," I declared. "She's probably just taking a nap in those bushes."

And so she was. We hauled her up the bank and carried her out to the road.

The sea serpent, of course, got clean away, but you could see where he'd dragged his tail up the shore . . .

CHOOSING A STAR

The year winds down. The moon has just passed full, the weather grown lovely, albeit seasonal. Friday morning the perigee high tide ran over the retaining wall and flowed beneath our shop. I could have (barely) sculled the Whitehall over the wall and into the parking lot. Would have saved the effort of dragging her out at the launch ramp, but I figured Ezra and Melati might want to go rowing next week. Afterward they can help me haul her and stow her safely at home for the worst of winter.

Perhaps we can row her with two sets of oars, with someone seated in the stern for trim. A jaunt up the Mystic River would be a good outing: perhaps six miles round trip. We could cut behind Mouse Island and be in the river mouth in a matter of minutes. Both the railroad bridge and the little bascule bridge above it have plenty of clearance for boats that haven't a mast. Strange to think, I haven't been out in a mastless boat for months and months—not since I took my kayak up the Wood River. How the ratcheted days escape: click by inexorable click. Seems it was only yesterday that I was young and handsome.

The bascule bridge in the village of Mystic constitutes part of the Post Road that runs the entire length of the East Coast. On the east shore of the Mystic River lies the town of Stonington—my hometown, now, these past two weeks. On the west shore lies the town of Groton. So the village of Mystic spans two towns as well as a little river, but no one takes it seriously except town councils and building committees and tax officials. But to us common mortals, who cross the bridge half a dozen times a day, it makes no difference.

Just above the bridge, on the Stonington side (*our* side, of course) stands Mystic Seaport. Above that, the river spreads out and shallows. In Old Mystic, two miles north, it forms an open marsh that beckons to my kayaking blood to explore. In the village center, the river narrows to no more than a stream and passes beneath a little bridge that, once again, separates Groton and Stonington for all and any who care.

I'm sure I could paddle the length of the river in two hours. Perhaps I could even commute to work by kayak. Hmmm. Haven't done that in thirty years. Coming home might prove just a little arduous; especially the last bit—through Old Mystic. The river here scarce covers the stones and spreads but a few yards wide.

I ought to look for the source of our river—track her to her lair within the forest. Every river, no matter how imposing, has a source that's no more or less than a rivulet: a spring welling up among some mossy stones in some shady wood.

Just so, each of us springs from the merest droplet, and we merge with others and run and spread and make our ultimate way to the great Earth Sea in which we lose our identity and become as one with all the lives that have been. Every time we paddle the length of any stream or river, we replicate the journey of our souls. Your boat is no more than a droplet to the stream. In our youth, we swiftly surge and tumble and bound with a reckless exuberance. Our frail craft retains the numerous scars of our collisions.

Once we clear all the rocks and rapids, our pace decreases; yet our perspective broadens, as does the river. We aren't so much in jeopardy of capsizing as at risk of drifting, apathetically, aground. Nevertheless, inexorably, we are carried in one direction—into the future. Will we, nil we, on and down we wend; by day, by night, by season, year and decade. But I prefer this to the alternative: to have all come to a stark and breathless halt. Don't put down that paddle!

Once you leave the river mouth, be sure to hoist your sail—you're off with a freshening breeze abaft the beam and setting a course for forever—or as much of it as will fit between today and your demise. There's not a moment to lose. This breeze may not be propitious after a while. The doldrums may descend and leave you to wallow among the swells. Or else a gale may drive you to the bottom. Keep your hand on the helm.

Seize not only the day but the night as well. Choose a star and follow it. Don't wish upon it—follow it. Be assured: Its light will outlast your journey.

THE WHITEHALL

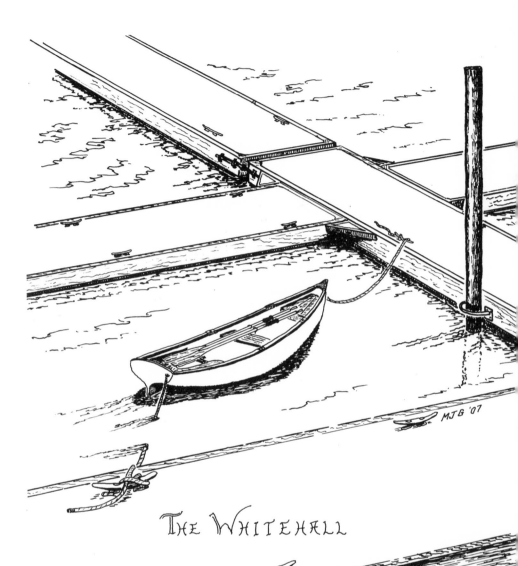

The Whitehall

Yesterday, I couldn't resist—I took my Whitehall pulling boat for a little row up to Mystic. It registered a mere fifty degrees—and we're talking January. There should be at least twelve feet of snow, making it tough for the woolly mammoth to get to the grocery store. And the temperature should be fifty below, not above. These shortcomings indicate global warming—the result of too many campaign speeches, no doubt.

My sister sent me a mug for Christmas that depicts the topographical effects of global warming. As the mug heats up (black, one sugar, please) the profiles of the continents printed on it shrink. Finally, the map shows what remains when both ice caps melt and all the oceans rise a hundred meters. The penguins, of course, all move to LA to wait on tables or serve as gondoliers.

Subsequently, the continental United States has a svelter profile. Aside from the Appalachians, the eastern half of the country remains submerged. But think of this: more ocean to sail; new harbors to explore. For those of you who focus on your portfolios, sell your land on the east coast and buy up all you can in the Alleghenies—it will soon be exclusive waterfront. Yes, global warming was designed with us boaters in mind. I suggest we make a contribution: All of you with sailboats—retrofit them with a pair of old 440 Chrysler V-8 engines. Don't even bother keeping them tuned up. You say you need a ring job? Dig the black smoke, Skipper! Open both throttles and put them little hydrocarbons to work!

I had planned to tell you about my row out of West Cove and into Mystic Harbor.

It is now two o'clock on Tuesday and I'm by myself in the boat shop. This afternoon, West Cove has become a glass in which the reflections of every line and spar reveal a second fleet, becalmed, at the piers. Beyond the breakwater, only the subtle urging of the moon, the merest mouthing of breeze, disturbs the surface. Marine forecast this afternoon: "Seas running three to five inches; wind out of the south by west at half a confiding whisper; sun, now over the yardarm, declining in stately leisure."

It isn't wise to let someone like me work so close to the water in beautiful weather. I grab my gleaming oars, an extra jersey, a cushion, some gloves, some water, a cell phone.

My little boat prances eagerly in her slip. I load my gear, cast off and step aboard. I run out my slender, varnished sculls until the hilts of their leather collars seat against the bronze oarlocks. A few short strokes and I'm clear of the dock and pulling for the channel. Past all the piers and the sailboats wintering wet: *Destiny* and *Awesome; Spring Tides* and *Current Sea.* I cross the channel toward Morgan Point, where a fisherman is loading his power-washed lobster pots aboard *West Cove III.*

The half-ebbed tide reveals weedy boulders all about. The slightest riffle of waning water betrays several just beneath the surface. Some folk hereabouts use four by fours to mark their moorings over the winter season. I strike one with the edge of my blade and knock off a chip of varnish. I do what I can to keep the industry busy. On my return, I'll scrape my keel over a well-submerged rock. (Half an ounce of bottom paint, please. Will that be for here or to go? Just stir it gently and I'll refinish her when I get home.) Yes, each of you boaters has a duty to make more work for your friendly neighborhood boat shop.

I head between Morgan Point and little Mouse Island. Around the point is the mouth of Mystic Harbor. Beyond the fishing piers stand some modest cottages of twelve or fifteen rooms and then the inactive lighthouse on the point.

This two-story cube of cut granite is surmounted by a massy wooden cupola. From the entryway, which faces the sea, a set of cut stone steps descends. Joined behind the lighthouse, a modern home rambles east toward Mystic Harbor.

I round the point, wink at the sentinel herring gull who wards the tide-lapped ledge, and enter the mouth of the harbor. The gull does not wink back. He reserves his humor for the little crabs who venture from beneath the bladderwort. I begin the two-mile pull upstream to the village.

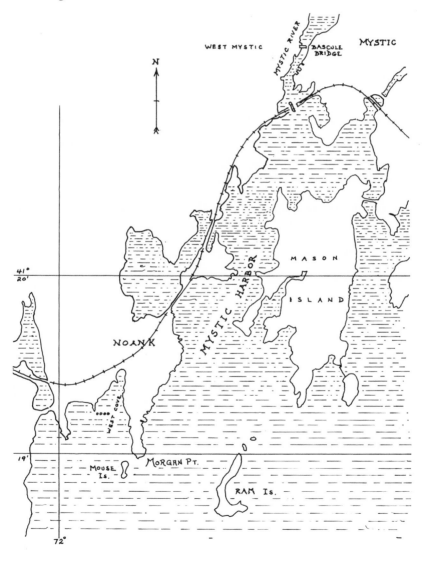

The honeyed sun dazzles. I don dark glasses; they dinge the glorious day.

The piers of Noank Shipyard front the first quarter mile above the lighthouse. The harbor mouth abounds with untenanted mooring buoys but, a mile away, at the foot of Masons Island, a thirty-foot cutter dapples on her tether—her tender trails astern. Someone must be aboard. It cheers me to know that other folk are on the water, feeling the ocean pulse beneath their feet.

By the time I reach the landing at the foot of Main Street I feel stiff. I pause; take a drink of water. I set myself and check the Whitehall's slow drift toward the sea. I put my arms and legs into each long stroke.

The half dozen ample boatyards in sight remain quiet. The Canada geese patrolling the shallows do not. "This harbor is ours, ours, ours, ours!" they holler. They regard me askance; my wings are going but I can't get off the water.

My hands begin to blister. My sailing gloves don't seem to provide much protection and I shuck them; I prefer the feel of the smooth, unvarnished handles.

Sixpenny Island—more of a marshy peninsula—juts halfway across the narrowing harbor. I pull toward the Masons Island shore to clear it.

The homes on Masons Island dignify the harbor. Perhaps, if someone thoughtfully leaves me several million dollars, I'll buy that great stone house on its prominent knoll with the steep lawn dropping down to the eighty-foot pier. It would be the perfect place to keep my dinghy.

I pass the head of Masons Island. After a brief expanse of open water, the mainland resumes, crowded with piers and slips. My muscles have begun to relax; the boat and I have blent. Bend, stoop, stretch, pull, straighten, relax, repeat. Forbear to think of rowing.

The harbor and river merge. I drift beneath the railroad trestle and glance straight up. The substantial control house atop the swing bridge could easily house the average American family: one and six-tenths children, seven-tenths of a dog, eight-tenths of a cat, about one-half of a goldfish. I'd inquire of the eight-tenths of that cat concerning the other half of that fish.

I near the bascule bridge on the old Post Road. On the west bank stands the old brick powerhouse—now become apartments. Then comes the low-lying Art Association, then more apartments. Rather classy apartments. Fronting the river runs a single pier—a boardwalk. PRIVATE, NO DOCKING, proclaim a dozen signs. Lastly is a slip reserved for *Valiant:* an eighty-foot, off-white excursion boat, now nuzzled up to the bridge.

The final two hundred yards of the opposite bank are reserved for public use. A miniature park separates the dinghy dock, then the "Riverwalk," from the winter-quiet side street forty yards off. A professionally dressed young woman snaps photos of me, rowing. Perhaps next week I'll adorn a page of one of our local papers: "Intrepid mariner braves the chilly water." I fend off another iceberg.

A stout and elderly matron, bundled in a heavy black coat and kerchief, staidly enjoys the sun from her wrought iron bench.

"A glorious day. A glorious day," she asserts to me. "God is good."

With half a dozen strokes I reach the small bascule bridge. The village of Mystic bustles up to the span from either bank. The river here is so narrow, you could toss a mackerel across it. Half a mile upstream lies Mystic Seaport: treasury of wooden boat and tall ship restoration. It is too late, now, to investigate the stately vessels moored at the massive wharves; to imbibe the fragrance of oak and cedar and tar and twisted hemp.

I back with my starboard blade and pull with my port. The White-hall slowly describes half of a circle. I run in my oars and gratefully drink some water. Now I slowly begin to drift downstream.

I run out my brightly varnished oars, set my feet against the rest, flex my knees, and stoop to my first return stroke. The poised blades glisten. The low-slung sun warms my back. It drenches the harbor in amber. I dip my slim oars into the stream. The Whitehall surges forward to greet the horizon.

I flex my knees and stoop to my second stroke. The poised blades glisten. The low-slung sun warms my back. It drenches the harbor in amber.

God is good.

THE CONNECTICUT

ANOTHER SPRING FRESHET

EAST HADDAM BRIDGE

The river inundates the low-lying banks below the old steel swing bridge. We shall readily canoe to the doorstep of our octagon on the island. The tide backs up the impatient river in vain—a mere three feet of brine cannot back up the spring thaw of New England. Abetted by the wind, the Connecticut in turn backs up the tide, the whole a slow but steadily seething mass. The river fills with boards and bottles, Styrofoam and Adirondack chairs.

In the parking lot behind the Riverside Inn, an abandoned blue Buick stands in silty water up to her wipers. The airstrip beyond has tucked its little planes away in their hangars. The pier is submerged;

only the weed-wrapped crowns of the pilings attest to its location. We park in the village and launch the canoe in the swollen creek that runs beside Creamery Lane. We canoe down over the runway. Not even the pontoon plane dares venture forth.

Below the airport, several cottages squat along the submerged dirt road that follows the riverbank. Though the cottages crouch on concrete blocks, the river rises within a foot of their thresholds. The residents have parked in the village and have come back home in their boats. Things normally kept in the yard—those hens, for instance—now sojourn on the porch. Canoes and dinghies wait patiently by the steps.

Just another spring freshet. The dormant gardens again receive fresh nutrients. Silt will coat everything, everywhere, for a while when the river recedes and noisome trash will abound, but no one complains. One takes what the river offers, both good and bad. The joy of living by running water far outweighs the sorrow. We pass the cottages, wave to the children sailing boats from their deck, and paddle off into the woods.

Amid the trees, the quietude assails one's ears—the little birds have forsaken the drowning underbrush. We emerge from the wood and enter Chapman Pond. Pond and marsh merge into one expanse of gray and turgid water. Poplar Hill, the second of Seven Sisters, bounds the inland shore of the pond. Our island bounds the other. Here, huge silver maples tower above the murky, presumptuous flood. They seem very little concerned. A hundred springs or more have they seen the river swell and surge and recede. They sigh in response to the wind, flex themselves and drink deeply.

We urge our canoe among them and over the path that leads to the octagon. Built on four-foot concrete piles, its floor stands eight feet above mean high water. The fourth step up lies exposed but wet, the third is still underwater; the river has crested. We unload tools, provisions, five gallons of water, and shove off again to explore. We find a few sturdy planks among the trees and tow them back to the house, where we make them fast. This occupies the remainder of the forenoon. What of it?

What is time to a water rat? What is time to the river? Only we humans obsess over days and minutes, hours and seasons. Life goes on—within us and without us. To thrive comes first: to be sentient, quick, responsive. Off we go, our paddles busily pushing aside the river. Our sensuous prow parts the water into halves. The river closes phlegmatically in our wake. We wend our seamless way downstream to the landing.

Gillette's Castle, aloof on its wooded hill, the Seventh Sister, frowns down upon the landing. The ferry, made fast in her slip with heavy hawsers, floats above the level of the road. We turn into Whalebone Cove, pass the ledge with its rusted ring that hasn't secured a ship for half a century. The creek leading into the cove has spread beneath the budding red maples. The cove beyond is a flat expanse of filthy water broken by the bedraggled plumes of eight-foot-high phragmites: the pampas grass.

We return to the river. The wind has died and the water has calmed a bit. We moor to the massive ring in the rock and share our simple repast. In the channel, some hundred yards off, the remains of an unfortunate boat, a thirty-foot skiff, drift downward to the ever-receptive ocean. A herring gull wheels hopefully above the ruined vessel. The sodden hull veers slowly about in the river. The sea heaves heavily round this whirled Earth.

ISLANDS

Most islands in our river look very much as yours do: narrow wooded sandbars that beckon to the birds. Canoe-shaped, they poise in the midst of moving water. They call to each voyager as would an oasis to one parched and famished. I find it difficult, when gliding on the river, guided by my paddle, by my slim ash paddle, to pass by an island with its lofty grove, with its birds and its breezes. It compels me to slow, to backwater with my paddle; the ash tree beckons to my slim ash paddle.

I run my narrow keel up—up, up the sand—and leave some fresh prints on this tentative shore. For all of this world is a shifting shoreline; we but the drifters, the dreamers, the watermen, who frequent these beaches, impatient to be gone. But now and again, one must pause to contemplate.

What metaphor has been so explored, so exploited, as that of the river: flowing waters, flowing lives? Nothing great thrives in the stagnant pool—nothing much prospers that does not change.

I tread the island deftly—used to smaller watercraft that rock beneath my feet. I poise in the midst of this microcosm and listen to birdsong well up from many perches. My resolution lurches. The arms of the silver maple arch overhead. The leaves of the cottonwood rattle in the breeze. Fragrant spicebush shelters in the shadows, and

I slip some new leaves into the pocket of my shirt. I nibble the blooms of the wild violet as the firm Earth woos me with its promises of peace. Of ease, of appeasement.

I stroke this smooth limb that the river left behind—driftwood from a world constantly shifting. The water is glistening. This waterman is drifting. Listen to the mourning dove's plaintive lamentation. She mourns for the watermen who perish on the river. She mourns for the watermen who perish out at sea. Curl up here amid the soft ostrich ferns and forget about the river. The Earth is your giver. Forget about the river. Linger in this thicket where the doe has reposed. Lay your heavy head here, wanton waterman. Forget about the river.

I stand up quickly, shake the drowse from my brow. It's time I was away. The river runs by with her message from the mountains; the river runs by with her tribute to the sea. I turn as the world turns, recede as the sea recedes, avid and glad as a boat upon the river. A shadow of arrested flight leans against the sky and I stop.

An osprey alights on a long dead limb overhanging the water and proceeds to groom herself—the four winds' daughter, disheveled and aloof. I stand without moving an enumerable while and listen to the river eroding the island from beneath my feet—grain, by grain, by grain. I stand without moving an innumerable while and listen to the river appreciating the island's other shore—grain, by grain, by grain. The island, most assuredly, is bound across the river—perhaps a foot per year. Is nothing ever still?

Where is the doe who lingered in the thicket? Where is the water that lately lapped the shore? The lush wind whispers. And the osprey is not there. I stoop and retrieve her long brown-and-white feather and plait it in my hair—in my long silver hair that shimmers as the river. I pause to admire the curves of my canoe and lay my hand on the swell of her prow. The lush water whispers. And then—*I* am not there.

WHALEBONE COVE

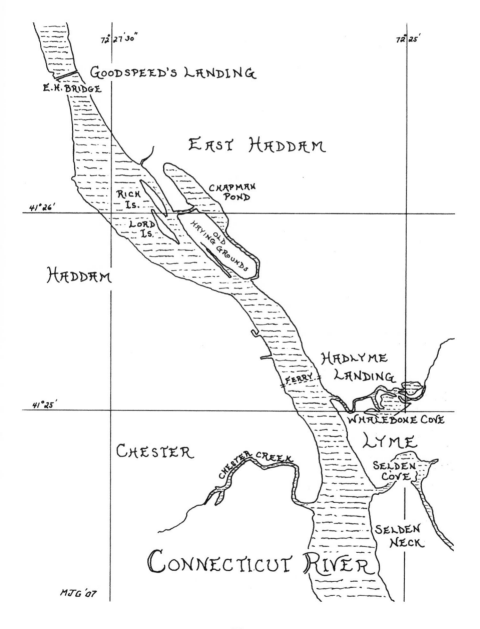

72° 27' 30"   72° 25'

GOODSPEED'S LANDING

E.H. BRIDGE

EAST HADDAM

CHAPMAN POND

RICH IS.

41° 26'

LORD IS.

OLD KRYING GROUNDS

HADDAM

HADLYME LANDING

FERRY

41° 25'

WHALEBONE COVE

CHESTER   LYME

CHESTER CREEK

SELDEN COVE

SELDEN NECK

CONNECTICUT RIVER

MJG '07

59

How shall I tell of autumn on the river? Can mere wordcraft depict the grace of an early October morning from my canoe? Now I drift dawnward—I left my island as day woke on the water. The inside of my aluminum boat is agleam with condensation. I am warmly clothed. And now a glimpse, a glimmering, as the valley breaks to a veiled sun amid a silver mist. I can scarcely see past the prow of my canoe. For half an hour, I think there will not be anything ever again save mist. Then an edge of the veil lifts.

Twenty yards east waits an oil tanker, her engines throbbing; she waits to cross a river that can't quite be seen. First I see only a ghost of her superstructure, then the red and white of the pilothouse, then fifty yards of black and gleaming steel. As I glide by, an easy hail away, I touch my cap, and her taciturn skipper nods his acknowledgment. Then, once more, I am clear and on my own—I will meet nobody else between here and the landing.

The fog burns away, there is not a bit of breeze; there is but the spiritual glow of emboldened sun. Every last wisp of fog is burned away. It is gone. The new light reveals the sensuous hills on the eastern bank and the broad bottomland on the western. Between the two, a steely, sinuous, great, long, moving mirror as a dozen colors leap from the wounded hillside into the water. The tanker's skipper empowers his engines and shatters the dawn with a warning from his horn. He follows the channel across the river and continues to crawl upstream. A mile more and he blows his horn for the old swing bridge to open. Then she is gone.

The dawn is so still I can hear a fish jump a quarter mile downstream. Ahead, the ferryboat sleeps in her slip. When I was a lad, her labors commenced at six o'clock each morning. I pass the landing—it is much too early to think about going to work—to be walled in by wood no longer living. I turn my diminutive craft into the creek and work my way slowly against the tide and current.

The creek is muddy and six feet deep and sixty feet across. Its slippery banks boast broken trees and tangled, strangling vines to the water's edge. Rose and briar and bittersweet suffice to keep a waterman from the shore. But the birds adore it. Now they are busy proclaiming another day. I paddle with power; I scarcely disturb the surface. The kingfisher clatters by me, swoops around the bend and disappears. The water roils round the cottonwood snag. Now I'm past the woods and amid the marsh. Cattails, pickerelweed, iris, wild rice. And, all about, the too intrusive phragmites—pampas grass. A monstrous dragonfly dries his wings in the sun. Very soon will his little season be over.

The creek has narrowed to half its former width—it now fans out—it ramifies into lesser creeks that twine toward shore to be fed by freshwater streams. This particular marsh is small—perhaps half a mile across—a sanctuary within a ring of woods and houses and road. I am hemmed in by cattails. The wan sun has finally dried the mist from my canoe. It has dried the four stiff wings of the dragonfly.

Now a pair of swans and two brown cygnets paddle down a narrow passage and vanish. During nesting time the aggressive cob will challenge any intruder. He will ramp up in the water and beat his wings and, if ignored, will stoop upon canoeists and batter them. Now he is wary. He has no wish to be seen. He and his family would prefer to forage uninterrupted. These are not half-tame harbor swans who go from boat to boat demanding breakfast. These are wild creatures— like myself.

WHITE RIVER JUNCTION

Our canoe slid down the Connecticut River, prow high and proud, with a following wind and a bit of current and a broad expanse of northern New England scenic brilliance—the maples aflame with October. We'd camped on an island, cooked our ample breakfast on a meager fire, which we'd doused with a bucket of river before departing.

The current was slow, but we were in no hurry. Half of canoeing is losing yourself—emptying out all the stupefying facts and responsibilities and refilling the space with perception: flight of blackbird, flow of water, splash of smallmouth, cry of heron; sheen of stone beneath the keel, sough of Zephyr through the forest. And then, for a moment—nothing save the river. The mediate fact of progress along the water—the result of gravity—the whole of the river dropping down New England—falling from the Connecticut Lakes until it reaches Long Island Sound.

And so we, too, had decided to drop—to fall—to tumble from the heights of the Appalachians down to that terminal moraine calling itself Long Island—separated the entire length of Connecticut shore by a finger of the Atlantic—ten miles wide and a long day's sail in length. Deep enough for commercial shipping, filthy enough to destroy the oyster fisheries.

But here, between New Hampshire and Vermont, runs its tributary: a rural, a strong, and a beautiful river. The effluent from the paper mills mostly under control, the textile mills gone south a lifetime ago. And today only us—we two, it would seem, and nobody else for miles and miles and miles.

About midday, the river forked about the head of an island. We chose, unwittingly, the east, the New Hampshire, side. The fork became constricted, the water quickened. Just ahead, the river backed and roiled. Boulders abounded. We beached our boat on a granite ledge that stretched down into the water and walked about to stretch our legs and spy out the course to take us safely through.

Sumners Falls, they call it. The drop is not significant, but the rocks create what's known as standing white water—water rebounding against submerged boulders. When it meets the oncoming flow, this creates significant waves. They hold your canoe in one place and fill it with water. During the spring torrents, these falls are vicious; whirlpools and rapids have accounted for several deaths.

Beneath our feet was an epitaph carved in the granite: UPON THIS SITE, ON SUCH AND SUCH A DATE, DID SO AND SO FROM SOMEWHERE LOSE HIS LIFE. Deeply graven, done with professional tools, these words had lasted scores of years already. We looked at the words, we looked at the river, we spoke in collected voices.

We decided to carry our baggage below the rapids. We donned our life jackets, tossed the canoe back in, and jumped aboard. Yes, it was rough, and we shipped a good bit of water and scraped some rocks. We dumped the water, retrieved our dry gear, and embarked again.

Mile after mile, stroke after stroke, we made our way south toward Massachusetts, made our way down to the flatlands—down to the sea. By midafternoon, we were weary. But the breeze followed after, pushed us down the river.

Both of us knew how to sail. Rolled up with our gear was a little nylon ground cloth. My partner folded the ground cloth on a diagonal—bandanna fashion—then balanced on the forward thwart, stood on the doubled loose corners of the tarpaulin, and held the other corners outstretched. A lateen rig, no less. I tucked the long paddle under my arm and steered by twisting the grip. Off we sped—roaring along at three knots. A couple of times, the mast very nearly tumbled into the river.

After three-quarters of an hour, we spied another island. We furled the sail, the mast sat down with aching arms, and we laughed at our improvisation. We steered for the isle and set about making camp.

UNNATURAL CRAVINGS
FOR CIVILIZATION

SELDEN III

A friend of mine owned a little restaurant just up Chester Creek, where the making tide bulges beneath the causeway and the haughty swans nest amid the cattails. Two main roads intersect there, so business prospered—at least during the clement seasons.

It never mattered to me, back then, what time of day or time of year prevailed. I secluded, most months, in a little shack on an island in the river. I hadn't a neighbor in any direction for half a mile or more. To call the summer idyllic equates to painting strawberries red. Winter proved more primal, stark, austere. When twilight dragged the premature day behind the hemlocked hills, I lit my Coleman lamp and read or sat on the frozen riverbank to watch the dark congeal.

When overwhelmed by evening's length, I fostered unnatural cravings for civilization. Then I would tuck my slim canoe into a fold of the river. I owned a small kerosene lantern with a corrugated lens. It didn't suffice to see by; it served as a running light. Most of the time I found it quite superfluous. After all, Chester Creek lay only two miles downriver, with nightly traffic nearly nonexistent.

A mile up the meandering creek I could haul out my canoe behind the restaurant.

Within I found warmth, hot food, and a cheerful waitress. Having regaled myself with each of these, I would venture into the village and listen to the musicians at the inn or visit with friends. It proved a welcome change from rocking on my cabin porch and waiting as the crippled night crept past. Then I would walk the mile back to the darkened restaurant, thence to enjoy a three-mile paddle isleward.

Chester Creek can grow very dark and lonely deep winter nights. Some nights so dark, I needed to lean down into the water and count the turtle tails to know where to turn. When I reached the river, I only hoped the tide had finished ebbing.

Fighting a northerly winter wind, as well as the current and tide, requires one to put aside all reluctance to exertion. But when the incoming tide backed up the river; when the placid wind lay curled amid the rushes; at times such as these, I relished a free ride home. Then I might paddle gently, steer and muse, admire the night.

Two towns from the sea, the river runs slowly here, a quarter mile wide with woody banks, occasional stately houses, narrow islands. On the Chester shore, the ferry—fast in her slip till April—rubs her rail affectionately against the creaking pier. On the Hadlyme side, the castle broods, two hundred feet above the black, black channel. On a new moon night, the castle appears a denser form against the impenetrable mass of darkness above.

With a full moon at zenith, the south running river becomes a shimmering ivory path dividing the dusky shores; the taller oaks reach silhouettes against the spangled sky. Then sentience grows to its grandest. Just inhaling, on nights like these, proves more than enough to justify life on Earth. From the castle, one can nearly touch the moon.

One calm winter night, when the stars seemed small and extremely far away, I met an oil tanker coming downriver. I could hear the throb of her diesels through the thin crisp air before I ever saw her. I removed my mittens and fumbled a wooden match to light my lantern. Halfway across the river, I had more than sufficient water beneath my keel for an empty tanker. Here she came; she rounded Lord Island, ignored the channel, and rumbled straight down the river.

About then, her wakeful pilot sighted my tiny glimmer. Moments later, his spotlight dazzled my eyes. Yes, a canoe, by golly. At two in the brittle morning. What sort of fool would venture out at this time of night, at this frigid time of year? Ask rather, at this intensive time of life?

CHAPMAN POND

There used to be an old abandoned house by Chapman Pond. This is a lovely, long, shallow pond, half a mile in length, which merges with a mile of tidal marshes. To the east of these is a wooded hillside; to the west a low, wooded island and then the river. The pond and the river confer by estuaries. The wet parts of the marsh are filled with cattail and wild rice; with pickerelweed, bulrush and yellow iris. The dry parts with viburnum; with wild rose and mallow. The island is a sandbar, and some silver maples there have grown so stout that you and I together couldn't reach around them.

I was fortunate to own a few acres on this island and had built myself a cabin there—a wildwood retreat for my wayward soul. The pond was my neighbor, the marshes my larder, the river my goddess and the island my shrine. And my nimble, swift canoe was my closest friend. Across the pond, the hemlock-clad hill rose slowly toward the local road, a quietude away. There still remained the vestige of an old woods road coming down to the pond and leading to the house at the water's edge. This was a small, two-story structure with a mortared stone foundation—a proper house half a century ago. Now it was empty, the windows smashed and graffiti of the biker clubs scrawled across the plaster. I'd explored the house. It was merely a shell; a tiny square dot on the town assessor's map.

But one day, one summer, as I paddled to the island from the ferry landing, I could see a column of dark, dirty smoke climbing up the clean air beyond the pond. No fire truck could navigate the unkempt woods road. The police came by boat, but there was nothing they could do except keep the blaze from spreading to the hemlocks using handheld sprayers. When it was over, nothing remained save a smoking foundation. And a crumpled gas can and a large melted ruin of stolen goods.

And the overdone remains of what had been a man. A lot of excitement for our little town. There was much speculation with few results. Nary a witness. Not a house about for half a mile in any direction—save mine, of course, and no one ever thought to ask me. And not having been aware of this business, my answers would have been to no avail. Had they asked me where the osprey made her nest, had they asked me where the trillium modestly blossomed, I might have answered. Had they asked me why the black snake watched my woodpile, why the phoebe perched upon my door, I might have responded. But what could I have told them about the world of Man?

The police brought out a launch that they towed with their patrol boat, piled it high with the stolen gear, and took it all away. They were no more than halfway across the pond when the launch capsized from overloading. The water, there, isn't more than up to your ears, so they managed to retrieve nearly everything. A good thing, too. For the carp has no need of any more distractions than he has already, the great blue heron no need of the sight of man-made rubbish as she glides above the pond to her cottonwood tree.

Finally, all of the men were departed, and the marsh and the pond were quiet again. Except for the four hundred red-winged blackbirds nesting 'mid the rushes—clucking and cackling and singing of the summer. Except for the kingfisher swooping down the estuary, chuckling to himself. Except for the splash of the snapping turtle dropping from her hole in the sandy bank. And the muted rumble of the oil tanker, laboring upriver; her plaintive horn calling for the old swing bridge to open.

In the evening I emerge with my nimble canoe and wander by the marshes. I listen to the squawk of the lovely night heron, watch the bats come wheeling across the pond, and hope that forever there will be some wilderness—even though men and their idiocy persist.

RUDY

Selden III

It was a squeeze fitting me, Brother John, his wife Marla, and all our gear into my thirteen-foot Grumman canoe. Not to mention Rudy. Rudy was their elkhound and was great in a canoe—except when he wanted to take a walk, which was only every five minutes. We'd put the canoe, and him, in the back of the truck; the three of us climbed up front.

The truck smelled comfortingly of lunch and dog and red oak stove wood and coffee. Brother John—who wasn't my brother—pushed aside his long hair and shifted gears.

"Yep. We're gonna catch us some trout today. I sorta got that feelin'."

We launched the canoe by the ferry slip while Rudy got the kinks out—after our two-mile drive—by galloping round and round the parking area. Brother John never bothered to lock his truck. Thirty years back, in a village small as ours, nobody ever locked up. Besides, Brother John's truck didn't have a driver's side window.

"Anyone steals my chain saw's got it comin'," said Brother John.

We paddled downriver about ten minutes, cut up the creek, and were soon amid the marshes. It's tidal there, and the trout don't like it much. We passed the deep hole where all you do is let down some bait to pull up a perch, a bullhead, or maybe a bass. It's a good spot to know if you need a few fish for supper.

Another half mile, the water ran clear and fresh—the bottom all sparkly gravel instead of mud. Here you catch nothing but brookies or maybe a perch. Wild brook trout are the Lord's own answer to flavor— there's nothing compares to a fresh one just out of the skillet.

I'd fished the stream out back of our barn as a kid and I'd had to think as a brook trout before I could catch one. There'd been too much brush to consider casting flies. Then it was strictly a boy and a worm and a trout. It wasn't much different, now.

We each baited up while Rudy, employing a tried scientific method, determined that even a dozen worms were more than enough for breakfast. Marla wasn't squeamish at all when she baited her hook. I was in love with Marla—and Brother John knew it. I never exceeded occasional brotherly hugs, so all of us got on well.

I had tried very hard to fall in love with her sister in upstate New York, and taken her paddling all the way down to the dam alongside the cheese works. The creek was slow without many riffles in it, and our sole concern had been down in the lower hundred, where two dozen heifers had capered into the shallow ford to greet us.

"It's all right," she'd assured me. "They just want to play a bit."

I'd felt the gravel grate against our bottom and envisioned two dozen Holsteins in my canoe.

"Paddle!" I'd urged, and we'd scooted among them and fled into deeper water.

Later, we'd nearly made love on a grassy bank, but thought better of it. Her dad would have chopped me for silage to feed the bull, who needed a high-protein diet for *his* line of work. Sometime, when the kids aren't around, I'll tell you all about *that* little canoe trip.

Now I watched Marla reel in a lovely trout and explain to Rudy how improved it would be by grilling and how much the hook would disagree with his nose. Rudy was one of those dogs who need convincing. Besides, he felt he was being much ignored.

He decided to take a little walk on the gunwale. A gigantic splash you could hear halfway to Christmas alerted us to the fact that the crew had jumped ship. We stowed our rods with a sigh. Rudy was hanging on to the gunwale and thrashing. Our rail dipped under and the creek poured in. Marla's appreciative trout applauded loudly.

We carefully paddled the few yards to shore, bailed the boat, and stood in the muck to hold the canoe so Rudy could bounce back in. He gratefully shook himself an inch from our faces and spoiled our single trout by treading on it.

But he fell out only once the whole way home.

WINTER AMUSEMENTS

Find yourself an ash or spruce pole about twelve feet in length. You can buy a length of closet pole or cut yourself a sapling and peel the bark. Dress one end with a rasp and pound on a metal ferrule. Voici—a punting pole.

"Now what?" you ask. "I don't own a punt."

A canoe is better. You *do* have a canoe? Good. If it hasn't a keel, you can punt in the shallow water about the marshes and scare the birds. But—if you happen to have an old flat-bottomed, aluminum canoe that has a long sharp keel—better still. You can punt across the ice— it'll track quite well.

Now give a good shove with your pole. If you find yourself lying on the ice, your legs waving gently in the breeze as your canoe skitters off, you've done it wrong. Flex your knees more. That's right. Over snowless ice, you zip quite quickly. With your weight distributed by the canoe, you need scarcely any ice to support yourself.

If you break through or come to open water, try not to tumble out. The water gets a mite chilly this time of year. If you do fall in and manage to drown yourself, don't come crying to *me* with your complaints.

After an afternoon scooting over the frozen salt marsh, drifting downstream on ice floes proves relaxing. Paddle back out to the river. Take aim at a heavy slab of drifting ice and paddle as hard as you can. If you're by yourself, sit in the stern. Your bow will be just high enough to ride up over the edge. Your canoe will want to roll as it runs up onto the ice. Try your best to discourage it. Swimming season doesn't begin for a month.

Now you're ensconced on your own little floating island. If it's large enough, you can venture out and explore. If not, relax—drape yourself over the thwarts, lean back, and contemplate Time and the River. An ice floe on a brisk winter day needs a true connoisseur to praise it. Lord knows that we northerners need to get our money's worth out of winter.

Remember to lash a spare paddle between the thwarts and carry a dry sack with plenty of extra clothing. If you haven't drowned by suppertime, you may want a change of socks. By nightfall, perhaps, you'll have cooled off.

Not cold enough, yet? Then treat yourself to an evening paddle by moonlight. You can find some open water in the channel. When it gets below zero Fahrenheit, the ice tends to form on your blade with every stroke. Think of the advantage: a heavier paddle develops your shoulder muscles. Come spring you'll be in better shape than all your canoeing friends.

This open water seems just a trifle crunchy. You should have brought a Coleman lantern to keep yourself from freezing. It could also serve as a steaming light to alert this oil tanker plunging downriver right at you. Her great steel prow comes crashing through the ice. And her skipper does *not* expect a canoeist this January evening.

Move that little boat, buddy! You frantically shove apart ice floes with your paddle. The tanker rumbles past you into the night. Maybe *now* you've had enough of nature. Hopefully, that big pot of soup simmers on the back of the wood range; maybe a loaf of hot bread has just come from the oven.

That's right, lad—keep dreaming. The last thirty yards to the island consist of huge shards of ice broken up by the tide—some of them on edge. As you stumble through them, dragging your canoe, you pause to look down and watch that icy water pour into your shoe. Fortunately, you no longer have the ability to appreciate such amusements: Everything below your knees belongs to somebody else.

Thank goodness your cabin lies just beyond those trees. Time to sit on the wood range and wrap yourself around a hot mug of supper. It would be fun to feel your fingers again. Just hang your wet wool socks from the warming oven—they'll impart a quite redolent odor throughout the cabin.

And no, she *doesn't* want to feel how cold your flippers have gotten from playing walrus, thank you. *She's* been tucked in with a good book since you departed.

GIRAFFE

The three of us left Mike's landing with our usual expedition—something of an accomplishment with a toddler. We loaded the canoe and set off for the island.

From Mike's cottage to ours is less than a mile down the slow side of the river—a backwater behind two other islands—the muddy banks strewn with cottonwood and silver maple snags. Birds predominate: statuesque cormorants, quiet black ducks, stately great blue herons; flitting catbirds, hovering ospreys, chattering red-winged blackbirds.

In the midst of all this stood our cottage: an octagon framed with chestnut from an old barn we'd demolished; sided—board and batten—with western red cedar. Twenty-four feet across the flats, it had a steep roof with a cupola and dormers. The building stood four feet up on concrete posts.

And everything we brought by boat. All the wood we worked by hand. Yes, I was mad in those days and a poet. We stayed in the woods a couple of days at a time, commuted home via canoe—or sometimes raft—and raised our son to become a water rat. He now has his lair near the riverbank and runs a halfway house for wayward canoes.

The morning I have in mind, we slid downstream—the three of us and Giraffe. 'Raffe was made of rubber and squeaked and stood about six inches short. He'd become a consummate waterman that summer, and knew the river as well as any giraffe *I've* ever met.

One can never learn respect for the river too early—even an old, slow river such as ours. There's a bit of tide, just over two feet, on our stretch, but the current runs less than a knot and the tide can shove it all the way back to Hartford. The shad go up as far as the Enfield dam—I suppose for the view.

When the tide ebbs, you can get to our place from Mike's, upstream, in maybe twenty minutes. When the wind comes ripping down the river in autumn, fighting back upstream when the tide ebbs becomes a challenge: You paddle and paddle and watch as the leaves change from green to gold and gradually drop from the trees. On these days we chose to surf downstream to the ferry landing and walk up the hill to home. None of this has much to do with Giraffe.

Halfway down to the island, Giraffe took a notion to jump into the river. Why an otherwise stable creature would do such a thing I've pondered for many years. As I paddled stern that day, I fished him out and returned him to my son.

"Really, Giraffe—you ought to be more careful," I admonished.

A minute later, over the side he went. And we thought Giraffe could be trusted. I grabbed him by his ear and gave him a lecture. You've probably heard it once or twice if you've messed about in boats. All about the inadvisability of being left behind. My son regarded this little speech with the mischievous impunity of toddlers. No sooner had he regained Giraffe than he gave him a diving lesson.

This time, after I fished him out, I took a more stern approach.

"What goes over the side hazards incontrovertible, irretrievable abandonment," I reproached him.

One can always impress a giraffe with polysyllabism. I restored him to my son a final time. He cocked his arm with a grin.

"Three to get ready and four to go," I sighed. And Giraffe, despite my warnings, flung himself into the tide as his grand finale.

"Goodbye, Giraffe," I said and waved farewell.

"'Raffe!" cried my son.

"Goodbye," I repeated. "Give my regards to Europe."

"'Raffe!" cried my son, and watched as his erstwhile friend deserted us—gaily kicking his little legs as he struck out for the channel. Today the river—tomorrow the broad Atlantic!

It was quiet the remainder of our passage. But since that day, I've never had another giraffe jump out of my canoe.

HAMBURG COVE

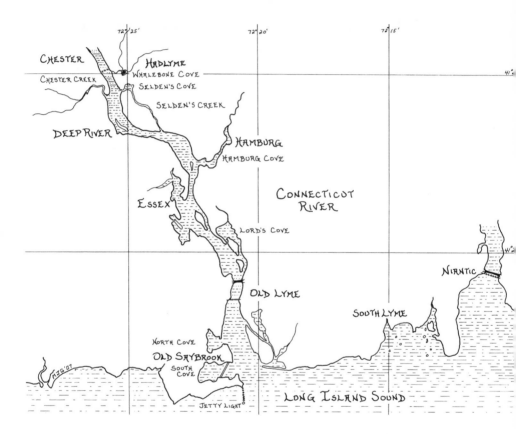

Hamburg Cove is a sheltered, secluded, and quite unspoiled place. I probably shouldn't even tell you where to find it. I live in the next village over—a pleasant six-mile walk on a winding road through the woods. On the west side of the road, long stately drives lead downhill toward the water, where massive houses look out over the river. There—that's all the hint I'm giving you.

Toward the end of the road, you emerge from the trees onto a breezy hillside cleared for dairy farming, and the most magnificent view of Hamburg Cove. By the head of the cove nestles a village with a Congregational church (what other denomination would you need?), the grange hall with its tiny fairground, and a humble, two-bay firehouse. A local family owns the cobblestone garage (your local Rover dealership) and the deep-water marina. From the little pier for transients and offloading, a short walk uphill leads to the family's store.

This store has been presided over by a local matron since I first toddled up to the candy counter. Her store contains dollhouses as well as comestibles, and in the corner you'll find a few cartons of old, unreadable books. The scarred pine counter is long and deep and crowded with glass canisters. The lazy overhead fan creaks at every rotation. The wide pine floorboards creak response underfoot. You can buy a ball of string or a head of lettuce or penny candy or a tinted postcard depicting the local farmers getting in hay.

Outside the store stands a pair of gas pumps. When I was a lad, you needed to crank the handle and pump the gas yourself. The new pumps run off electricity, but if you expect *Her* to come out and tend to your buggy, think again. You want service like *that*, you'd best go across the way to The Landing and honk your horn for Jimmy.

The Landing resembles the general store about as much as a horse resembles a hay rake. It caters to those people who like their comforts. It employs four people full time—more on weekends—and boasts a butcher shop, a liquor store (with a separate entrance, of course) and the tiny post office. You can purchase the *Wall Street Journal*, the *New York Times*, and little tins of caviar and pâté. On weekends the smell of hot scones and bread embraces you at the door. Sunday mornings, the cars are so thick in the parking lot that you can't get near the gas pumps.

Down the hill behind the two stores the small marina bustles. The mechanic rebeds a stanchion on a Bristol 29 alongside the pier.

A white-haired man applies an eighth coat of varnish to his dinghy. The boatyard dog employs himself by keeping a folded sail as flat as possible.

The water knows better than to cause a ripple that might disturb the few dozen elegant boats asleep on their moorings. The type of boater who makes a wake or has loud engines never seems able to find this cove on his chart. You aren't encouraged to raise your voice hereabouts: even a normal conversation carries across the water.

My Grumman canoe meanders the cove accompanied by swallows. I have friends who rent a cabin atop the hill behind the farm, accessible (with four wheel drive) by half a mile of rutted tractor road, or by the water. Of course, once you tie your canoe to the elder bushes, you have to climb a steep footpath with your groceries, but when did a bit of heavy breathing ever hurt anybody? Another friend keeps his thirty-foot twin-hull houseboat in the cove. Being poor, he can't afford to moor at the marina, but arranges to anchor off the meadow just where the brook spreads out to join the cove: a lovely, secluded, idyllic spot where the grassy track peters out beyond the barns.

The mile-long channel from the cove out to the river alternately spreads and constricts between the wooded hill to the north and the low shore to the south. Here occasional reclusive homes and a summer camp shelter amid the maples. You would never notice the camp but for a boathouse overflowing with brightly colored canoes. Where you enter the river, a wooded island is hove to just offshore. On it stands a compact, half-timbered house. They sledded the building materials out to this island over the ice with oxen. But that was back before the glacier receded. Things have changed. When Hamburg Cove appeared as I've described it, my truck had running boards.

THE ONE THAT GOT AWAY

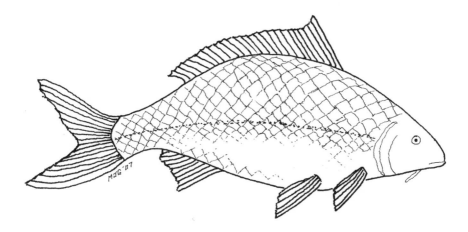

Think of fishing in reverse. Think about a large fish catching some-one—maybe me—for breakfast. Of course, I would have fed him the young lady first. Beauty before age, my dear.

We were fishing from my canoe in Whalebone Cove. It's a lovely small tidal marsh with deep estuaries, but not brackish enough to discourage freshwater fish. We'd anchored by the deep hole where the two largest streams converge.

I'd brought my spinning rod equipped with eight-pound monofil-ament, a can of lively nightcrawlers, and the young lady. I haven't necessarily listed these in order of importance. Without the night-crawlers, this story would have been different, and you'd need to hide this book under your mattress.

We had my little Grumman canoe. The distinctive dent in the bow came from that time she leapt off Wally's truck as we drove back to the barn. The wind got underneath her and there she went—doing a spectacular flip off his '56 Ford. We had tucked the stern inside the tailgate, rested the gunwales on top of the cab, and run two short pendants from the forward thwart inside, pinched in the rolled-up windows. It might have worked had we used longer lines and knotted them together. Hindsight is fine—until you pull up your pants.

The little canoe bounced once in the road and settled amid the chicory flowers along the verge to ponder her new career in modern dance. Had anyone been driving right behind us, this episode would have merited a full page.

This afternoon, we practiced a bit of alchemy: attempting to convert the bait into supper. It isn't especially difficult: Even a minnow can do it. I never bothered with floats or sinkers. The way I look at it, when a worm falls into the river, he starts at the surface and ends his life at the bottom—presuming he makes it that far.

I didn't care if I caught a bass or merely an ugly bullhead. If all else failed, we could always eat rice and beans. We enjoyed messing about in the boat; the fish enjoyed messing about in the river. Occasionally, we swapped roles. Often the fish lucked out and absconded with the bait. If you caught a fish with every cast, you couldn't stay out on the river as long. No point in that. Down and down went nightcrawler number four.

No one seemed the least interested. I let him lie on the bottom while I finished my peppermint tea. Suddenly I felt something down there—fooling about with my bait. I waited a moment, then I set the hook. Snagged, by golly. Must be a sunken log. Oh, well. I could cut the line or pull until it broke.

Suddenly the log began to move. Good, I thought—I've yanked a chunk of sodden wood from the bottom, and now it wants to travel with the tide. I attempted to reel it in. The rod bent double. Then the clutch slipped; the line began to leave the reel—there was something alive down there! Something quite large. I increased my drag. This fish was not impressed. He stopped, he started, he stripped off most of my line.

The young lady weighed our anchor. This behemoth towed us toward the river—against the incoming tide. As he hadn't any plans for the afternoon we excursed at leisure. For a while, I thought it might be a snapping turtle, but a snapper would have bitten through the line.

For twenty minutes I played a losing game of tug-of-war. He towed us half the length of Whalebone Creek. He never came up from the bottom. Sometimes I paddled over him and bent my rod as far as I dared in vain attempts to raise him. Eventually, he took a round turn on that cottonwood snag down at the bend—you know where I mean—and went about his business.

We have some good-sized carp in the Connecticut—a friend of mine hoisted out a forty-pounder. Infrequently, someone catches a sturgeon. One got tangled in Uncle Joe's shad net back when I was a boy. They run to hundreds of pounds. Who knows what monsters lurk at the bottoms of rivers? Makes you think twice about dangling your toes over the side of your boat.

With heavier line, I could have forced him up and made his acquaintance. Then again, he might have decided to add canoe to his menu. I tell everyone I was glad to be the one that got away.

That isn't true. Had I landed him, I could have stretched this story out and filled another page.

A THREE-DAY PADDLE

I dropped my canoe into the Connecticut River at Hadley—nearly ninety miles above Long Island Sound. I carried a minimum of gear and a maximum of fresh, home-roasted granola (my personal recipe) and a spare paddle. There's quite a large dam at Holyoke, a few miles downstream, and a low, abandoned dam at Enfield, Connecticut. Aside from that, just slow dreamy river and the joy of escaping modernity for a few days.

Not having anything as prissy as a canoeing guide in my possession, I kept to the west bank coming into Holyoke. The undeveloped east bank had the portage trail—but little things such as that never bothered me.

I hauled out at a tiny park in the city and carried my canoe down a long flight of stairs, along a street, and stashed it in some bushes by the river. Then I retrieved the rest of my gear. So what if some people gawked? Wouldn't be the last time. As a professional water rat, one gets used to folk staring and grinning and shaking their foolish heads in disbelief. My advice? Tuck your tail into your trousers and no one will ever know your derivations.

The first night I spent on an island. I don't know who belongs to these islands up and down the river. Most of my life, I owned a few acres on one of them. I try to stay inconspicuous wherever I make camp—build the least fire possible and clean up after myself.

I didn't carry a tent. When it rained, I inverted my canoe, wrapped a ground cloth around it, and pegged the corners. Or strung a line between two trees and improvised a shelter. You know the drill. As long as you carry something to ward off mosquitoes. I've found that an AK-47 works well—except up in Maine where they breed them especially large to discourage tourists.

The second day, I approached the Enfield dam. I considered running the sluiceway—with a kayak I might have attempted it. My little canoe would have plunged underwater and taken me down with her. Adventure is one thing—suicide another. I portaged down the steep bank.

Connecticut remained rural along that stretch of river. A mile away, shopping malls pandered to highway traffic. My third morning, I shoved off early and found myself gliding between wooded shores, ten or fifteen miles north of Hartford. Quiet, pristine; birds in the trees, fish in the river, "God's in his Heaven, all's right with the world." (How often does one get a chance to quote Robert Browning?) By ten o'clock the back of my throat made sure it was July.

Along the west bank lay a narrow hard mud beach—a good place to disembark and stretch my legs. And what did I see? A six-pack of beer with four full bottles in it. Who would have left four bottles of beer behind? How could they know I'd come by to see that they didn't go to waste? They were warm—extremely warm—but extremely wet. Halfway through the third bottle, I entertained doubts. Warm beer on an empty stomach wouldn't appeal to me now. Thirty years ago, almost anything went. I'm glad it's gone.

The next ten miles I floated down the river. So did my little canoe. I presume we made contact at least a part of the way. I arrived in Hartford just in time to collapse. Across the river from the high-rise financial district, a park appeared. I hauled my canoe beneath the welcoming shade of a silver maple. I had paddled fifteen miles; the high sun dazzled; the plate-glass towers danced with one another.

After I stuffed myself with bread and cheese, I looked at beer number four and decided on water. Then I stretched out to rest. I never heard the eight-lane traffic, three hundred yards away. But after a while, something—or maybe someone—kept nudging my foot. My eyes, with a bit of effort, came unglued. A policeman, size double extra large, towered above me.

"And would ye be feelin' aw right, me lad?" he enquired solicitously.

THE OLD HAYING GROUNDS

Having collected eight watertight steel drums, I purchased some carriage bolts and proceeded to build a small raft. It sufficed to carry a pickup truck load of lumber. We had begun to build an octagonal cottage on an island, and needed to transport the lumber the final mile.

Back when Grandpa was a lad, he could have driven his team across the ice—the glacier hadn't totally receded from Connecticut in those far-off times. Nowadays, with global toasting, the woolly mammoth seldom emerges before Christmas.

I decided instead to build a raft of rough-cut rafters from an old barn I had dismantled. I ran them once through the rip saw and bolted them together. Not everyone in my neighborhood, population three hundred, could boast a raft made entirely of chestnut.

I constructed an X-shaped frame between two uprights, aft, in which to lay the steering oar, which would double as a punt pole. My deck consisted of the thwartways stringers necessary to hold the drums in place; after all, I would stack the raft knee-deep with lumber during the downstream passage.

Rafting on the river requires waiting on the tide, and hoping the wind will blow in the right direction. Most of that year we lived our lives according to the sun and wind and tide. We couldn't bother even to wind our sundial.

When anyone asked what time we'd return on the morrow, we'd think of the river, its ebb and flow, and answer, "Well, maybe about midafternoon—if the wind is out of the south."

We lived pristinely, with the scantest of commitment to civilization. On the island, we rose with the sun, worked until it became too hot, bathed in the river, ate our lunch on its banks, and napped in the shade of the huge silver maple to which we made fast the raft. Occasionally, a boat would come by, and we'd have to scamper about to find our clothes.

We hadn't a pier at the island—the only place deep enough to moor the raft against the bank was on my neighbor's land. We merely tied up to the maple tree and passed the boards ashore. Then we carried them on our shoulders the last hundred yards to our clearing. At that time the wheel had not yet been invented.

Neither had cellular phones. Nor had we a radio: Neither the Beatles nor Tchaikovsky ever dresses appropriately for the wild. Our music was the soughing of the breeze among the cottonwoods; the phoebe calling to her mate from the spicebush by our door; the long-drawn note of the oil tanker, requesting the steel swing bridge to open, up at Goodspeed's Landing.

In the evenings, we lit our Coleman lantern and scribbled or sketched in our journals. During fair weather, we cooked on an open fire. We wrapped potatoes and onions in foil and set them among the coals. We foraged for wild salad. Occasionally, we invited a fish to supper. A simple life, as idyllic as anything found between two covers.

Sometimes we waxed domestic, and shooed the voracious deer from our vegetable garden. For diversion we took our little canoe and went foraging in the salt-marsh pond that spreads behind the island. Above us, the osprey poised in the sultry sky to study the water and, from the reeds, the blackbird practiced his ancient, ancient air. Otherwise, it verged upon the serene.

In June we picked cattail flowers that we mixed with egg and fried on the iron skillet. At Solstice we invited some friends—they had canoes, of course—and built a quiet fire out on the sandbar. We feasted on fish and cattail cakes and homemade dandelion wine. We danced on the sand and toasted the longest day of the year, and toasted the constellations.

Later, we drifted upon the silent, moonlit river in our canoe, and noted the lights in darkened houses along the farther shore: the flickering lights of television—bringing a facile reality into people's jaded lives.

THE SWANS

Here is your world—see to it when you can. It spills over with miracles—with death, with life, with loss, with parturition. Even now, in constrictive winter, one can find the latent bud on the maple.

I canoe amid the ice floes on the river. I ply my paddle judiciously —a jagged slab of floating ice can tip me into eternity; my coat and boots will drag me to the bottom.

This world is my curriculum. If I study hard, I may earn, at last, a degree of immortality. Here the sun, the river, the wind, range about me, displaying their various tempers and proclivities. Today the chill breeze gathers her robes about her, stalks to the sea. Tomorrow the predaceous gale will seize the river in his roaring jaws and shake it from its bed. On such a day, to test one's mettle is merely to play with Death. I, myself, prefer to play with Life. I shall sit by the fire in my cabin and keep my journal.

The breeze descends the river from the north. The tide shoves its imperious way upriver. Wall-sized shards of snowy ice surge steadily to the sea. I slowly, patiently, work upstream to the island. The frigid water ripples by my hull. Whom does moving water not transfix? I remain as entranced as the native in N. C. Wyeth's portrait *The Crystal Depths,* who drifts alone in his birch canoe, scrutinizing those depths, his journey forgotten. Wyeth's lordly, rich-hued hills shout loudly.

Today if I drift I regress. This afternoon I contemplate opaque depths: This river so many flashes of charcoal and pewter. These muted hills recline. The silvery limbs of the white oak implore the heavens. The risqué gust lifts the green skirt of the hemlock to reveal her pale petticoats. A pair of black ducks arises from amid the tawny rushes. The smolder of the wintry sun smokes the quilted sky. I go in beauty.

Cycles both broad and brief amaze me. I anticipate no explanation of many. Why should I care when the river compels me, the sea commands my respect? The moss-rimmed pool in the forest shows me a vital world in miniature. It has no need to compete with the Mediterranean. You cannot find a body of water more mediterranean.

My sojourn, though brief as ten and threescore summers, assures me perception. All about, the world flaunts transition. Nothing remains the same; yet all remains. The blackbird sings but a handful of seasons; always will blackbirds trill amid the cattails. When Man has had his way with this Earth and Earth, in turn, has had her way with Man, blackbirds will return to sing of summer.

I steer my canoe through the estuary that leads to Chapmans Pond. The water runs quickly, here. I'm wary of a clutching snag and lean into my paddle to avoid it. The time for words, enunciation, comes later. This snag is now and real and lethal. Once a cottonwood leaning to her reflection in the river, now she leans to shelter the torpid carp. Now this snag can seize a dreamful waterman and feed him to that carp.

The estuary opens into the shallow, ice-clogged pond and the frozen marshes. No sign of progress accosts me. Beneath the hill, by the far shore, a lone foundation crumbles. Come summer, rambling rose will bring it beauty it never knew when it raised its unsightly ruin.

The sky, the marsh, the pond: All reach to embrace me. As I embrace them. One day I shall return to be a part of each, of all. All about, this avid world is, and was, and becomes.

From the pond two swans arise, susurrant and swishing. I hark to how their wingsong lingers as I listen. On the wind their wingsong lingers as I listen . . .

Sailing

BOATS I HAVE KNOWN

BLOCK ISLAND

Block Island lies about ten miles off the sandy Rhode Island shore. It is pear-shaped about its north–south axis, about three miles broad at the south end and maybe six miles long. The southern end rises to sandy bluffs—about a hundred sixty feet above the resounding surf. The view is superb; on a clear day, one can just glimpse Bermuda.

A dozen years back, they moved the stately brick lighthouse and adjoining residence back from the brink of the precipice the Atlantic had undermined.

The narrower northern end of the island also has a lighthouse, but here the sands accrete. The lowlands at the waist of the island surround a sheltered harbor a mile in diameter: Great Salt Pond.

Old Harbor is opposite, on the eastern shore. A pair of breakwaters provides the only resistance to the ocean. A few fishing boats and the larger ferries from Point Judith dock there. Passenger ferries from New London dock in Great Salt Pond. Nearly everything comes via ferry, including thousands of tourists.

Perhaps eight hundred people winter over—many of them wealthy retirees. The farming and fishing folk who settled here in colonial times have all but disappeared. Pleasure craft cram the pond all summer. Taverns and restaurants, hotels and boutiques do a thriving business four months out of the year. Restaurant prices are hardly higher than on the mainland; everything else costs half again as much, for goods and services need to be ferried over.

Great Salt Pond is a happening unto itself. It boasts a nine-foot channel and deeper basin providing anchorage, moorings, and slips for hundreds of vessels. The harbormaster and two private launches stay busy all day long. An entrepreneur selling fresh-baked goods from a bumboat wends the haven, singing out his wares in Portuguese.

The road from the village, lined with restaurants, continues onto the pier, where one can also buy bait or blocks of ice or rent a bicycle. The permanent tavern on the pier provides an elliptical bar set up alfresco during the summer. Two bronzed and bearded fellows offload cases of beer from a pickup truck. Just next door, outside a little café, the grilling of fresh sea bass steaks requires close supervision by several dogs and children.

At the next pier over—a quarter mile downwind—the pump-out station deals with sea bass steaks from the previous week. The Coast

Guard cutter that plies Block Island Sound strictly enforces dumping regulations. We passed her as we sailed in on *MoonWind*. She cut across our bows at half a mile, cruised to the southern end of the island, then turned and steamed right at us. I expected to be boarded to have our plumbing inspected—a not unknown occurrence in these waters—but on she went in search of more fulsome prey.

We rounded the bell at the harbor mouth by six o'clock, dropped our sails, and chugged about the basin. We found a suitable anchorage near the shallower, northern shore—far from the ceaseless bustle of the marina. There were eight feet of lucid water, a firm bottom, and room to swing. On a Wednesday night the pond has ample space.

We drew our Whitehall pulling boat alongside and tumbled into her. Off to explore and find a bit of grub. After a leisurely fifteen minutes admiring good old boats, I backed water alongside the fueling pier. On either hand, in numerous slips, people sipped Martinis in their cockpits. I backed the Whitehall up to a cabin cruiser.

"Where can I beach my boat?" I inquired.

"Over there," grunted a portly, red-faced gentleman, pointing with a three-quarter-empty bottle. "Just drive around behind these piers. There's a little basin there with a sandy beach."

"Drive?" I asked, as I leaned on my oars. "Drive what?"

"Just drive your boat around these piers," he repeated. He enunciated slowly, as you tend to do when speaking to someone simple.

"All right," I replied. "Thanks for your help. Good evening." And, spreading my glistening, slim spruce oars, I proceeded to "drive" away. A quarter mile later found us thirty yards from his boat—but across the road. The sun was low and the sky was red as we eased the Whitehall up on the sand above high water and went in search of supper.

FALLING IN LOVE

My earliest recollection of boating concerns dining aboard a wooden sloop moored in the Connecticut River, probably at Essex.

My father was engaged at the time in building fishnet machines and manufacturing netting. Nylon had made its debut during World War II and now replaced cotton in every field imaginable. Though stronger than cotton and totally rot-resistant, certain knots tied in nylon tended to slip.

My father modified fishnet machines to tie a different knot. The government granted him a patent. He already owned a machine shop to build textile machinery. He teamed up with a local net and twine mill, and they pioneered the nylon fishnet business. Of course, someone discovered that the patent hadn't validity in Japan. They shipped nylon to Japan, made it into net, and returned it at ruinous prices. My father cut some of his losses: He brought away three fishnet machines that he set up in our barn.

The entire rack of shuttles followed a cam in order that the loop formed from the previous knot pass about the bobbin. This movable rack of shuttles, eight or ten feet long, completed its machinations with a crash.

Up and over and through and back to the bottom—Crash! And again. And then again. At every cycle, the beam jerked another long row of knots from the loom. Gill nets for shad, shrimp nets, seines, and drag nets; yards and yards of netting.

One of the mill owner's middle-aged sons had a boat. It was certainly a sloop, probably thirty-five feet or more, for it had what seemed to me a commodious cabin—the grown-ups could all stand up, and six of us managed to squeeze around the table. I remember all the brightwork. It was a wooden boat, of course. In the early fifties, builders had just begun experimenting with fiberglass.

My father, though adventurous, was never a river rat. He spent four years in the navy during the war and served aboard ships both in the Caribbean and the Pacific. He progressed from engineering officer to navigator to executive officer, often serving in more than one capacity. At the close of the war, he served as executive officer on the *Patrick,* a troop transport. That ship made three round trips from San Francisco to Calcutta. He logged more miles aboard in one year than I shall ever log my entire life.

But he never slogged barefoot in the river; never waded in the surf; never fooled about in little boats. My mother would never, willingly, get her feet wet, although she was nimble enough before her accident. It amazes me, in retrospect, that my parents spent several days aboard a large chartered schooner—as passengers—just after they married. But both of them had entered sedate middle age by the time I came along.

My father encouraged me to have boats, but never had any interest in joining me on one. His idea of a pleasure cruise entailed a ship hundreds of feet in length with hundreds of sailors ready to his will. I grew up with naval terminology ringing in my ears.

In the morning he roared, "Lay below."

He always cooked us marvelous hot breakfasts.

At night he ordered, "Pipe down!" and "Hit the sack!"

Then he would climb "the ladder" and tell me sea stories. Stories of running high-octane aircraft fuel among the islands in the Caribbean late at night, skippered by an ex-rum-runner who knew every shoal passage from San Juan to Port-of-Spain. Their fuel was so explosive that they didn't carry lifeboats.

Stories of being in Halsey's Seventh Fleet in the Pacific. Being on an auxiliary, he never engaged in action, but he told me of the typhoon that broadcast havoc among the fleet. At one hundred thirty-five knots, the wind tore their anemometer from the mast. They were on their beam-ends half the night. Making his way across the boat deck from the bridge, he nearly perished beneath the waves. This was on the *Cebu,* a repair ship, four hundred forty feet in length. The boat deck was probably twenty-five feet above the waterline.

Stories of steel warships notwithstanding, I fell in love with this varnished sailing boat. I must have been about four years old: a sprat, a minnow, a young salt; wet behind the ears, but not wet enough. This was my first experience on any boat whatsoever. From there I regressed to rafts and rowboats, canoes and sailing dinghies. Now I have a sailboat of my own. My smaller boats have achieved some sophistication.

At nearly three score, I seldom pick seaweed from between my toes or dump sand from my cuffs. Yet, as ever, I find myself drifting and dreaming, though my weather eye now watches a far horizon.

PETITE CHOSE

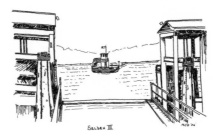

SELDEN III

From the time I became a teenager until I bought an old Rhodes 18 a few years later, I used to sail my plywood pram, *Petite Chose*, up and down the lower Connecticut River. If I didn't plan properly for the tide, or if the wind abated, the Powers at home expected me to, somehow, contact them.

Cellular phones waited to be invented; phone booths grew miles apart. Mostly, I just tacked among the powerboats and barges, and hoped that I wouldn't lose too much way when I needed to come about. Occasionally, I made it home for supper.

I also took sailing lessons over in Essex, and sometimes motored my little boat to those. Taking my motor when rigged for sailing seemed superfluous; perhaps I was a purist even then. But I always remembered to carry a pair of oars. Sometimes they proved as significant as my lunch.

I recollect a day that I sailed to Essex. It blew a bit—whitecaps roughened the river—but, after all, it was only four miles each way. I had a bailer—a bleach bottle with the bottom cut off—and I wore my life jacket for a change, instead of sitting on it. What could go wrong?

I'd stepped my wooden mast through the thwart and stayed it in every direction. But I hadn't any reef points. Consequently, with that much wind, I either surfed or dipped my rail and hung on for dear life. I couldn't have asked for better.

I arrived at sailing school in record time, and saw all the Bluejays straining at their moorings. The committee boat plunged at the pier and, on the veranda of the clubhouse, two dozen children, glum with disappointment, waited for their parents to retrieve them; sailing class had been canceled. Just because of some frivolous little whitecaps.

Chortling, I wended among the bobbing fleet, zipped inshore as close as I dared, waved my superior hand to everyone there, and managed to come about without quite capsizing. Pride prevented my bailing my pram until I was out of sight.

On my way home, the wind commenced to whistle. Opposite Selden Creek, the channel spreads out the entire width of the river. An oil tanker bore down on me with no intention whatever of changing her course. Arrogant boys in sailing dinghies do *not* have the right of way. Even I knew this. As I headed away, a gust knocked me down; I heard my weather shroud part. The mast snapped like a stick.

In a trice, my pram became a tangle of sail, spars, and rigging. I lurched about with no control whatsoever. The tanker, running downriver empty, had plenty of windage problems of her own, but yawed a bit and cleared me by twenty yards. Shaken and tossed, I managed to secure my rig, and lashed it to the thwarts.

Out with the oars, mate; pull for yonder harbor.

Yonder harbor proved a private basin designed for an eighty-foot cruiser—presently at large in search of amusement. Enclosed by a wall of massive planks, the basin boasted a hundred-foot pier that stood about six feet high: the perfect accommodation for my yacht. I found a ladder, made fast, and scrambled ashore. Just ahead stood a lovely, six-room granite house—the caretaker's cottage. No one answered my knock.

I climbed the hill and came to the manse itself: a twenty-room granite Federal commanding a mile of river. A gray-haired lady came to the door—a lady of elegant bearing, exquisitely groomed. She eyed my ragged cutoff jeans and wet bare feet before she deigned to usher my wild self in. She graciously allowed me to call my father.

Then we sat in the library—a little room with about ten thousand volumes—and waited for my parent to come and claim me. The lady scarcely spoke a word; she never left the room. It was obvious that the likes of me should not be trusted with anything near so precious as a book.

THE JET 14

Fortunately, I attended "the School by the Sea" for those four tumultuous years preceding college. Rather than bore you with chemistry class and hormones, I'll tell you about the sailing fleet at the school.

In addition to a ninety-foot schooner, they had close to forty boats of diminutive size. The school owned Cottontails, Puffins and Silver Terns, Mercurys and Woodpussies. And they had just purchased three new Jet 14s—planing boats that scarcely kissed the water during their flight. Built of brightwork battens laid on a bias, they were light and sleek and strong and extremely swift.

They hadn't coaming but only a hand-span width of decking to sit on. This decking was invaluable when you heeled; your lee rail could submerge several inches without a cupful coming into the boat. The centerboard trunk ran most of the length of the narrow cockpit and housed a formidable steel plate. The genoa was a "sweeper" and had a window in it. On a close reach you could keep up with an airplane.

Thankfully, the hefty hiking straps allowed the crew to drag their ears in the drink. An ample hinged extension to the tiller allowed the skipper to steer from underwater.

The day I remember best, the breeze tore ragged holes in the harbor. The launch driver—one of the masters—cautioned us as he dropped us off at our moorings. I gladly crewed for Jim. A senior on the sailing team, he had confidence and experience. Off we went and, immediately, got our boat on a plane.

We skimmed the whitecaps out to the point, where the small-craft warning crackled at the yacht club. But no one ever paid attention to that—every year it stayed up the entire season. Today it had valid reason to be aloft. Outside the harbor, in Buzzards Bay, the breakers piled up. We wisely made the decision to stay inside. Here we had a basin a mile across—and more than plenty of weather to learn our limits.

Sure enough, we looked astern and saw that one of the other 14s had gone over. The launch came charging out from the pier to help. The wind picked up; our sails ran with spindrift. The foot of our low-cut genoa dragged in the water; the chilly spray ran down inside our shirts.

Towing the swamped boat, the launch crossed ahead of us. The two boys huddled, shivering, in her cockpit.

"Sailing has been canceled this afternoon!" the master bellowed.

"What's that, sir?" we hollered politely and, porpoise-like, leapt the next wave and sped away.

The master picked up his megaphone, but the wind stuffed all his argument down his throat. He should have been pleased: only our two boats remained at large.

"Head for the outer harbor," I suggested.

There we reveled for thirty minutes before the launch completed her work and returned to harass us. The wind neared twenty knots. I played the genoa carefully as we teetered on our beam-end. Hiked far out, I could see a few inches of centerboard clear of the water.

When we came about, we could see the second 14 heeled far over; too far over. Water poured into her cockpit; her mast dug into the sea. The two boys stood on the centerboard to right her, only to have her continually knocked down. The launch came pounding through the swells to her rescue.

The wind screamed; our rail was buried six inches but our boat stayed dry. Life grew glorious—there went my favorite hat. We flew to the mouth of the harbor and circled the schooner, lifting and plunging massively at her mooring.

The launch returned to pursue us, driving through the choppy seas at her uttermost twelve knots. She could nearly keep up with us. The master gesticulated and bared his teeth. Being upwind deprived us of his lavish commendations. We settled onto a broad reach, our hull half out of the water. Our rooster tail diffused the rays of the avid sun and flung a rainbow about us. We fled in regal splendor.

IN NEED OF A BREEZE

JETTY LIGHT
OLD SAYBROOK
CONNECTICUT

When I was young and quite, quite mad, I took my carvel-planked Rhodes 18 from Deep River to South Lyme. Merely fifteen miles. You cruise down the lovely Connecticut River the last few miles to Long Island Sound, go out past the lighthouse at Lynde Neck, and follow the channel beside the impressive breakwater down to the second lighthouse—the Jetty Light. Thence you head east, (did I mention I hadn't a compass?) avoiding Long Sand Shoal, and follow the shore until you round Hatchett Point. A few fierce rocks in a mile-wide bay designate this the harbor. You anchor wherever seems likely and take your chances.

Everything went swimmingly from the start. I had the tide behind me as I departed. I hauled up my main, and the halyard jammed in the sheave. But the sail had ascended eleven-twelfths of the track, so I made up most of the difference employing the downhaul. Up with the jib, off with the mooring pendant, and away!

Ah, freedom! I was eighteen, invincible, and also perfectly stupid. My first mistake was leaving so late in the day. How long can it take to sail fifteen miles? It wouldn't get dark till nearly eight o'clock. (Did I mention I hadn't a light?) Toward the mouth of the river, the wind turned fluky. My main remained as shapely as a watermelon in a hammock. I headed up and slacked the halyard; yanked on the luff and the main descended a yard. Then I tried to haul it back up.

Wake up, son—you might just want to undo that downhaul first. This time, it jammed immediately: The halyard had jumped the sheave. Sometime, I admonished my clever self, you need to reeve the next-size-larger line. Now I had more slack than I could possibly take up with just the downhaul. Without a reef point in sight, I decided on the alternative: simply—to climb the mast. I had all the requirements: two hands and two feet. The climbing didn't prove difficult, but the boat heeled over, then heeled over some more, and, just as I passed the spreaders, began to welcome the river in over the rail.

So much for that idea. North of the railroad bridge, against the Old Lyme shore, a gas dock juts into the river. Out at the end of it stands a little shack. By this time—half past six—business was done for the day. I moored alongside, climbed the pier, and managed to clamber up to the roof of the shack. With me I had brought the recalcitrant halyard.

Now I balanced twenty feet off the water. I pulled on the halyard, and the boat rolled toward me until I could grasp the mast. What could be more simple? Then the boat rolled away and nearly twitched me from the ridgepole. Whoopee! Suffice it to say, this little game went on for twenty minutes until I finally managed to clear the sheave.

But the wind had died. (Did I mention I hadn't a motor?) Still, the tide and current would carry me to the sound. I flopped my way down the channel past both lighthouses; the ebb tide took me eastward toward Hatchett Point. Off I went—no light, no paddle, no motor, no compass, no common sense whatsoever.

A few hours later, drifting at nearly half a knot a couple of miles from shore, I noticed two things: The night, though clear, was also surprisingly dark. Fortunately, the shipping lane lay a mile or two beyond me. *Un*fortunately, I'd also forgotten to lay in any provisions. My stomach began to complain of cruel neglect.

"Supper!" it cried.

"Shut up," I consoled it. "We've only five miles to go. All we need is a breeze."

Then the tide changed. Very slowly, my little boat drifted back westerly for a second and better view of the Jetty Light. I paid out my fifty feet of rode: it scarcely reached the bottom. Oh, well. Eventually I had to fetch up somewhere. Most of that sleepless, dark, and ravenous night my anchor bounced along the sandy bottom.

By breakfast time (by *what* time, mate?!) my hook held fast just off the mouth of the river. Then the tide turned again; the breeze awakened. I rubbed the last bushel of Long Sand Shoal from my blurry eyes, hauled my Danforth, and sailed down to South Lyme in only two hours. I anchored out, sloshed the last hundred yards to shore, and squished on up to the village to find some breakfast.

LITTLE BEACH

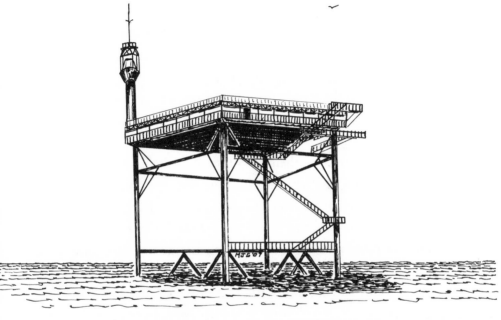

BUZZARDS BAY TOWER LIGHT
BUZZARDS BAY
MASSACHUSETTS

I used to spend some time at Little Beach in Westport, Massachu-setts, between Gooseberry Neck and Slocums Neck. Most of Little Beach has either dunes or shingle, though at certain times there emerges a sandy foreshore. The gale giveth, the gale taketh away. Behind the beach lie hundreds and hundreds of acres of shallow water—Allens Pond. It has a little natural breachway, where the water dashes through a gravelly chute and shoves a miniature sandbar toward the ocean.

Most of Little Beach remains a bird sanctuary, and signs posted everywhere concern the proprietary rights of terns and plovers. The terns have read these notices and cheerfully enforce them. Even so, two miles of foreshore provide a relaxing walk, and mile-wide Allens Pond a relaxing paddle.

The road itself remains private—the gate at the top of the drive requires a key. As you come down the rocky drive, high stone walls on either side block most of your view and, hopefully, keep the cows where they belong—on the other side. A quarter mile brings you to the low point of the meadows and the Cow Gate. Again, you have to disembark, open it wide, advance your car, disembark, and close it. Heaven help anyone not securing this gate. The local farm frowns on folk who encourage their cows to bask, naked, on the beach.

Past this gate, the briefest causeway crosses a four-foot conduit conveying a tiny estuary back to Allens Pond. Here we often lurked to catch blue crabs. Another half mile of sandy drive brings you to a cluster of modest cottages and trailers. Beside the farm, only these few acres are privately owned. Beyond lies over a mile of sanctuary.

Little Beach lies opposite Cuttyhunk Island—gateway to Buzzards Bay. West of Cuttyhunk rears Buzzards Light. Two successive lightships kept vigil here from 1954 till '61. Now a formidable Texas tower carries the torch. Huge vessels venture up the bay that leads to the Cape Cod Canal en route to Boston. Adventurous souls have gone as far as Gloucester. People I trust have told me there is even a deal more coastline north of that. Seems far-fetched, to me. Who would want to live that far from New England?

One can get into plenty of trouble here in Buzzards Bay.

It all began when I borrowed a little Sunfish and, launching it through the gentle surf, clambered aboard and aimed her for Cuttyhunk, eight miles away. The sun was bright and the water wet; what more could a sailor want? Of course, I left my Eldridge's behind. Also my sextant, GPS, and radar. I did remember my clasp knife. If shipwrecked, I could use it to cut down coconut palms to build myself a raft. And—horrors!—unravel my bathing trunks to lash the logs together. A man's gotta do, they say, what a man's gotta do.

As usual, I hadn't the need to do either. Perhaps, next time, I'll dispense with my bathing trunks. But maybe I ought to bring that Eldridge's with me. Give me something to read while perched on the bucket. It seems to have pages and pages just about tides. Those are the things in the water that keep the moon in orbit. I've never quite understood just how they work. You mostly can't see the moon during the day, so they can't be very efficient.

But it seems I snagged my daggerboard on a whale. For every mile I made due south I made about ten miles west—toward New York City. I've been to New York—there's lots of neat stuff to do there. But New York Harbor gets a bit scary when you're huddled on a shingle holding your bandanna spread to the wind. Some of those big ferries get pretty aggressive. Fortunately, by the time I passed New Haven, the moon had risen. It chased that ocean home to Massachusetts where it belongs. I made Little Beach in plenty of time for breakfast.

I must admit, no had really missed me. Except, of course, the owner of the Sunfish. He tried to explain the tides to me, but I told him that all a real sailor needs is a capful of breeze. Besides, I confided, now that morning had pulled the sun from the sea, we didn't need to worry much about those pesky tides. They had dragged that silly moon clear back to Cleveland.

RIGGING THE CANOE

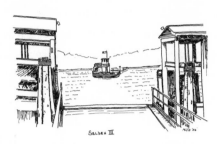

SELDEN III

For a time I didn't have a sailboat. Except for the twenty-seven-foot Rhodes Caller in my barn. I couldn't see how I could ever finish working on a wooden boat and afford to keep her in the water and raise two boys at the same time. So she sat there for several years, and I picked at her when I could.

But I needed to feel the wind in my face and, much as I enjoyed canoeing, well, you have to admit it isn't quite the same. Up in the bow of my Grumman, on the keel, sat this funny little wedge-shaped aluminum clip. What else but a place to step a mast?

Are you old enough to remember wall-mounted crank can openers? A wedge-shaped flange on those can openers slipped into a wedge-shaped bracket that screwed to the wall. One of these brackets perfectly fit the flange on the keel of my canoe. I screwed it to the base of a six-foot pole to serve as a mast.

I fashioned a board to fit across the gunwales just above the step to support the mast. This board had a deep U-shaped notch facing aft and a gate across it to keep the mast in place. This gate was secured by a pin: an eye bolt on a tether. Out with the pin, open the gate, kick the base of the stick forward to disengage the tapered clips,

116

and behold! You could drop the sail and unstep the mast in less than half a minute. This proved handy when landing on a shore overhung by trees.

Two lengths of closet pole hinged at one end and secured to the mast with cordage and I had a lateen rig—easy! Now for a sail.

I went to the local sailmaker and encountered a young man there willing to teach me. He gave me a sack of lightweight scraps of Dacron—foot-wide strips—bright red and brighter blue. He showed me how to add some draft by trimming the strips to be wider in the center. Sailmaking 101. I stitched up a sail, set grommets along the luff and foot, and lashed it to my spars.

Making a rudder and tiller proved no big deal. Make the rudder larger than you think you should: You can always trim it down. Gudgeons and pintles were a bit of a challenge: the gudgeons most of all. I had some eighth-inch-by-three-quarter-inch aluminum strap in my shop that was soft enough to bend. After a couple of tries I made some passable hardware and mounted it astern.

Then I thought I'd be clever and make a pair of outriggers. There I failed. I formed two wooden skis about six feet long—each having a little keel to keep it stiff—and depended them from a bracket across the gunnels. When I tried them out, the lee outrigger dove well beneath the surface and caused the most horrific drag; the canoe slewed hard to leeward.

I thought I would try two lengths of sealed-up tubing next—something more buoyant. Before I could put this into practice, someone offered me a set of real leeboards. I clamped them to the gunwales and sailed away.

She handled quite well in light air but, when the breeze got over ten knots, you had to fight with the helm and slack the main. The mast seemed too far forward. I went out one day on the river in a stiff chop and knew right away I had too much sail on her. I headed back to shore on a broad reach.

She began to porpoise. One good gust and the bow went completely under. She swamped in a matter of seconds. I furled the sail, unstepped the mast and immediately my canoe began to roll. The leeboards didn't help much.

Have you ever sat astride a barrel weighing several hundred pounds and just awash in a two-foot chop and tried to get it to move with only a paddle? All the while it rotates and you have to shift yourself continually or you end up in the drink.

It proved more fun than falling off the barn, but not by much. I made at least two inches of progress with every stroke and never got rolled into the river more than twice in a minute.

Fortunately, my grandmother (on my father's side) was a muskrat— and my beard has always shed water.

SANS SOUCI

Before I knew better, I purchased an old wooden sloop. She was a twenty-seven foot Rhodes Caller, built in '47—my natal year. I took this as a good omen—a significant one at least. It signified, all right. It signified that I'd left my common sense beneath a rock and hadn't the chart to locate it ever again. I'd worked on a couple of wooden dinghies and a small, carvel-planked sailboat and thought that this would be just more of the same. This is where you're at liberty to laugh.

Naturally, you always get what you pay for in this world—except when you get less. I got less. An old man owned this boat. He "parked" it at a pier for use as a summer cottage. He named her *Sans Souci,* and kindly translated for me: "We don't give a care." And, apparently, he didn't. Being fond of bright colors, he painted the teak cockpit lockers, the canvas deck, and the cabin top bright blue. With house paint. It was lovely. If you like that sort of thing.

After three gallons of "Zip Strip" she looked a bit improved. I also stripped the very-far-from-brightwork. Of course, the stripping compound raised the grain. I rediscovered sandpaper. Sleeves and sleeves of sandpaper. Then I learned about varnish. And about little badgers; how they spent the best years of their lives to make us brushes. Then I refastened the planking and painted the bottom. The inside of the boat would have to wait.

That first year I owned her, I kept her on a mooring in the river six or eight miles above Long Island Sound. She had a small gas inboard—a "Blue Jacket Twin." My first time out, I played around the mouth of the river one breezy afternoon. As I headed home the wind decided to die. The tide flowed against me; the dark flowed everywhere else. I started the engine. It purred, it roared; it crouched and prepared to spring. I shifted into forward—but nothing happened. The key securing the propeller shaft to the coupling flange had jumped out and hidden in the bilge amid the unmentionable filth of thirty years.

I dropped anchor and made a call for assistance. When the launch arrived, I found my anchor irretrievably snagged. I cut my rode and allowed the launch to tow me across the river to a marina. These generous folk attempted to charge me tourist rates to tie up for the night. I had already emptied my pockets for the launch driver. My anchor sulked in the mud across the river. I won't tell you the cost of the little key to repair my propeller shaft. I could have filled my entire cabin with little keys for what I spent to be rescued.

The very next week I declared I would rebuild that engine. Who knew what else would fall apart on the next trip? They had shoehorned that Blue Jacket Twin into my boat. After securing my topping lift, I rigged a chain falls to the boom and hoisted my engine through the companionway with an eighth of an inch to spare. I swung it out over the pier and lowered it gently onto a sturdy hand truck and made it fast. A friend helped me drag it ashore to his pickup truck. In those days they built engine blocks of massy cast iron. That little engine, including the transfer case, weighed well over three hundred pounds. My hand truck weighed about forty. We rested its handles on the tailgate, stooped low, seized the entire load, and heaved. This nearly deprived me of further connubial bliss.

I rebuilt that engine and scraped and painted the block. I even cleaned out the bilge before I replaced it. This greatly enhanced my taxonomy—I met some primordial slime. I never did find that little length of key stock. Nor did I find a twelve-millimeter wrench I'd dropped into the bilge. Wrenches are not adept at hopping over frames—their legs are much too short. Nor have they the agility to wriggle through limber holes. I believe that wrench was caught and eaten by the gremlins who lived in my bilge. You should have seen what they did to my poor old bilge pump . . .

CUTTYHUNK

The first leg of our journey took us from Cataumet (this side of Cape Cod) to Cuttyhunk Island. We sailed less than thirty miles—the length of Buzzards Bay—but we didn't leave Cataumet till after lunch. I wished I had more time to look around.

I resist traveling with others. Someone else always decides when to come and when to go. As a water rat and a writer, I want to inquire and peer and mess about. What makes travel interesting is talking to people and looking at their boats and poking into coffee shops and marine consignment stores and walking the shady lanes in elderly villages overlooking harbors. If I have a notebook and a pencil, I can get lost for hours. Other people try to overtake places as quickly as possible. Perhaps they enjoy a sense of accomplishment.

"I went from point A to point B in only four days and eleven minutes. Pretty darn good, don't you think?"

Well, I *do* think—which, at least, poses complications. Because I think, some mornings it takes me four days and eleven minutes just to get to work.

We planned to expend at least a week to deliver this Cal 34 to Hampton Roads, Virginia, camping out at marinas along the way. We frequently found ourselves sailing dead into a wind that wasn't blowing. Until we arrived in Chesapeake Bay, we had the motor on nearly all the time. There a mellow breeze met us. Our final day we encountered a serious breeze and made ninety miles in twelve hours.

All the way to the Chesapeake we encountered haze. This delightful phenomenon restricts visibility to barely half a mile—give or take a thousand yards—and keeps you constantly peering at apparitions and wondering if you ought to alter your course. Our boat hadn't any frills such as GPS—a rarity at that time. We had loran, but none of us knew how to use it.

We worked with a compass, charts, and binoculars; along with parallel rules, dividers, a wristwatch, and a pencil. When you haven't a knot meter, you calculate your speed after two fixes. Whatever else you need for coast-wise navigation, ask Mr. Eldridge. Now take a bearing on that light you can't see, plot our position, and pipe down.

When you can't find any aids to navigation, position becomes problematic. Yes, the next marker should appear about over there, almost anytime now. It should resemble a bell buoy, adorned by the number fourteen in large white numerals. If you squint, sailor-like, long enough through this haze, you'll most likely find it. If you don't, well, the next one you won't see ought to say number sixteen. Yes, right about there. No, lad. What you see sticking up through the haze is only our Samson post.

Nonetheless, we managed to find Cuttyhunk. We happened to choose the weekend of Independence Day to begin our little excursion. Inside the basin we discovered about a million vessels rafted together in groups of a thousand or so. To circle the harbor we had to butter our rub rails. We couldn't access the only pier and the only means to shore and the crowded village. But staying aboard improves one's self-sufficiency. We had supplies for a week and plenty of fuel and water. We escaped and anchored outside in the company of a score of other latecomers.

We dropped our hook in the drink, and the current assisted to set it. We paid out plenty of scope and thought about supper. The skillet had just gotten hot enough to terrify the onions when the island decided to move a tad to the west. We looked out the port-hole and there it went—on its way to New York. Gravelly bottom, Skipper. We started the engine, hoisted the anchor, and set it again with more scope. We tried a different anchor. On the fourth attempt, it held. And no one else's anchor dragged during the night. A good thing, too. I've always objected to sharing my bunk with a sailboat to whom I haven't been properly introduced.

THE EAST RIVER—1977

HELL GATE

Nothing amazes me more this trip than entering New York City. Our Cal 34 feels like a bathtub toy. We douse our sails as we motor upwind from Connecticut. We pass Sands Point and Hewlett Point, round Throgs Neck, and enter the East River—a fourteen-mile crooked strait separating Long Island from The City.

We dimple beneath the Throgs Neck Bridge, then the Whitestone Bridge. Here Rikers Island broods with its gloomy penitentiary; to the south spreads LaGuardia Airport. Just ahead rears the railroad trestle across Hell Gate—a sensual arch surmounting a thousand-foot span. We pass beneath the Triboro Bridge. We look to starboard and can see up the Harlem River to the footbridge, carefully painted a vibrant purple and yellow.

Ahead these bridges connect Manhattan to Brooklyn: the Queensboro, the Williamsburg, the Manhattan. Traffic thunders above us. Look! The Twin Towers—the glorious World Trade Center. Towers, indeed! Monuments to futurity! Fully a quarter of a mile in height, they dwarf the rest of Wall Street. They throw off the rays of the sun in royal splendor. Surely they must grace Manhattan forever . . .

The lower river is serried with piers and rife with water traffic. The din of The City whelms our senses. Here, to port, stands the Brooklyn Navy Yard—decommissioned in '66 and now a commercial complex. Just ahead vaults Roebling's amazing venture—the Brooklyn Bridge—in 1883 the longest suspension bridge the world had seen.

But it isn't safe to gawk too long—here comes a freighter right at us. Prudence dictates giving her right-of-way. Her keen stem springs with tree-like grace to at least the height of our mast. We slip by eight hundred feet of pulsing steel, humbled by the immensity of her hull. Now we pass the financial district; abeam stands Battery Park—the very tip of Manhattan—and, suddenly, twenty square miles of New York Harbor open wide to receive us!

Water traffic abounds—ferries and tugboats scuttle in every direction. To port lies Governors Island. To starboard, the mighty Hudson River empties its mile-wide waters. Up the west shore of Manhattan jut massive piers—scores and scores of piers. Cranes offload the produce and manufactures of a hundred nations to tempt the ten million appetites of The City.

Transatlantic cruise ships, smart and luxurious, keep company with enormous freighters streaked with rust and guano. An outgoing vessel blows three, long shattering blasts as she backs into the Hudson, and two attendant tugboats grunt and strain to turn her prow toward the sea. An aircraft carrier anchors off New Jersey—at a mile, the men on her deck appear so many ants. Two Russian freighters raft together, waiting on their assignments—Cyrillic figures adorn their lofty bows.

And there stands grand Miss Liberty—gift of the grateful French people. The arm that bears that torch shall never tire. Behind her, just upstream, lies Ellis Island, where one set of my grandparents passed through immigration a century ago.

A ferry, astern, screams loudly in indignation as a square-rigged brig leans silently up the harbor. We haul up our sails. They fill; the running rigging creaks as we gently heel and reach south toward the Narrows—gateway to the Atlantic. To the west reclines the borough of Richmond—Staten Island; to the east, the borough of Brooklyn and old Fort Hamilton.

Above us rears an engineering marvel—the Verrazano-Narrows Bridge. At its completion in '64 it boasted the greatest suspension span in the world: four thousand two hundred sixty feet. Its decks soar two hundred feet above the water. Its two massive towers stand seventy stories high. As we pass beneath this modern Colossus, it daunts our frailty, thrills our imagination.

Now we cruise down the coast of Staten Island; the Verrazano remains in sight for mile after mile. The day has worn and we set our course for Sandy Hook, New Jersey. New York City? We were so busy sightseeing we forgot to eat our lunch . . .

THE C & D CANAL

CAPE MAY LIGHT
CAPE MAY POINT
NEW JERSEY

We'd come up Delaware Bay to the mouth of the river and entered the C & D Canal without a hint of adventure. Our Cal 34 had brought us here from Cape Cod via New York City. We'd coasted New Jersey without tucking into the Intracoastal Waterway at Barnegat Bay. Our chart told us that ten feet of water ran through the inlet, but the swells ran six feet, the tide was out, and we drew over five feet.

We chose instead to run down the shore to Atlantic City. It began to rain. We moored in the dark and spent the night on board. The following day there was no wind; we puttered down the coast. The sea sloshed gently. The haze kept visibility under a mile. We made a slow passage, only advancing to Cape May, the southernmost tip of New Jersey. In the morning, the harbor held ugly brown jellyfish each large enough to fill a ten-quart pail.

We headed northwesterly and motored up Delaware Bay. The haze persisted. We finally encountered a bit of breeze as we entered the canal, but we kept the motor at half throttle. The Chesapeake and Delaware Canal runs westerly, connecting to Chesapeake Bay. A London Bridge type of railroad trestle straddles the canal, a huge tower on either shore. Just ahead, the deck of the bridge began to descend as we approached.

I slacked the main until it luffed. The span stopped—midway down. We tried to call—our VHF was filled with bumblebees. We proceeded slowly beneath the trestle. Shadows covered our boat.

Once again, the bridge began to drop. Our mast stood over forty feet tall—well above the height of the railbed.

"I thought he was going to let us through."

"We're not going to make it—turn around!"

"Trim that genoa! Here we go!"

I wound our little inboard until she screamed. We scooted under; necks crooked back as the sullen steel descended. We heard the machinery frantically clank to either side as we passed between the towers. The breeze picked up.

"Seven knots, Skipper."

The gap between the dropping deck and our masthead quickly dwindled. Ten feet. Five. Moments later, we heard the trestle crash into place behind us, thirty feet off the water.

Our sails swelled. I throttled her motor back to idle and shut it down. Two minutes later, the Norfolk Southern thundered through at seventy miles per hour. The rails rang in her wake. Then, once again, we could hear the red-winged blackbirds trill in the rushes.

We made some modest progress through the canal before we became benighted. We discovered a long commercial pier that fronted one bank, jammed with pleasure craft. Only one berth remained—about four feet longer than our boat's length overall. Parallel parking a boat requires some practice, but we tucked her in—nearly without mishap.

At the very last minute, our bow pulpit bent the flagstaff on the fantail of the sailboat just ahead of us. The burgee of some distinguished club leaned till it kissed the deck. I jumped to fend off as our helmsman backed her down. The flagstaff snapped. I can't understand why it wasn't designed to withstand five tons of pressure.

We had just made fast when out of the pierside restaurant lumbered a florid-faced man. He flailed the air; his chest heaved.

"I'm going to sue, I'm going to sue!" he shrieked.

You wouldn't think neurotic people belonged so near the water. We finally placated him with fifty dollars and he stalked back to another round of cocktails, abristle with rectitude. The four of us voted to have our supper aboard.

The following morning, we cast off our mooring lines at break of day. That forenoon we cruised in beautiful Chesapeake Bay. We reached down the western shore, hove to for a cooling swim, and made our next berth tucked behind Solomons Island.

We were fast in our slip well before it was twilight, and the captain and I took a walk into town for provisions. As we waited to cross the busy main street, a car whizzed by containing a couple of fellows about my age.

The driver waved from his open window and shouted, "Hey! Hey, Matthew!" They disappeared round the bend.

"Who was that?" the Captain wanted to know.

He knew I lived nearly four hundred miles away. I watched the car recede and shook my head.

"You got me, Skipper. I haven't the slightest idea."

THE CAPE DORY TYPHOON

WATCH HILL LIGHT
WATCH HILL
RHODE ISLAND

My little Typhoon grew anxious to spread her wings. Fifteen knots or better tore through the sound. The wind backed up the tide, and the waist-high swells surged eastward. What fun to reach along the shore at two knots over hull speed! This crisp day in September, with the sun at full strength, my little boat tugged at her pendant. She was like the dog who brings you her leash, all aquiver in joyful anticipation. "Let's go, let's go, let's go!"

So off we went, the main and genny full to their brims and straining. We dashed down Fishers Island Sound toward scenic Watch Hill, a mere seven miles away. It seemed but an hour; nay, a mere blink of time, until we passed the lighthouse and the reef off Fishers Island. To the north of us lay Rhode Island—no stern and rockbound New England coast but merely sandy dunes. Nothing lay to our south except Block Island, several miles away. After that—Brazil. I stayed a mile offshore and surged along with the ebb. Returning might be a bit of a problem, but by then the tide would have changed. Why worry about it? In three hours' time, I'd surfed some twenty miles; ahead of me loomed the breakwaters at Point Judith.

It was time to return. The tide had changed; my Nantucket sleigh ride was over. I came about and realized what awaited. Now the tide and wind fought against each another; the swells had all become chop. To keep my course parallel to the shore required heading dead into it. The little Typhoon began to plunge and shudder. The spray came aft and I realized I had left my foul-weather gear in my truck. Fortunately, it was warm. Comparatively warm. I eased her off the wind a point and the pounding nearly ceased.

Unfortunately, my course now lay toward the beach. Every time I came about I was heading for Cape Hatteras. Fairly soon, I would need to choose whether to make two long tacks to the sea side of Fishers Island. Fishers Island, six miles long, runs parallel to the shore. I would need to reef to weather the passage outboard of the island. And sailing around the island would add ten miles to an already arduous journey.

I would be benighted before I could round the farther end where the passage back inside always proves rough. "The Race," they've named it: the entry point of the North Atlantic into the fifteen hundred square miles making up Long Island Sound. Rip tides up to five knots and a merciless chop spell danger for a sloop three fathoms long.

The sanest way, by far, was to hug the mainland. But that meant pinching and heading straight into the broil. The only third choice seemed to be to get out and walk. I started my little outboard. Two miles later the engine sputtered and died—my fuel had water in it. After exhausting my store of expletives, I resumed my wearying course against the weather. After four hours of pounding and getting drenched, I'd clawed my way back to Watch Hill. It would take me three hours to cover the final eight miles, but already the sun was lapped by the thirsty sea. Without GPS, I didn't fancy threading a rockbound channel in the dark. I pounded through the spindrift; the shore went by amazingly slowly, yard by reluctant yard.

Another mile and then I could round the point and shelter this night in nearby Stonington Harbor. A thousand yards more; a hundred. At last! I finally fell off and, angling through the whitecaps, raced for shore. The final mile I sped on gilded wings. Within the breakwater, seas ran about six inches. At the first marina, I received an invitation to share a slip. "My neighbor won't return until next week—here—pass me your line." I expressed my thanks, wrung myself out, and dialed my patient wife.

I never knew you could hear somebody roll their eyes by phone.

THE FAR SIDE OF THE SUNBEAM

I've a casual acquaintance who owns a Bristol 24: a handsome boat with a pedigree of distinction. Unfortunately, his upper weather shroud parted while he reached across the sound this summer. First his mast bent, then the entire rig went by the board. The mast, stepped on deck, decided to step off. He pulled the clevis pins and had the beast alongside for a couple of minutes but, before he could gaff it, it threw the hook and plunged to a cool fourteen fathoms where it now cavorts with the lobsters. The rest of the season he languished on his mooring. His home away from home, I suppose, but not as thrilling as leaning before a voluptuous young breeze.

The month before last, he bounded into our shop.

"I've found a mast!" he exclaimed.

Just up the road a piece is a facility that deals in secondhand vessels—mostly sail. They take donated boats and sell them; the proceeds go to the local university. Unfortunately, this yard lies twenty miles from the ocean. Whatever you purchase needs to be trucked away. Most of the craft are surprisingly worthy, and prices are negotiable.

There he found a Bristol 24—a sad old boat considerably under the weather. So much so that her owner had decided to sell her piece-meal. Spars and sails and rigging? Not a problem. Except—my acquaintance had only a little car and couldn't transport his new mast. After seeking help and being refused, he came to me. Wednesday morning, I strapped a tall wooden horse in the back of my truck and lashed a sixteen-foot ladder to it and the top of my cab to form a scaffold. The mast would extend but seven feet beyond each end of the ladder.

I spent awhile securing it all, tied a red flag astern, and off we went. We fetched up at the marina all-a-taut-o, and carried the mast down the snowy pier and laid it atop his boat. We agreed it would not be fortuitous to slip on the ice and fall in. Now he needs to check continuity of the wiring; inspect the rigging; affix a new antenna—all the usual off-season chores that add savor to the mix that we call boating.

Meanwhile, in the shop, we've cleared the deck for the Petrel That Has No Name. Number 33—the very last boat of this design to make her maiden voyage out of Noank. Her spars will go aloft to have their varnish; her sails and running rigging are tucked away. Another bird come home to the nest after many years away. Petrels seem to wing their way back here to be refurbished and have new sailors installed. We run a halfway house for needy Herreshoffs. I'm proud to report that all have recuperated.

For a short while, back in the seventies, I worked at a yard that built a number of well-designed sailing boats. I wanted to learn ship's carpentry. What they needed, however, was a millwright.

"Oh—you can run a lathe, and weld and make repairs?"

"Yep."

"Very good. This way, please."

But it wasn't to be my way. The first day on the job, my boss inquired, "Have you ever installed a toilet?"

"Yep."

"You're our boy," he said.

So there I knelt, by his office, connecting a brand-new thunder mug to the plumbing. I searched and searched but I couldn't find a single through hull fitting.

I also repaired the sprinkler system, fabricated pulley guards, made stainless keel bolts, fitted propeller shafts, and poured lead keels. People have pointed out to me that fumes from that molten lead have addled my brain. I reply that every little bit helps.

After a while, getting filthy for gas money ceased to amuse me.

"You expect to have fun and get paid as well?" they asked. "Sorry we can't accommodate; the door over there opens out."

The best sort of door invariably opens out. You can reach the latch if you try. I know the wolf has her lair just the other side. But who minds a wolf when the wind freshens and the seagull calls from the far side of the sunbeam? When your rail dips to greet the swell and your sails strain to lift your hull to Heaven?

SIPPICAN HARBOR

Once upon a time, a sailboat got chartered for the weekend—perhaps out of Fairhaven, or maybe Mattapoisett. Grandpa doesn't always remember things the way they actually happened. That's why he's had such an eventful life.

We sailed her up and down Buzzards Bay and ducked into some of the picturesque harbors just this side of Cape Cod. We ended our outing in Marion.

Tabor Academy, in Marion, is my alma mater: a preparatory school or simply "prep." It prepared one for college—which in turn prepared one for a suitable career. Or an unsuitable career. As Thoreau remarked, beware of any enterprise that cannot be undertaken in one's old clothes. I have a three-piece suit just as you have; I even enjoy getting dressed to kill on occasion. But I never feel like killing anything after I put it on; not even my supper.

Most of my life I've spent in ratty jeans, just messing about. And the older I get, the less I feel inclined to stop messing about. I'm more inclined to roll on the floor with the kitten than worry about a portfolio; more inclined to fool about on one of my small boats than work for a living. It may not be remunerative but it's generally rewarding.

My fondest recollections of Tabor—where I boarded for all of my self-conscious high school years—involve sailing little boats around and around in scenic Sippican Harbor. Now I'd returned, ten years later, to do it once again. I still loved to sail and cared even less about what the civilized world thought about me.

That day the colors at the Beverly Yacht Club, out on the point, snapped as though they meant to snap the stripes right off the flag. Every spring, they run up the small-craft warning for Buzzards Bay; it never comes down all season. Even inside the mile-wide harbor we made five knots among the moored boats, which numbered in the hundreds. Our charter hadn't a jam cleat or a cam cleat or anything so handy for the main; one either held the sheet or belayed it on the horns of an old-fashioned cleat.

If you ask for trouble someone will always oblige you. Who would have guessed that the tiller would snap clean off?

One moment I zipped along, entirely in control; the next moment I zipped along, entirely out of control, staring down at a long length of ash in my fist. Our boat rounded up at a truly alarming rate and tried to make precipitate acquaintance with another sailboat tethered to her mooring.

By the time that I cast the mainsheet loose, the two boats had grown rather intimate, though the moored boat resented the mess we'd made of her rub rail. Having an inboard, we couldn't steer without a tiller; we needed to get towed. The wood had parted an inch away from the fitting; surgery would be called for.

Our outing ceased abruptly. No one had cell phones back then— we roused out a grumpy someone with VHF. When we'd made it to shore, we placed calls to both of the owners, then to all the insurance companies, whose answering service messages assured us of prompt response come Monday morning. Next we needed to get our boat to the doctor to be fitted for a prosthesis, then find ourselves a lift back to our car. After that, we still had a two-hour ride.

I've had more rewarding experiences, but it could have been worse, of course. When I see all the wrecks of beautiful boats in the aftermath of hurricanes in the Gulf, I just shake my head and sigh. But one can't ascribe malicious intent to what are mere acts of Nature. With all the woe already in this world, it amazes me why any should actively seek to perpetuate more. Nationalism equates to exclusivity: the overweening conceit of narrow minds.

Every day I repair boats. Most of my patients suffer from nothing worse than the natural effects of aging. Would that every physician could say as much.

DREAMTIME

MORGAN POINT
NOANK
CONNECTICUT

Today I've knocked off early; my wife has come down to the boat-yard, and we join our friend on his blue-and-white sloop *Dreamtime*. He hasn't bent on the sails as little wind ripples the harbor. He tips his outboard down and we cast off. This first week of April the air feels warm for a change.

Our cove, West Cove, has a breakwater halfway across its mouth to keep out the worst of the weather. Just beyond, the mooring field comprises four or five acres. The channel runs between the mooring field, to the west, and Morgan Point and Mouse Island to the east. The granite lighthouse, a literal house, on Morgan Point no longer beams or beckons.

A stone's skip beyond the point lies little Mouse Island: a water-worn acre of rock with four stunted trees that share a cupful of soil, and three firmly rooted cottages. It has no well, no electricity, no deep water for mooring, but you'd need a deep pocket to purchase a cottage there. At low tide you could walk to Morgan Point, though some inconsiderate person has left numerous boulders strewn on the bottom that impede pedestrian traffic.

We round Mouse Island on the outboard side; pass the point and enter Mystic Harbor. Ram Island divides the mile-wide harbor mouth. Enders Island, with its massive seawall and cut-stone monastery, guards the farther point. Above it, across the causeway, Masons Island forms the east bank of the harbor for more than a mile.

The mouth of the harbor bristles with moorings; both banks sprout marinas. This time of year, desuetude prevails. We hear scarcely a sound save the rising breeze and the rinsing of small water. We ascend the harbor and admire the houses, which were built with this end in mind. The harbor constricts to become the Mystic River.

After twenty minutes, we come to a swing bridge—the railroad trestle—clearance about eight feet. Above, the village of Mystic straddles the river. Old and refined, Mystic boasts a tiny bascule bridge that opens to water traffic at stated hours, though not at this time of year. On the riverbank above the village stands Mystic Seaport—renowned for its array of antique vessels, including a square-rigged whaling ship, and its maritime museum. In the Seaport's shops, master builders restore old boats and teach their craft to others.

Today we stop at the railroad bridge, explore a marina, run briefly aground on an errant mud bank, meander back down the river. A long, lean shell, stroked by eight young women, zips from beneath the trestle and hurtles by. A white launch, run by the rowing coach, follows in her wake. A Bertram 50 slips from behind a pier and gradually overtakes us. Her skipper, high above in his pilothouse, is far too focused on The Beyond even to acknowledge our presence.

At the harbor's mouth, we leave the channel and skirt the back of Ram Island. Privately owned, it comprises twenty acres, has a large house and barns and a sturdy pier within a sheltered cove. As we enter the cove, three horses foregather hopefully to greet us; a flock of guinea fowl patrols the beach. We drift a few minutes, then slowly turn and depart—to the obvious chagrin of the horses, who have far too few diversions for their liking.

We motor back behind the island. I stand on the bow, my arm around the headstay, and keep my weather eye alert for rocks. The wind has picked up and I'm glad of my heavy jacket. We clear Ram Island, pass behind humpy Whaleback Rock, cross the channel and round Mouse Island again.

Within West Cove, the barge methodically dredges the marina. The yard crew repairs the water mains. Ashore, two sailors, their collars turned up, scrape old paint from their bottoms. The yard skiff busily shunts boats from winter to summer slips. But no one here is out in a boat for the fun of it. Few people find early April conducive to ". . . messing about in boats. Simply messing."

A TRUE STORY

UNIDENTIFIED LIGHTHOUSE
FRENCH COUNTRYSIDE

It blew like fury all night. This morning the storm tore out of the west at fifty knots; it gusted double that. When I arrived at the shop, the boss shook his head.

"It's much too windy to work," he said. "We'd better go sailing instead."

We rigged my sloop with a storm jib, took two and a quarter reefs in the main, and cast off from the mooring. I never knew that I owned a planing boat. We flew our sails wing-and-wing; our keel came completely out of the water; our wake would have drowned a whale.

The wind increased to force fourteen; the lubber's line strained until it nearly parted. We pitched so severely, we nearly spilled the last of our fluid dynamics. The seas grew tremendous. We rose with each swell until we could see Cincinnati, then surfed down the fronts. In ten minutes' time we had passed Cape Cod and were on our way to Europe.

"Just keep your eyes open to pick up the Eiffel Tower," I said and, sure enough, there it was on the horizon.

Four more waves and we entered the English Channel. The next wave swept us over the isle of Jersey; the next, over Guernsey; the next, over Alderney. We had cows in the luff, and cows in the leach, and cows in the aspect ratio. I uncovered a pair of sleeping Jerseys tucked up beneath the jib sheets, and a big fat Alderney had her tail caught in the relative bearing. Tomorrow I'll tell you how all of those cows got home.

We rounded Le Havre and went up the Seine on a wave so large that it left us stranded on top of a café table in Montmartre. A good thing, too. It was nearly noon and we had four Guernseys wedged five ways in the galley.

We started with café espresso and croissants, then digressed by way of a zesty omelet. After lunch, we wrung out our socks and hung them from the spreaders; with waves so huge it was easy to reach that high. We moored my boat to one of the waiters and climbed the Eiffel Tower.

The view was superb: I could see my lovely wife hard at work— earning money to support my boating habit. That always cheers me up. My boss believes that his wife shouldn't have to work—he keeps her busy sanding and scraping his boat. What would we do without the ladies, God bless 'em.

By this time it was getting on for dinner. Knowing how well the

French can roast a duck, we cast our net from the tower and snagged a couple. Then we took the boat to Spain for some oranges. You can't have duck in France without an orange sauce. The tempest had worsened—we sank so low in the troughs of the waves that our keel nearly snagged the Greenwich meridian.

We returned just in time for the chef to prepare the sauce. The ducks were most appreciative. We washed them down with plenty of vin ordinaire. Washing ducks is just one of my many talents. Some day I'll have to tell you a few of my others.

After dinner they brought us a bottle of cognac. The French believe it's a cure for "mal de mere." It must have worked; I can scarcely feel a thing. It certainly simplified the navigation. All we did coming back was follow the tiller.

To head home entailed sailing dead into the wind: Tacking would have wasted at least an hour. We had no choice but retrace the way we came. I put the rudder into reverse and set a course stern-first dead into the storm—wung out all the way.

The wind exceeded force twenty; the suction was intense. It sucked us back to our mooring in two hours flat. I bailed the tender and, pulling hard, caught a small wave that set the dinghy down in my pickup truck.

I parked in the yard. When you look out tomorrow, you'll see the boat and know that I've told you the truth. I made it home just in time to tuck you in. I would have been here sooner except the oars leaked.

That's what Grandpa's been doing all day. See—I can prove it— here's a piece of the orange peel in my pocket. Now that's your yarn for tonight, children; pipe down and go to sleep.

MOONWIND

A WATERWOMAN

MOONWIND

My wife suggested I write this. When first I met her, ten years ago, she was not a waterwoman. I decided to convert her. Now, ten years later, she still is not a waterwoman. However, she now has become an aspiring waterwoman. Progress. That's what we like to see.

At first, I borrowed my son's canoe and took her paddling on the most placid water imaginable—a large salt-marsh pond a few miles down the road—Ninigret Pond. Half of its thousand acres, shallow enough to wade in, encouraged her to get in and out and slog about, clamming, way offshore. She soon learned to deal with the canoe—an unstable, white-water model. After a while, we switched to flat-water kayaks. Besides stability, they offer back support. The double paddle, easier on one's arms, allowed us more range.

I told her about sailing. I'd sailed growing up, but hadn't owned a sailboat in years. One of her sisters had a powerboat at a marina in Connecticut and, occasionally, invited us for a ride. Perhaps we could buy a boat and keep it there, my wife suggested.

One day, while driving, we passed a curvaceous young sailboat on a trailer—taking a nap in the sun. I slowed a bit to bestow my admiration. A Cape Dory Typhoon, eighteen feet, six inches long, she had a full keel and cuddy cabin. Such a pretty lass, I remarked.

A couple of miles later my wife responded, "Let's buy her!"

We bought her. I did the survey myself. Though basically sound, she needed lots of TLC. (No, dear—that doesn't stand for Totally Lost Cause.) Eventually, we got her into the water for half a season.

My wife proved quite observant. "It tips," she yelled. "The ocean is rough," she cried. "Turn it around and go back!" she screamed. "I'm much too young to drown!"

Relax, I told her. This is how little sailboats behave. And it isn't rough at all—there's often a two- to three-foot chop when the wind backs up the tide.

"Turn it around!" she commanded. "We . . . are going . . . Back!"

Aye, aye, Skipper.

By the end of our second season she began to relax a bit, as long as the wind didn't exceed ten knots and we didn't go more than a mile from the shore. The cuddy cabin made her claustrophobic.

"No way will I ever sleep down there in that cave!"

The Porta Potti she admired from a distance. It definitely ranked as very second-rate sculpture.

"Thanks anyway," she would say, "but I can wait."

There seemed only one plausible solution. Yep—you guessed it. We purchased a larger boat. The little Typhoon found a new home in New Hampshire. I bought an old Chris Craft sailboat: a twenty-six-foot Pawnee. We named her *Moon Wind*.

Now *this* is the cat's pajamas. We even have curtains. We have not only headroom but also a head. With a door. And a galley with an icebox. And a table where she can sit down to eat a meal. We have running water. And lights. She can curl up on her bunk and read a book in the evening. The boom is so high, it doesn't ever hit her in the head. A lifeline runs all the way round the deck.

We spent a couple of weekends on her. Everything went smoothly. One of these years, I'll promote her to bosun's mate. When the boat doesn't bounce, she helps me take in the sails. But whitecaps fill her with terror. Heeling more than fifteen degrees is tantamount to drowning.

But progress looms on the horizon. She's learned what some of these nautical terms denote. "Head up" has nothing whatever to do with posture; "shoving off" is not euphemistic for overboard disposal of carping wives. She's even learned that "reaching" has nothing to do, most of the time, with cookies.

She can handle the helm in calm weather. I've taught her to come about and to trim the sails. One of these days, I have no doubt, she'll learn to use the outboard.

What's that, dear?

Oh, well—it was just a thought . . .

LITTLE NARRAGANSETT BAY

STONINGTON HARBOR LIGHT
STONINGTON
CONNECTICUT

We had a wretched time fighting with the outboard. It had started easily and taken us out of West Cove without complaint. We'd set our sails for Stonington and killed the little motor, tipping it up and out of the water as usual. The breeze was ample and out of the west and we had no need to tack the whole way down. We rounded up off Stonington and steered to pass behind Sandy Point and enter the channel that joins with the mouth of the Pawcatuck.

Drawing four feet, we hadn't but a few yards' breadth of safe water between the green, lighted buoy and the shoals and, summertime, the traffic through here can be daunting. Prudence dictated, "Have the motor running." I flopped the motor into the water, pulled the cord twice, and it started. It ran twenty seconds and died. Again, with the same result.

We passed the last red marker and I jibed her about. I swore at the motor—got it started once more. It caught, it kicked, it sputtered, it grunted, it forswore service to all of Mankind, forever. I taught it a new word and gave my attention to the tiller. With the wind dead astern, I slacked the main. The genoa flapped twice and crossed to starboard—now we were wing-and- wing. "Wung out," as the old-timers say.

The boom nestled against the shrouds. I stooped, peered beneath it, and spied a big Bayliner steaming straight at us. Evidently we would meet at the narrows with only the scantest clearance. On her foredeck lazed a bathing beauty, clothed in little more than her natural endowments. On our present courses, my topping lift might catch in her halter top. With no room to turn, I straddled the tiller and hauled in the mainsheet, sailing by the lee for the merest moment.

The bathing beauty blinked as the shadow of my sail interrupted her tan, and the skipper fixed me with a baleful glare. Had we leaned a bit, we could have shaken hands.

"*Sail*boats," I imagined him mutter. He shoved his throttles forward as he passed the mark, and the Bayliner leapt with a growl and a roar. I slacked my main quickly, wallowed once in his wake, and rippled down the channel with nary a sound.

We rounded 22 at the mouth of the river and headed for the lee of Napatree Beach. I brought her up, shaking, dropped the Danforth, and, just to be safe, paid out my whole rode and set a second hook. I never like using just one anchor when staying long enough for the tide to change. Much too easy to foul your anchor and end up dragging and drifting. This time of year, a hundred small craft share this anchorage, and some are more savvy than others.

Just upwind, a larger sloop was joined by two sisters, and the three of them rafted together for the night. The sunset proved magnificent, the water placid. We lounged in the cockpit and savored our supper. I lit the anchor light and we both turned in. At five AM, I slid open the hatch and watched the sun climbing Watch Hill. When I looked about, it seemed to me the three boats were closer.

"I need some coffee," I thought to myself.

I went below and did the needful, started the coffee, and put on my shoes. When I came on deck, the three sailboats were just off my quarter and closing quickly, their one anchor dragging. I uncleated one anchor but didn't cast it off. I hadn't any time to fetch a buoy for it, let alone bend it on, but I hated to lose it. Straddling the taffrail, the rode in one fist, I seized a stanchion of the nearest boat and braced myself to keep us apart. Not a big deal—just twenty tons of boats and my anchor trying to pull me overboard.

"Hello!" I hollered. "Is anyone below?" After a moment, a hatch was raised and a tousled countenance squinted out.

"Is anything the matter?" he asked.

REBUILDING HER RUDDER

It's frustrating not having my boat in the water. June has arrived, summer approaches, and poor *MoonWind* sits, disgruntled, on her poppets, and reproaches me for my obvious lack of concern.

"Boats belong in the water," she complains, "not propped up here on this knoll looking out at the harbor."

I meant to be kind, but so much work remains. This spring I had her bottom sandblasted. After loving her for a year and a half, I got to see what she looks like, totally bare. Quite healthy and graceful for a slim young thing just turning thirty-five. Her hull appeared sound, even the leading edge and bottom of her keel. A few small chips in her gel coat, but no evidence of her having climbed any reefs.

Her worst affliction proved a multitude of tiny blisters. Sandblasting left thousands of pocks; she resembled a target attacked with number six shot. These I troweled flush with epoxy filler, sanded fair, then troweled and faired again. Next I applied barrier coat: a thinner epoxy, the consistency of honey. After two coats, the finish appeared lumpy. This I blamed on the roller—even though it had a close nap and was recommended for bottom paint and resin. Two afternoons with an orbital sander made it smooth again, also more fair. I applied a final two barrier coats with smoother rollers made of fine, fine sponge.

Meanwhile, I had her rudder off to inspect what seemed to be serious cracks around the base of the shaft. This entailed removing the rudder head, digging a hole beneath the rudder, removing the stainless bearing housing from the base of her skeg, and dropping the rudder into the hole until the rudderpost cleared the hull. Miraculously, the three, slotted, flat-headed bolts consented to back out of the housing with minimal effort.

Of course, the hole was two inches too shallow and several inches too narrow on the first try. I needed to hoist the rudder back up and block it with a short beam that bridged the hole. I discovered how heavy my rudder was. I couldn't hold it up with one hand while I inserted blocking. I needed to use a lever, then block the lever, then block the rudder. I had to dig out the rest of that hole, which was mostly stones, with a trowel, as there wasn't any room to use a shovel. Eventually, I prevailed.

It appeared the water had migrated up the shaft and followed the lowest cross pin most of its length across the width of the rudder.

I opted for invasive surgery. I took a long reciprocating saw and cut a trapezoidal wedge eight inches high and ten inches wide around the rudderpost. The last foot of this stainless-steel shaft then resembled a fleshless bone. I scored it with fifty-grit paper and replaced the cross pin with a length of stainless rod secured with nuts.

My rudder had no core: only solid resin. I ground the cut edges half an inch deep and faired them back about four inches on each side. On one side I laid a piece of matting large enough to bridge the ground-out area, and bonded it with vinyl ester resin. Matting first to provide a stronger initial bond, as the matting lies flatter than cloth, providing more surface. Next a layer of cloth, which provides more transverse strength.

I laid up only a couple of layers on the first side to bridge the gap and keep the filler in place. After my bridge cured, I flipped the rudder over and began to fill the huge gap with vinyl ester compound mixed with chopped fiber. Small batches prove better, as the pot life is fairly short and thorough mixing is imperative. Every half inch or so in depth, the filler must be allowed to cure completely; otherwise the heat from the chemical reaction, if trapped deeply, can cause cracking. My rudder was over three inches thick at center.

After using well over a gallon of filler, I'd brought the repair within a quarter of an inch of the original surface and built up the lead edge around the rudderpost. I bonded the first layer of matting straight into the final layer of filler before the latter cured.

I wrapped fabric around the rudderpost as well, adding layers until the repair was just proud of the original. I flipped the rudder over and built up the other surface. I ground away the excess fiber and resin and checked fairness with a batten. I continued to fill and sand fair for most of a day. Then I sanded down the entire rudder. I applied four layers of barrier-coat epoxy, two at a time, sanding gently between them with two-twenty paper. I then rolled on two layers of gel coat, sanded them smooth, then applied four coats of bottom paint.

With the help of a friend, I hoisted the ninety-pound rudder into place. One of us held it up as the other secured the lower bearing bracket to the skeg.

This entire process took most of a week of filthy, intensive labor. Had I known how much work was involved, I would have opted to hire a mermaid to swim beneath my boat and steer with her tail.

LATE LAUNCHING

MoonWind has finally been launched. About time, too. Everyone reminds me that half the regular boating season has passed. I look at it a bit differently. I've no intention of hauling my boat for at least two years, and she'll spend her winters at the pier behind our shop. There are lovely days for sailing right up to Christmas. And next spring I can sail before the crocuses come up.

I sandblasted her bottom; filled and faired; gave her three coats of primer, then an indicator coat, then three coats of ablative bottom paint with extra paint at the waterline and all the leading edges. Then I attacked her topsides: sanded it to the gel coat, puttied, faired, primed, and sprayed. Once again, she glows a hunter green. I replaced the rub rail. I rebuilt the rudder. I never imagined that days could have so many hours.

At least she's resumed the water. I uncovered her back in April, and she's been underneath two enormous maple trees through flower time and seed time. There were sticks and leaves and compost on her decks. Enough to house a number of wriggling tenants and provoke my interest in spontaneous generation.

As soon as the riggers brought her to the pier I went to work with soap and brush and hose. After two hours, most of them on my knees, she appeared presentable. Water squished from my sneakers. My sodden jeans embraced me. At least she looked more like a boat than a discarded vegetable cart.

The halyards and lazy jacks and topping lift were all in a tangle: bundled to the mast with a length of shock cord. The boom lay on deck. I spent another hour detangling all the lines and rigging the boom. By twilight, I secured the main hatch, adjusted my spring lines, and trudged back to my truck. I have a list of projects half a page long.

Fortunately, I can actually sail the boat before doing most of them. I have a cutout transom for an outboard—previously framed by a loose assortment of weathered wood and dented metal. I've replaced that with teak sheathed in sixteen-gauge stainless. Now I need to trim the entire cutout with nine small pieces of teak, then varnish them until I can admire myself in their reflections. I also need a new forward hatch, for which I shall have to build an enclosure, and a new deck pipe for my anchor rode, and a chain stopper, and, and . . . Most days I choose to ignore my list and go sailing.

I haven't a lot of brightwork on this boat. Nineteen-seventy, *Moon-Wind's* natal year, proved a good year for the trees—the boatbuilders left them alone to dream quietly in the forest. The hatch frames, the companionway, the drop boards, the grab rails, and the tiller constitute the extent of brightwork on deck. Below, only the ladder, some cabinet trim, two pin rails, and the fiddles require varnish. Don't get me wrong: I'd enjoy owning an all-wood boat—the pride of the whole marina. But I also want to sail. And my job at the boat shop demands a good deal of time. So does writing. I spend more hours writing than sailing. This problem needs rectification.

Life becomes a tradeoff. I want to sail, but I need to repair other sailors' boats a number of hours each week. Then the mundane obligations of living intrude: eating and sleeping, for instance. Living aboard one's sailboat and having neither house nor vehicle nor job, and needing none, would be hubris—the most arrogant presumption—and therefore suitably punishable by the gods. One would be drowned by Poseidon early on and die extremely happy.

As this option doesn't affect most of us, we allocate what portion of our time we can afford—a few afternoons, a few weekends, perhaps a few weeks—to lose ourselves in that Heaven we know as sailing. Were Gabriel to offer me my very own cloud tomorrow, well, all I should say is, You'd better rig her for single-handing, brother. . . .

MYSTERIES OF THE DEEP

NORTH DUMPLING LIGHT
FISHER'S ISLAND SOUND
NEW YORK

Why anyone would want the drawstring of her pajamas to get hung up on the corner of my forward hatch cover is beyond me, but my frivolous genny does it whenever she can. I scrambled forward to free up my straining jib sheet.

"Just take the helm for a minute," I said casually over my shoulder.

"Me?" squeaked my friend.

"Just don't run down that schooner," I added. "I've just replaced my rub rail."

"What'll I do?" she cried.

"Just keep her steady as she goes," I answered.

"What does that mean, 'steady'?"

"Just keep her headed straight for North Dumpling—give or take a mile."

By this time I had a half nelson on the genny, which had been having a grand time trying to knock me overboard.

"Okay, now you can sheet it home," I said.

"But the schooner," she cried. "I don't want to hit the schooner."

"I was being facetious," I answered, stepping down into the cockpit. "That schooner is nearly a mile ahead and heading for the Race."

"How could I know?" she asked.

"Waterman's intuition," I said, taking a turn on the winch. "Head off a bit—you're pinching."

"I haven't touched you," she said.

I shoved the tiller gently a point to windward. "There," I said. "Now slack your main a trifle before I set the jib."

"What does that mean?" she asked.

"Slack," I said. "As in, 'loosen.'"

"You mean I should let it out?" she asked.

"Just until it begins to luff, then trim it," I instructed.

"What does that mean—'luff'?" she inquired.

"It's merely a quaint Germanic term of endearment," I said. "I thought you'd sailed before."

"Oh, yes," she replied. "Last summer, I spent a week with my friends on their thirty-six-foot whatever. And I used to own a little catboat thing. It was so much fun. The man in the sailboat store showed me how to pull on the string to make the sail go up. Then you just climbed into it and it went."

"But you managed to sail her back to where you launched her?" I asked.

"It didn't matter," she said. "Wherever I landed, I'd just get out and walk it back along the shore until I found my car."

"Ah," I said. "But you must at least know by now how to jibe and tack."

"Oh, yes," she affirmed. "That's when the boat wants to go the other way. Even the thirty-six-footer kept trying to do that. I'd turn the wheel one way and the boat would tip way over; so I'd turn the wheel the other way and the boom would go flying and everyone got excited."

"Uh-huh," I said.

"They were very patient with me," she continued. "Now I understand how to hold a course."

"Speaking of which, you're falling off," I observed.

"No, I'm not," she replied. "I've got my feet braced against that thingamajig. I won't fall off."

I showed her how to head up a bit and keep the sails filled. My bulkhead compass constituted a Mystery of the Deep.

"What's wrong with your compass? All the numbers are backward," she observed. "Isn't the 'N' supposed to line up with the mark instead of the 'S'?"

"They planned it like that," I responded. "That's so when we come about to return home it'll show true north. It's much more important to know where north is when you're heading back to port."

She wrinkled her brow as she thought about that for a while. We quickly approached that outcrop known as West Clump, so I managed the genny and helped her to come about.

"There's just one thing I've never been able to understand," she confided. "Why is it, when you shove the tiller right, the boat goes left?"

I patiently explained how the rudder works.

"The rudder's the thing that hangs off the back of the boat," she said. "Even *I* know that." She hung her head over my transom. "But you don't have one."

"No," I said. "After you've sailed as long as I have, all you need is a tiller."

"You're pulling my leg," she said. "Without a rudder, the boat would just go backward."

My friend is not a visual person. Nor is she mechanical. Nor does sequential reasoning play a large part in her life. This is to be expected. After all, she's worked for the federal government for over twenty years.

THE MARINA

Some people have begun complaining to me that summer is over.
Not for a little while, I respond. Not until the Equinox.

"The *what?*" they ask, politely.

Then they go haul their boats.

Autumn begins the best time of year to sail—the breeze blows far
more constantly than during the hazy summer. It's not unbearably
hot.

"Look," they say. "The leaves have begun to change."

"Just get a few miles offshore," I reply. "You won't see any leaves."

Oh, well. Let them haul their boats. It gives the yard crew something to do and leaves the ocean less crowded.

I presently keep *MoonWind* docked alongside the walkway that
feeds the finger piers. The first hundred yards of the walkway they
designate the dinghy dock for those who keep their sailboats on
moorings. Everyone rows or putters by my boat and bids me good
day.

The boatyard launch has the first berth along the walkway after
the dinghies. She's large enough to hold a dozen boaters, plus a couple of dogs—providing they're friendly—and has a busy schedule

all summer long. Now, after Labor Day, launch service has been reduced to weekends. Even then, demand becomes sporadic.

Folk who need to come ashore to do their laundry and shopping, or perhaps go out to dinner, tune to channel sixty-eight and grieve in a public way. Some, of course, just want to go home after sailing. Our launch remains nondenominational: They've even been known to pick up people who just went out to their boats for a barbecue.

Then there are all the boaters who live "in town." Which is to say, they have slips at the finger piers. *Moon Wind*'s dock lies between piers F and G. H and I lie beyond. A hundred boaters pass me on the way to board their vessels. These are my neighbors, many of whom must stop and chat and tell me how good a job I've done—how spruce my sloop is looking.

I have so much work I need to do, replacing and refinishing brightwork, grinding out digs and crazes in the deck. Most of the boats at this end of the marina are substantial—forty feet or more. Some of their winches cost more than what I paid for my little boat. Their brightwork and stainless steel glow in the dark. *Moon Wind* will never become a yacht. No matter how many hours I spend, her Bakelite winches just won't take a polish. Yet these folk encourage me. It must be my Flemish coils.

A few of them live aboard all winter. Some of them sail south. Already this group has begun to make plans, to confer, peruse charts, hoard extra engine parts. Key West, the Bahamas—where shall we go *this* winter? It must be tough—giving up all this beautiful icy weather to bask in the sun. Come on, folks—New Englanders were born and bred to suffer—builds character and curbs that degenerate urgency to relax.

When the need to sail descends on me, to garner my quota of wind and spray, *Moon Wind* answers my call. Yes, she'll stay in a slip this winter. I paid my dues this year. I spent the first two months of the season to overhaul my bottom, to rebuild my rudder. Next spring,

I'll start sailing before the daffodils peek from beneath their coverts, when people still carry snow shovels in their trunks.

For now, I'm still stripping brightwork and yapping with my neighbors, each of whom has advice to share as to which finish to use. They also share cheering news about the weather. There's a hurricane off Cape Hatteras, they inform me—may be up here by the end of the week. Just maybe.

Once every fifteen years we get a bad storm. Once every fifty years, we get our comeuppance. Hurricane Carol, in '54, was the worst in my short memory. The hurricane of '38 demolished southern New England. The breakwater at the mouth of our marina might make a difference—at least in a moderate storm. It stands about six feet above high water. Then again, it consists of loose-piled rocks. As the man says at the fairgrounds booth, "You pays your money and you takes your chances." And a parting word of comfort from my boss concerning hurricane damage:

"As long as the hole isn't larger than the boat, I can fix it."

And he can.

AUTUMN EQUINOX

Sailing off to Block Island today on *MoonWind*. Were the weather any more perfect, I'd puppy-roll in the parking lot and kick my legs in the air. I plan to return tomorrow and meet with Paula. The round trip consists of forty nautical miles, as the gull wings. Regrettably, tomorrow's forecast omits any mention of wind. Hopefully, on Monday, I shall find some work in the boat shop. Otherwise, I'll have to search for something remunerative to further amuse myself.

Or else go sailing again. I haven't visited Cuttyhunk for a while.

This past week, I did very little save mess about with my boats. Hauled out my Whitehall dinghy three days ago and scrubbed her little bottom. Pleasant for her, but scarcely sufficient to pay to put gas in my truck or buy the groceries.

Now everything's stowed; I can shove off anytime. I'll curl up here in the cabin for just a few minutes and finish this page. May as well start the kettle . . .

MoonWind needs her grab rails varnished again. And a new light fixture in her galley. The Whitehall needs a bow piece and some trim across her transom. And her varnish touched up. Summer has surreptitiously ebbed away. I've gone out in my kayak only that once during the freshet back in April.

Can the seasons have changed as quickly as all that? Winter, spring, summer, and, suddenly, autumn again. What sort of cycle is that to tempt a person? Autumn begins today, and these journals have grown and multiplied; sprouted and bloomed, blown and gone to seed; scattered themselves across the fertile pages of periodicals.

Finally under way—after a fashion. Clear of West Cove but making perhaps half a knot—my GPS disdains to display such absurd attempts at progress. I have the tiller secured, an apple in one hand, mechanical pencil in the other. I may need my motor to chase down a breeze, as only six hours of daylight remain to traverse some twenty miles. My Whitehall basks smugly astern; *she* has two fresh coats of jade-green bottom paint.

Fortunately, it is slack tide, or else I might drift backward. In that case, would all these tentative words unwrite themselves? Tide will soon ebb—taking *MoonWind* eastward toward Block Island. Now her sails wrinkle, begin to fill. The sound of water flowing by both boats soothes me as no other voice has ever done—save that of the fluting brook behind our barn when I was a boy. My sails go slack. The jib sheet sags in the drink. I can think of worse ways to spend an afternoon.

There are plans afoot to make a bosun's mate of the tortoiseshell kitten just rescued from the road. She appears no more than a few weeks old, but has proved herself, in twenty-four hours, trusting, gentle, affectionate, playful, and conscientiously conservative—making regular small deposits to her box.

Having wasted an hour poking along, I give up and start the motor. As the sea runs smoothly through Wicopesset Pass, I opt to save a mile by taking it. Some days the whole Atlantic tries to fit through Wicopesset; those days I sail around. As I leave the shelter of Fishers Island, a presumptuous breeze accosts me. I line up the passage marker with the red-and-white bell and head for the Cape of Good Hope. Would probably make it, but perhaps not in time for breakfast.

The breeze increases incrementally and I finally kill my motor. I've spent three hours traversing the first eight miles. Making three knots with fourteen nautical miles to cover with four hours of daylight remaining. I could berth in the dark, of course. Great Salt Pond will not be crowded on a Thursday in late September. The wind picks up and then picks up some more. *Moon Wind* shoulders the sea aside and leans against the sky. If the wind grows more zealous I'll have to douse the large genoa jib, hoist the small working jib, and reef my mainsail.

Halfway across Block Island Sound, on a broad reach, the tide astern, I surge along at hull speed and more—close to eight knots a few times—though scarcely wetting my rail. Glorious! Seas run only three feet with just a few whitecaps. I let out the straining sails another few inches and *Moon Wind* soars.

Despite no sign of a squall, I need to know if the weather intends to worsen. I tune in the VHF weather channel. The computer-generated female voice emits not the least emotion. Yes, she assures me— the water is wet and the wind is in a hurry. Seas will be high enough to meet the sky but seldom higher. The sun is due to be replaced by the moon and the night will be dark. I thank her kindly and send her on her way. I pity the fellow who has to live with her.

I chance the weather and race across the water. The blue and indistinct profile of Block Island begins to resolve into bluffs, low shores and beaches. I hold a course for the waist of the island and soon distinguish the light tower at the mouth of Great Salt Pond. Another half hour reveals the wildly clanging bell buoy just outboard of the light. When close enough to read her number, I start the motor, heave to, secure the helm, and clamber carefully forward to drop my sails.

The wind has abated just enough to allow me to work on the

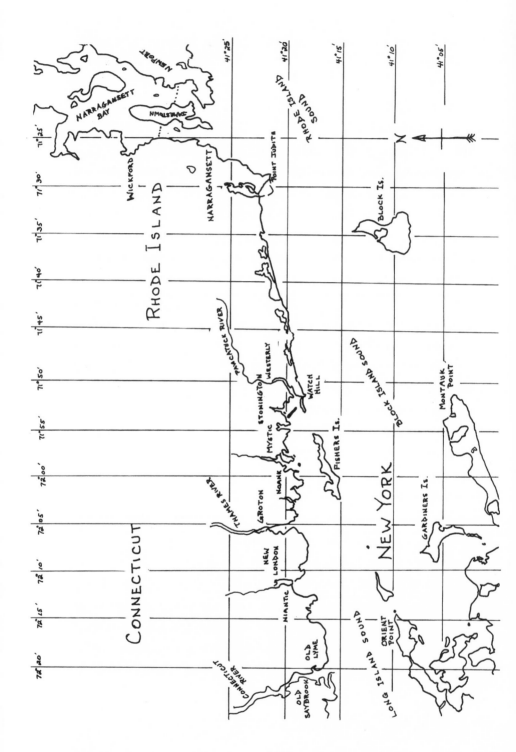

plunging foredeck without pitching overboard or receiving baptism. I wrestle the furious genoa jib to the deck, take a wrap with a shock cord and secure it. The mainsail flaps, as would a huge white seabird in distress, as I gather and enfold her and pinion her wings to the boom. I employ the least restraint. Motor, sails, and anchor should all remain ready, all of the time, to keep *MoonWind* off the shore.

I feel no urge to go ashore, myself. I have come here merely to make the passage: to abandon myself to sailing. I've been ashore here a number of times; I'm content to remain aboard.

I chug up the channel, find a berth, set my hook, and become all-a-taut-o well in time to enjoy a magnificent sunset: battlements of purples and reds, shocked with gold, from San Juan to New York City.

Strong breeze most of the night. Probably pretty fierce outside the pond. Go on deck twice during the dark to check my anchor. The first time I find the chafing gear has shifted. A split rubber sleeve about a foot long surrounds the line to protect it. This has splayed open and slipped, so I find myself hanging, naked, over the bow to resecure it. With most of a moon, I never think to switch on the foredeck light. Good thing in retrospect—I might scare my neighbors. Or make them laugh.

A couple of hours later I check again. How reassuring, on poking my head out the hatch, to see that the shore remains as far away as previously, and that no other boat has closed the gap between us. A dragging anchor can spoil a good night's rest.

By dawn the wind subsides to a steady breeze. I wash up my breakfast things and set them on the green towel on the drain board. Before departure, I stow everything securely in racks or cupboards or lockers. I convert my double bunk to the table and settles, roll my bedding and shove it deep in the quarter berth. Through the gaping main hatch and companionway the morning streams in, regaling me with breeze and sun and salt and the sounds of water.

Halfway across Block Island Sound on my way back to Connecticut. Lively lush air as I make about five knots, but with four-foot seas running dead abeam, *Moon Wind* rolls and the heaving horizon leaves my stomach queasy. Nibbling on an apple finally helps. Secure the tiller with the "tiller tamer"—an adjustable bridle—and find it satisfactory for a change. It usually needs continual adjustment. I set *Moon Wind* a course of 330, quite close-hauled, and she steers herself for three hours. Except when I meet a dragger and have to zag astern of her. A cloud of adoring seagulls follows her wake, and I tack again behind the last of the birds.

Back on port tack, *Moon Wind* rolls with each successive swell but rights herself and swings back onto her course. Unfortunately, I need to steer about 310 to make it back to Watch Hill but, in this business of sailing, I find the wind to have a will of its own. Consequently, I'll fetch the shore about three miles east of the lighthouse and about ten miles from Noank. Were the winds of this world cooperative, would there be any point to sailing? Self-reliance, patience, and acceptance are virtues I associate with sailing. Whether these are prerequisite or acquired lies open to debate.

The wind has commenced to veer and weaken; the tide has turned against me. After a couple of tacks that waste an hour for the sake of a mile made good, I yank on the cord and motor into Fishers Island Sound. The wind continues to veer—a sign of high pressure. A large blue sloop, following in my wake, has found some wind; but I power home the last few miles at half throttle, just enjoying the view. The big sloop overtakes me. An hour later, she passes the mouth of the Thames and disappears. What if I simply followed her? Passed by Noank and headed for New York? Hung a left at Manhattan and set a course for the islands? Probably be late for supper and have to sleep with the cat.

After the tall white lighthouse at Watch Hill comes Napatree Beach—a long, barren sand spit parallel to the shore. Before the '38 hurricane, herds of summer cottages huddled here. Behind Napatree spreads a mile-wide sheltered bay into which the Pawcatuck River empties. From the east bank, Watch Hill, Rhode Island, enjoys an uninterrupted view of most of the civilized world. On its west bank, Stonington, Connecticut, shelters behind two breakwaters. Most of us have our breakwaters. Some of us are so well sheltered that never a wandering bark makes a port of call, and we risk never savoring sandalwood or green tea.

Opposite the shore extends a string of rocks and shoals: the tip of Fishers Island. Wicopesset Passage is the first of four passing through this treacherous stretch of water. When heavy winds abet the brunt of the tide, ferocious seas rear up among the rocks. When this occurs, you sail down to Watch Hill and around the reef.

For the next six miles, the stately summer homes of Fishers Island complement those of the low Connecticut shore two miles away. I pass the stubby lighthouse on Latimers Reef. Whitened rocks ward the distant Stonington shore. There stands Saint Edmund's Retreat on Enders Island, connected to Connecticut via causeway, with its tranquil granite buildings and formidable seawall. On a calm day, the sea whispers by this wall with no more noise than the whispered devotions of the votaries of Saint Edmund. On a stormy day, the sea reminds these votaries of the latent wrath of God.

Motoring by Ram Island, which divides the gaping mouth of Mystic Harbor, I can just discern the pair of comfortable horses among the trees. Rumor has it Ram Island will one day be left to the state of Connecticut. Who will care for these horses when that happens?

Between Ram Island and the lighthouse at Morgan Point, the channel wriggles its way into Mystic Harbor. Just beyond Morgan Point lies rocky Mouse Island. The foremost of its three cottages clings limpet-like on the ledge, defying storm after storm. Until the next Big One. Then Mouse Island, once again, will be but a barren acre of sea-worn rock. Ultimately, we all succumb to some great storm that bares our souls forever.

I round Mouse Island and enter the channel into West Cove. This runs down the western shore of Morgan Point and terminates at our lift slip. Our marina, across the channel, dominates the head of the cove. First appears the mooring field, then the breakwater. Then finger piers splay, providing accommodation for four hundred boats.

As I leave the channel and pass between the breakwater and the outermost pier, I throttle down and proceed with utmost caution. I draw the Whitehall alongside and secure her fore and aft; she must ride outboard of *MoonWind* at my dock. Just before rounding the head of the pier, I hop up onto the afterdeck, air horn in hand, wary of darting dinghies. I round the pier at an idle and traipse down to my berth.

Everything secure by seventeen thirty. Rig the mainsail cover, bag the jib, put my binoculars, chart, and cushions below and hose down *MoonWind*—especially her anchor, caked with mud. Every vessel cooperates on a highly secretive mission: We dredge up Block Island, fluke by fluke, and bring it home to West Cove. Eventually, we'll dine at the island's restaurants by strolling out on our pier. Having contributed my bit, I stroll ashore to have a lovely hot shower.

Discover a large contingent of antique cars in front of the

Seahorse restaurant, just opposite the head by the sail loft. Vehicles from the early teens and twenties predominate, including a Willys-Overland, a Hupmobile, and a bright red Rolls-Royce. Mystic Seaport, just up the road, hosts an antique auto show tomorrow. For now, more people are outside the bar than inside, but this proves merely a passing aberration.

Join a local skipper in the 'Horse for a Margarita. He sails off for the islands next week on his Beneteau 42. Hurricane season rages on, I remind him. "Yes. I know," he grumbles. Rita, crouched off Galveston, roars and lashes her tail before she springs. The television above the bar delights in the horrors to follow.

This skipper's intention of stowing three hundred feet of three-eighth-inch anchor chain in his forward locker precipitates a lengthy debate with the old salt the other side of him about stowage and ballast and trim. I excuse myself, return to *Moon Wind,* and square away the cabin. My cell phone jangles. My wife and first mate, Paula, is on her way to the harbor. With the Pusslet.

Daybreak. I'm settled in my cockpit at the pier, wrapped around a monstrous mug of coffee. Rather chilly, and had to towel the condensation from my seat on the locker. I wear a thermal windbreaker and a watch cap. Come noon, I'll be in shirtsleeves.

The Pusslet, below, terrorizes the cabin and dances on Paula's head. She climbs and leaps and flings herself just about anywhere. On the Beaufort wind force scale she registers as a squall—perhaps force eight.

Spend this morning scrubbing the bilge and visiting with numerous passersby. Scrubbing the bilge proves so much fun I scarcely want to stop, and Paula nearly turns the hose on me to cool down my ardor. Soon afterward, breakfast with her sister aboard *Tara.* We leave the Pusslet rigorously disciplining a dirty sock in the quarter berth, and saunter down to pier A.

Their Egg Harbor 33 powerboat has a commodious cockpit; six

of us surround the table easily. Miss Kelly, age seven, is too busy fishing for snapper bluefish off the finger pier to attend to breakfast. Although she has a couple of strikes she brings nothing to the table, and has to content herself with pancakes and bacon. We loll about the remains of our meal and share the languorous morning. Miss Kelly rows among the piers, chatting with the neighbors.

Returning to *Moon Wind,* we notice the launch driver has ferried the same young woman out to the mooring field and back some half dozen times. Just along for the ride, seemingly. Later, they have their heads together—no doubt conferring about marina business. Launch service ceases today, and this young man rejoins the yard crew to help haul hundreds of boats. One day a week he devotes to college courses. A sculptor, he hopes to pursue a career in teaching—but first a master's degree is required, for which he needs a portfolio. Meanwhile, he must power-wash hulls and ferry sailors to and from their moorings.

Why mariners should want to haul their boats now, in the pride of the year, mystifies me. People no longer live by sun and moon, by wind and stars, but by some slyly contrived conventions known as clocks and calendars.

"Deadlines!" they shrill. "Deadlines!"

I, myself, should prefer to have a liveline. Something by which to secure myself to this world.

Everyone seems intent on saving time. Where do they invest all those precious moments? Have they started accounts from which they may withdraw upon retirement? Imagine how many moments you might accrue; but would they be compounded by your interest? Alas, the many moments whose acquaintances I have made were wont to spoil—one could not keep them long under any conditions. Freezing reduced them to torpor; drying only produced pervasive wrinkles. Moments, as vine-ripened strawberries, must be enjoyed immediately. Tomorrow will find them regrettable, their sweetness dissipated.

Another sunrise at West Cove. The water between the finger piers has calmed to mirror stillness—every boat has a doppelgänger lurking at waterline. Were I to look down at the water, what should I see? A young old man? An old young man, perhaps? Foliage quite gray and growing white; curious visage tanned to pensive brown; aura slightly blue from fond regrets. The wrinkles on that face might prove no more than the wrinkles left by a tickle of breeze upon the mirror. But, lo! Whose mooring line has secured my restless leg to this brawny piling? A trick of the light, no doubt. A trick of the light.

From the stern of a cabin cruiser in her slip, two men avidly cast for bait—hooking four-inch mummichogs and saving them in a bucket. What sport!

Who hooks us, I wonder? This bucket confining us has a broad horizon. We seldom perceive we have any limits at all. One of these days—or hours, perhaps—some Fisherman shall pluck us from our complacency and use us to bait a truly formidable hook. The reel will scream as He casts us adrift and trolls us the length of the Universe.

A cormorant surfaces noisily; a mummichog squirms in her bill. The cormorant has no need for a bucket. A moment later, nor has the mummichog.

For now, the harbor sparkles, the warm sun beams, the whole marina reclines with scarcely a sigh. Except for considerate fishermen who depart with muffled internal combustion and a minimum of wake. The mummichogs—Narragansett for "they go in great numbers"—also depart. Those bait fishermen should have employed a tethered cormorant, a ring about her neck to prevent her swallowing.

I put my hand to my throat. There's no ring here. *I* can swallow anything I fancy. I'll have a large slice of Autumn Equinox, thank you, slathered with sunshine . . .

BOATING SEASON

RACE ROCK LIGHT
THE RACE
NEW YORK

Went for a brief sail yesterday—after all, it registered sixty degrees and the sun nearly shone and the breeze pushed hard: about twelve to fifteen knots. Enough to wet our rail. I bent on the working jib so I wouldn't have to fight the helm so much whenever a puff laid us over. The first mate abused a windward stanchion with a grip like a Stillson wrench. I believe the water that ran down her nose was spray, but figured it more prudent not to inquire. I spilled considerable wind and thereby avoided open mutiny.

The motor performed well after having been temperamental the last time we went out. I've been running it a couple of times a week and that always helps. Outboards don't like being left unused too long—they tend to get sulky; feel slighted and resentful and, consequently, often aren't responsive. I've often found roses and loving platitudes effective. In drastic cases, I've had to resort to theater tickets and dinner in dim-lit bistros.

We didn't see many vessels in Fishers Island Sound—three or four sailboats; a few small powerboats fishing off the rocks; and a dark-hulled trawler steaming along the far shore with both her booms tucked up. We went as far as Middle Clump, tacked to the west, and beat to Seaflower Reef. The wind whistled out of the south-southwest. As balmy a day as we're likely to have this late in the boating season.

Is there a boating season? I know most pleasure boaters prefer easy living except for the die-hard fishers—the type who anxiously wait the weekend and bounce on board before the sun wakes up. These are the guys in their oilskins with thermoses of coffee and their dogs, pounding out to blue water in search of tuna. Maybe the dogs help track the fish to their lairs. You can't have too good a nose when it comes to fish.

When we reached the steel beacon at Seaflower Reef, I came about and headed back to Noank. Beyond the reef, the sound had a nasty chop—the influence of the rips pouring through the Race. Coming home on a broad reach, we had the surf on our quarter. I had to steer small to keep her on course but it wasn't in any way arduous. Outside of West Cove, I hauled in the main, then flung the tiller over my shoulder, jibed her, and headed in.

Our mooring field, totally void of boats, had nothing save little place markers bobbing in the water. Across the channel, by Morgan Point, some stalwart craft remained. One of these, a gaff-rigged, wooden sloop built on the lines of a Down East fishing boat, has low freeboard at her waist and lots of shear, a generous bowsprit, and a boom extending well abaft the transom. A totally open boat, and maybe a wet one, but also a worthy craft in a heavy sea—provided you reef before it gets too snotty. Her sails remained well furled but uncovered. I trust she goes out occasionally to taste the spray and flatten out her wrinkles.

With a bit of luck, the weather allows us out a few more times. I can't resign myself to covering *MoonWind*. Perhaps I'll just rig a tarpaulin over her cockpit. Soon the snow and ice will whelm the shore, but now the sun is shining. Last year I sailed *MoonWind* till Thanksgiving; then I had her hauled. This winter she stays in the water— where a boat belongs.

One of these winters, I'll leave the ice-clad water behind and descend the latitudes. I'll need new charts of the East Coast; I gave most of mine to the young fellow who outbid me for that twin-keel sloop at our local boatyard auction year before last. We met at Carson's diner a few weeks later.

"I'm off to the islands next week," he told me. "Come along for a shakedown tomorrow—let me know what you think of her."

He and I and his lady friend spent a tentative afternoon, skimming about the sound. She answered her helm better than I expected, and probably proves quite stable in heavy weather. I gave them three orange life jackets, four books of well-thumbed charts, and ample license to feast upon the world.

Hopefully, they save me a generous helping of wind and a goblet brimmed with sunshine . . .

THE ART OF RUNNING AGROUND

LATIMER'S REEF
STONINGTON, CONNECTICUT

Running aground in calm weather is not a big deal. I usually do it once every season just for the sake of practice. You never know when you might need to get hung up on a rock at short notice. Occasionally, I practice running a friend's boat aground to demonstrate my technique. After all, if we've been placed on Earth in order to learn, the evident corollary is that some of us were dropped off—perhaps on our heads—in order to teach. Running a friend's boat onto a shoal is just a way of showing you care about his, or her, education.

Getting off—well, that's something we all need to practice. I suggest beginning one's education with small craft. While almost any boat will eagerly go aground, those weighing more than a couple of tons may or may not cooperate when it comes to going afloat. With a little boat, as a last resort, you can always climb over her side, put your shoulder against her flank, and heave.

I'll quickly enumerate the commonest causes of going aground. Blindness, drunkenness, arrogance, ignorance, stupidity, stupidity, and stupidity. Blindness and drunkenness are often grouped together as coexistent afflictions. Arrogance and ignorance—insistence on ignoring the chart, for instance—run a close second. Stupidity covers a multitude of shortcomings: stupor, stupidness, and stupidiferousness. I suggest that, rather than count the syllables in this last word, you pay attention to your chart and scan the horizon for aids to navigation.

Last year I went sailing with a friend. I'll call him Bob because, no matter how many times I shove him under, he always pops back up to the surface. We took his Able 20 out for a little jaunt to clean some marine growth off her bottom. We followed the shore of Fishers Island, inboard of the Clumps. When we pulled opposite the marker by West Clump, I fell off to round the rocks on the outboard side.

"Just come about," suggested Bob, "and pass behind West Clump. There's plenty of water if you keep at least ten yards off."

Well, I came about and passed behind the rocks.

"A bit farther off," warned Bob.

"I'm pinching her now," I replied.

"You ought to just make it," he said, looking over the side. "Boy, look at those rocks down there. Maybe you ought to . . ."

Crunch!

"Maybe I should have," I said.

Fortunately, some judicious shoving with a six-foot boat hook while Bob swayed *Dreamtime* by hanging off her shrouds sufficed to free us. Now we know our limiting factors exactly. A boat drawing three feet, two inches, should keep at least forty-one feet, fourteen inches off the backside of West Clump when the tide is five-eighths full on a Tuesday. We dutifully entered all the pertinent information into his log. We even made a mark on his boat hook for future reference. One can't be too careful.

There's something about West Clump that attracts small boats. Last summer we took out *MoonWind*—my son and his wife and little boy, ourselves, and another couple. We sailed down to Seaflower Reef and returned between the Dumplings. (Or the Cupcakes, according to Paula.) We ran alongside Fishers Island, but north of the Clumps. East, Middle, and West Clump reside a mile or so apart and are marked by cans on the outboard side. Any two marks can be connected by a straight line at any time. Staying outboard of this line comes highly recommended. At high tide, the Clumps are submerged and, on a calm day, scarcely a ripple betrays their whereabouts.

"Head away from the can," I warned my son.

He lackadaisically moved the helm an inch.

"No—like this," I demonstrated. "See the next green can?"

The problem was not with his eyes but with his mouth. He was busy explaining the newest innovation in wind technology and, gradually, resumed his former course.

"Fall off," I warned. "You're really close to West Clump."

"Okay, okay," he said. "I don't see any rocks."

"Not at high tide," I countered. "Fall off some more."

"You mean," he said, "like . . ."

Crunch!

Doing two knots, we didn't harm poor *MoonWind*, but we startled the whatsis out of some napping barnacles. I dropped the sails, flipped the outboard motor into the drink, and yanked on the starter cord. Some days she starts on the second pull. This was not one of those days. As soon as I reminded that motor of the lovely young four-stroke languishing in the motor shop, hoping to replace her, she decided to humor me. On the fourteenth pull she started.

I ordered the entire crew to come as far aft as possible. With six consenting adults in three square feet, we were probably breaking most of Connecticut's Blue Laws. I threw the motor into reverse and we scraped our way clear of West Clump.

"Party's over," I hollered. "Raise the main!"

"More rocks!" shouted the crew. "We want more rocks!"

"Belay that, me hardies!" I hollered. "Raise the genny!" A mutinous crew can make for a long afternoon.

We straggled down to the stubby lighthouse at Latimers Reef. This perches on a pile of quarry stone and hasn't a proper landing since the light became fully automated. I had the helm now. (Can't trust them kids, nohow.) Fifty yards off, I prepared to jibe and head back to the harbor.

"Closer, Grampa," urged our three-year-old. "I want to climb on the rocks." Like father, like son. Needless to say, I jibed and hurried us out of there. *Moon Wind* had no desire to climb the lighthouse.

The other couple, who had spent their afternoon on the foredeck, snuggling, expressed their thanks for our invitation.

"We must admit," they confided, "that going aground was the highlight of our excursion."

My son endured his flogging with scarcely a whimper.

CAN YOU TAKE A LINE, PLEASE?

Yesterday it reached forty degrees; cold enough to discourage most boaters and rather rough outside the West Cove breakwater. But four o'clock found me messing with my outboard aboard *Moon Wind*, changing the fuel filter, purging the line, replacing the thermostat—all the exciting things one does to ensure the motor starts up without difficulty. I haven't a great love for motors but I do know a few things. One of which is: Always suspect the fuel. Just as you wouldn't drink from a grungy old mud puddle, don't expect your motor to imbibe old fuel. If you do drink from grungy old mud puddles, pay no attention to this.

Though I visit the pier a couple of times a week to check the lines and fenders on several sailboats, I hadn't gone aboard my own boat for a month. My Whitehall gives me reproachful looks whenever I come out the back door of the shop.

"This summer *Moon Wind* resides on a mooring," I tell her, "and I'll row that lovely paint off your little round bottom."

The quietude on a mooring commends itself but a boat tends to

185

pitch a lot. This makes staying aboard only half as delightful more than half of the time. Sleeping aboard in a slip has none of the challenge that comes, free of charge, with a mooring.

How simple to get under way from a mooring: just raise your mainsail and cast off your mooring pendant. I won't miss motoring in and out of finger piers. The alternative—sailing in and out of your slip without power—only requires knowing how to maneuver in a tablespoon's worth of water. Especially when the wind turns fluky, when single-handed, or when other craft block your way.

Some mariners—occasionally even sailors (those are the ones with the earrings, dear)—don't observe when the wind provides your sole propulsion, and assume you can readily back down your boat at will.

Sailing backward requires heading nearly into the wind. By yourself, backing your main and putting your helm hard over while tooting three times on your horn, taking Poseidon's name in vain, and eating an oversauced eggplant Parmesan sandwich requires two mouths and at least two pair of hands—more if the eggplant suddenly panics and tries to abandon ship.

I've sailed into my slip a couple of times when the wind cooperated. A supple mainsheet that runs freely proves most useful; also having the main halyard accessible from the cockpit. I usually drop my jib before attempting close maneuvers. Even under power, when the weather turns rough, I've no compunction about hailing someone and asking him or her to handle a line.

Parking your yacht on top of the pier—or in another boat's cockpit—is generally frowned upon. It's imperative to learn how to heave a line accurately at ten or fifteen yards. Conversely, prepare to hand off your rabbit and catch a flung line to secure a plunging boat. In crowded marinas, even clearing a slip while under power may require assistance.

While lazing in our dock one day with an un-nautical acquaintance, a good-sized powerboat passed astern and headed for her slip.

Not seeing a second person aboard, I jumped up to help. Then the skipper's wife came on deck. By the way she straddled the pulpit, snatched their spring line from the piling, and cussed the boat hook, I knew she knew her business. I climbed back over our taffrail.

My acquaintance asked me what I had meant to do. When I explained that I would have taken a line or fended off, he looked at me, rather puzzled.

"Why should you care?" he asked. "It isn't your boat."

"No, it isn't," I said. But I thought to myself: If ever you owned a boat and kept her here, you'd find, on even the hottest day, an abundance of cold shoulders. I've discovered since that not many people ashore seem pleased to see him.

You'd better stow your egoism when you work on the waterfront. Wait till next time you try to berth single-handed, and the wind is slamming your bow against a piling. What a relief to hear someone shout, "All secure forward, Skipper. Pass me your spring line."

APRIL

Went sailing yesterday. First time this year and, though there have been more pleasant days, it certainly sufficed. *Moon Wind* stood ready to go; her motor started on the third pull and ran smoothly. The mainsail remains tucked away under its cover; the battery has a charge. But Bob decided to move his Able 20, *Dreamtime*, to her summer slip, two piers over, and, as long as she had to go abroad, we might as well jog about the harbor and clean the growth from her bottom.

He worked on the piers yesterday and today, restoring water to the docks, and opened up *Dreamtime* and started up her motor. He ran out the first tank of fuel, meanwhile flushing the motor with fresh water. At four thirty, ready to depart, he connected the motor to the second gas can, primed the carburetor, and pushed the ignition. Nothing. And then more nothing. Enough nothing to run down the battery. Turns out the gas had some water in it. He purged the fuel system and off she went—fired up and purred.

Meanwhile, I had gotten the sails on her, but the breeze blew directly up the channel. We motored out past the breakwater, fell off, and hoisted our rags. Had to tack a few times to clear Mouse Island as the light breeze and the tide tended to carry us back into West Cove.

We cleared Mouse, finally, fell off until we ran dead before the wind, and ascended the Mystic River, wung out with the tide behind us.

Rather overcast and maybe fifty degrees: one of those innocuous days when the whole world seems but shades of gray—drab and of little interest. But it only seems so. Lacking contrast, form and shade and composition take on more significance. When you learn to see with the artist's eye, you discern a dozen shades in any object where light and shadow mingle. With diffused light, you must learn to read a subtler sort of contrast and revel in sparseness. The sky and sea are met at the horizon; do they diverge, or converge? Even when the fog has enveloped your vessel; when your sail merges with the prevalent whiteness; even then, beauty surrounds you.

We never made it much past Sixpenny Island. The tide had trouble overcoming the current; the breeze abated until our jib could scarcely lift the sheets. We rippled up the river at a pace to please an artist, remarking the quiet homes and the few moored boats. And suddenly, over our shoulder, we noticed the sun reclined on the muted softness of Fishers Island. I dropped the despondent jib; we sheeted in the main and came about. The motor started immediately; the four small pistons pushed us down the river without complaint. The mainsail tumbled upon the deck; I unbent it and stowed it below. We rounded Mouse Island and headed into our harbor, the breeze again at our backs.

The mooring field contained but last year's stubble; not a shoot attested to the seaworthy crop to come. The fifty vessels fast at the piers seemed abandoned. The ferry, in between trips, had no one aboard. We discovered a work barge moored alongside the pier in the berth intended for *Dreamtime*; the yard replaces the steel hoops that attach to the pier and ride up and down the pilings. The berth astern held a boat from Fishers Island; the berth ahead had a single mooring line fast to a cleat.

Though the line seemed glossy, we chanced leaving *Dreamtime* there for a couple of days until the yard moved their barge. We tucked the Able into the berth ahead and plumped her pillows. Just as we finish securing, along came the owner—a twenty-five-foot Parker skiff with an enclosed pilothouse. Bob moved *Dreamtime* into a slip at a finger pier across the walkway. I helped them both to secure, and the three of us shared a pleasant chat on the pier before we headed our several ways to supper.

Amazingly, we didn't have any adventures all afternoon. We encountered no storms with waves breaking over our mast, we never piled our boat on the rocks, we scarcely drowned enough to make it worthwhile, and, worst of all, we were never rescued by mermaids. But I suppose someone needs to have such uneventful trips. Otherwise, we'd never be impressed by all *your* yarns.

A HURRIED DEPARTURE

Friday afternoon about half past four I decide to call it a day. At least the commercial portion of my day. Everyone else has left for the weekend. It's time to work on *MoonWind* and finish installing the forward hatch surround I've begun. Then the phone rings and I spend several minutes with a client. Meanwhile, one of the fellows from the marina comes by and patiently waits until I finish my call.

"That your green sloop in A-10?" he queries.

"That's right," I say.

"The people renting that slip for the summer need it tomorrow," he tells me.

"Tomorrow?"

"Tomorrow *morning*," he informs me.

After he leaves, I assess the situation. I need to go on my mooring tomorrow morning. I don't know whether the new tenants need to bring their boat a hundred miles or just from the next pier over. If the latter, they may be here at eight AM, rightly demanding my eviction. After all, my wet winter storage expired in April. Some mariners launch their boats early in April; others don't bother putting theirs in until Memorial Day. A few people's boating season won't begin until the Fourth of July. I had hoped to get everything done a bit sooner, but, as always, work and inclement weather interfere.

My outboard motor sits at home in the driveway. It needs grease and a new zinc before it goes into the water. I need to fit this hatch surround that I've built; having power would facilitate the process. *Moon Wind* has sanding dust all over her vee berth; I've considerately tracked it everywhere I could. Having power for the vacuum cleaner would help. As would fresh water for hosing my deck. I need to bail yesterday's rain from my Whitehall and row her around to my slip.

It takes me three hours to finish fitting the hatch surround, prep the deck, install it, clean up the caulking, cut a square of plywood for a temporary hatch and secure it to the frame. I arrive home for supper at eight o'clock, exhausted.

At seven AM, I begin again. I grease my motor and change the zinc. Fortunately, the motor, a Johnson 9.9, weighs but seventy-five or eighty pounds. I toss it into my truck. En route to the boatyard, seven miles away, I stop at the local station and fill two small gas tanks. I choose to drive down the flowering river road.

May surrounds us, overwhelms us, shatters us with her beauty. Bridesmaid dogwood lavishes her flowers. The redolent scent of lilac takes me home to my parents' house in Hadlyme. The temperature registered fifty degrees at daybreak and now ascends past sixty. By the shore, the seagulls sing merrily from the lofty pilings; the anemometers have taken the morning off. The boatyard slumbers peacefully.

I load my outboard into a dock cart and trundle it out the pier. I fit the motor into the transom cutout and bolt it on. Soon it purrs happily and pees a stream of water into West Cove. I leave it running all the while I vacuum and clean and generally square away my gear. I may need to make the hastiest of departures.

I secure my gas cans to the taffrail. I bail my tender, row her into the slip, and make her fast alongside *Moon Wind*. I disconnect, coil, and stow my shore power cord. As no incoming vessel approaches, I take the opportunity to hose down the deck but keep my weather eye open. I cast off my lines and fling them aboard. The cove has scarcely a ripple as I back *Moon Wind* out of her slip and head out into the channel.

I find my mooring, J-11, and snag it with my boat hook. Home at last. I shut down my motor and tilt it out of the water. I square away the deck, coil lines, bring my fenders aboard, adjust my chafing gear. I go below and stow everything securely. Here, outside the breakwater, the cove can quickly turn bumpy.

I load my tools into the Whitehall and pull to the dinghy dock. What a lovely morning; and scarcely ten o'clock. Time to go home, have a hot shower and a more substantial breakfast.

A-10 remains vacant. Anyone need a slip?

DRAWING FOUR FEET

Finally took *MoonWind* out for a sail today. Motoring up the Mystic River a month ago scarcely qualifies. So little breeze blew that we powered away from our mooring, and I hadn't even hanked on the jib. By the time I had both sails on her, we had halved the distance to Flat Hammock and found the diminutive wind. The tide ran out, toward the east. The breeze blew from the south at perhaps six knots. Hardly exciting but enough to keep full and by. The tide contributed its two cents' worth, keeping us under way at a couple of knots.

I expected more water traffic this holiday weekend, but a majority of the boats never left their berths. I suppose that everyone assumed it not worth venturing out with the waters so crowded, so nobody did and, consequently, they weren't. The sound had no more traffic than any other summer weekend. Yet most of the population came to stay aboard their boats, making parking at our marina problematic. As always at this time of year, more than ten percent of the fleet still stood ashore on jack stands. A few concerned sailors busily painted their bottoms.

We went as far as Latimers Reef then turned to fight the tide. Fortunately, the wind persevered and we made nearly two knots return-ing. For a couple of hours we enjoyed the delicious breeze. Then it suddenly ceased—without any warning. We found ourselves off North Dumpling with drooping sails. About four o'clock, every boat in Fishers Island Sound became becalmed. Mainsails came down, jibs were furled, and motors purred as sailors headed for harbors and drinks and dinners.

Coming across the sound toward Noank, my two-stroke motor sputtered and sneezed and gasped. So do I whenever I inhale gaso-line. I gave it what encouragement I could, gentled it the two miles home, and headed for my mooring. The tide by now had ebbed as much as it needed.

Suddenly, at the edge of the mooring field, our boat went bump as we passed over the only rock in the vicinity. I'd been told about this rock but never seen it—until about four thirty this afternoon. For-tunately, we draw but four feet of water. Unfortunately, this rock pro-jected within three feet and eleven inches of the surface. That the authorities haven't flagged it surprises me, though it appears on every chart. Someone told me that, during a perigee low tide, the sea breaks over this rock. On that same day, you can wade to the Bahamas.

The rubberized tug of one of the towing services moors not two hundred yards away, waiting to aid any mariner in distress. Had the tide been out another couple of inches, I might have gone aground but a few hundred feet from where my Whitehall dinghy swung on my mooring. Some folks would have kedged off the rock by buoy-ing up an anchor with life jackets and swimming it from their boat. For such a gala occasion, should it occur, I carry tow insurance.

Having a depth finder doesn't resolve the problem. Isolated rocks won't show up on your screen until you bounce across them. In shoal water, you need to exercise caution.

Those who live shallow lives often drift aground. Those who nav-igate the depths, whether of joy or sorrow, of intellect or spirituality, run the risk of encountering tumultuous storms. They also have the noblest lives and feel the grandest passions. Those who stay the middle course, who keep their noses pressed to their depth finders, never see the sunset—and go aground as often as anyone else. Read your chart and keep your weather eye open.

Last week I affixed a float with a whip to the end of one of the two pendants on my mooring. I found myself with the new float in my fist and the mooring buoy caught beneath my keel. Not a major calamity, though, and readily resolved. Scarcely as calamitous as having one's sunny enthusiasm pinched in the crack of dawn.

WATCH HILL

We've just returned from Napatree, the beach beside Watch Hill. Sailed over Saturday afternoon. New outboard works well—no complaints—but enough wind to round Sandy Point under sail and traverse the mile-long channel. Rounded up into the south wind, pushed the starter button, and behold! The little pistons danced up and down and drove us to the likeliest spot to anchor.

As usual, I set both of my Danforths from the bow, aligning us with the wind. Both Saturday and Sunday night it blew hard. The anchorage at Napatree provides scant shelter, though tucked behind a mile-long spit that separates it from the ocean. Even the south wind passing over this spit does not slow much.

My Whitehall gladly streamed astern, at least until the tide changed. Then she came alongside and begged to snuggle. I secured her fore and aft, provided three fenders, and turned into my bunk to be rocked to sleep. All night I heard the thumping of the fenders against the hull and the slosh of the bucking Whitehall. No matter how often I roused myself and laid aloft to reprimand that dinghy, she flatly ignored me. After my well-deserved hour's sleep, the insistent sun came up. I made a huge mug of espresso and poured it over my head.

All night, our new black kitten, Pye Wacket, walked on our ears and scampered the length of the bed to assert her affection. The rocking, pitching, and thumping affected her not at all. She used her box behind the companionway ladder, climbed like a sailor, and hauled on every rope's end.

Saturday night, July first, the sun broke through the haze for a last hurrah: a crisp-edged vermilion disc against a pink smear. Gradually, night enveloped the gleaming water. We had gone below to make up our bunk and . . . Bang! The fireworks began. At Watch Hill and Stonington, the darkened sky came alive with sparkling colors. The pop guns of each local village carried across the bay.

Twelve miles west, at New London, the Pequots and Mohegans provide the most magnificent show each year; but not until next weekend.

A couple of years ago, we anchored inside the mouth of the Thames on a Chris Craft cabin cruiser to watch the event. A mile up-river, hundreds of boats milled about to secure advantage. At a mile, the concussion and dazzle sufficed. The clamorous finale resounded as a monstrous battle at sea. The heady odor of brimstone rode the breeze. To come any closer would have dismayed our ears. High above, the bursting displays lighted the sky for miles.

This weekend, from Napatree, we could see a more modest display above the Thames put on by the submarine base. At twelve miles, the most impressive explosions could be covered by one's thumb. From the south, fifteen knots swept the noise toward Lexington and Concord, where it all began. The unaccompanied Lilliputian showers of red, green, and gold scarcely held our attention.

The eye of the mind tends to nearsightedness. A remote conflagration has little hope of competition with the flames in your fireplace. If not for sooty skies the following season, Europe would never have noticed Krakatoa: one of the most spectacular disasters of our era.

Sunday dawned bright and sunny. We lazed about and read and played with the kitten. In the afternoon, I rowed to Watch Hill; tied up at the dinghy dock. There I had a lengthy discussion on brightwork with a disembarking mariner. On the single street, persistent tourists proved the dominant species.

I squeezed into the secondhand bookshop and insinuated the narrow aisles to while a pleasant hour. Those volumes of most interest proved collectible and too dear. I came away empty-handed. I wandered among the cafés, looked into boutique windows, and dodged exhausted children intent on their ice cream cones. I visited the antique carousel and wished I could drop fifty years for fifteen minutes. The proud little horses had flowing manes to their fetlocks.

As the day expired, I mounted my prancing Whitehall and galloped throughout the fleet.

ONE CALM DAY LAST SUMMER

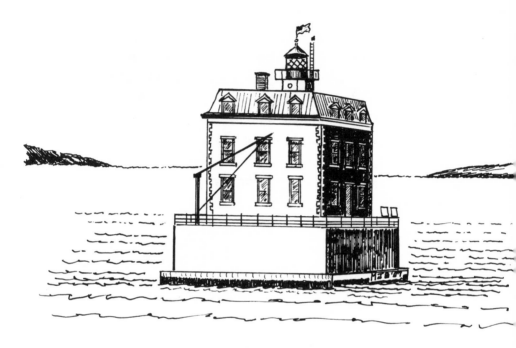

LEDGE LIGHT
THAMES MOUTH
CONNECTICUT

Off to Pine Island today. No wind, of course, this time of year, so motored all four miles. Tossed our anchor into the drink and ravished the hamper for lunch. Then a short nap and headed homeward again. Breeze threatened familiarity, so put up main and genny. They began to draw but, after twenty minutes, the wind fell foul, finally died, and we took our canvas in. Motored home the whole way.

A perfectly uneventful cruise but delightful in its way. This time of year one doesn't expect much wind. Everyone awaits the autumn and steady winds to carry them off adventuring.

Scrubbed the bilge and made a partition for the chain locker this week to ensure the rode doesn't sprawl about the vee berth and get entangled. A serious consideration should one's life depend on getting the anchor out without confusion. Only one's life depends on it— nothing important.

Also put up a towel rack. Little things add up to make life aboard not only safe and endurable but convenient.

Discovered that Noank Shipyard, up the river, will pump my tank for a measly five dollars. This, after trying to raise the government pump-out boat for over an hour.

The Littlest Pusslet came for a sail again. She seemed placid and accommodating—maybe the motion of the boat prevented her from expressing any longing for dry land. She shied away from venturing into the cockpit—until I took her topsides and let her look about. She wanted to bury her face in my arm until I showed her a rope's end. Then she consented to play and be a kitten. At least she hadn't any incentive to dive overboard and swim home.

Tuned into the VHF and listened to a man and a woman on separate boats discussing their course and aids to navigation on their charts. Neither seemed really sure about what they read or saw or thought they should have been doing.

"Are you taking that next mark to starboard?"

"You mean that one a mile ahead—where that boat is anchored, fishing?"

"Is that what they're doing?"

"That's the red mark, right? That bell sort of thing?"

"Yeah, I guess that's the one. Which side of it are you going?"

"I think we ought to go to the left. That is, if that mark's the entrance to that harbor where we're going."

"I guess so. Can you see it? There's a sailboat passing in front of it now."

"You mean that sloop?"

"Is that what you call it? I thought a sloop had two masts."

"I don't know. Just in front of that big white house on the shore."

"The one with all the trees in the yard, or the other one?"

"Which other one?"

After a while, one wonders how these people ever get home. What do they do if no one cooks their supper or brings them their slippers? Maybe this is the couple who persist in trying to make their landings sideways into their slip. We take their line and fend them off and accept their thanks that we know are offered sincerely. As long as they don't run into our boat more than twice a year we can deal with them.

Our guiding rule has always been: When large, immovable objects such as pilings approach, proceed slowly. Coming into our slip at half a knot, nothing too preposterous can go wrong. We seldom grudge acquainting our rail with a piling at half a knot. Acquaintances we've made in a hurry have sometimes proved more abrasive.

Having the Pusslet aboard always reminds us to take our boating seriously. Nothing can have worse repercussions than slopping the Pusslet's milk.

THE PETREL

The Petrel

A DISGUSTING JOB

I sauntered into the shop a few days back and heard voices in the office. The other two discussed matters of infinite importance as I could ascertain by their laughter.

"Here he comes," said my boss.

"Yep," I replied. "It's me."

"I have a really disgusting job I think you'll enjoy." He grinned. "Do you have a respirator?"

"Yep."

"Do you have some heavy neoprene gloves?"

"Yep."

"Do you mind climbing into a tank that used to have sewage in it?"

"Yep."

"That's all right," he chortled. "You won't have to do that, anyways. I need you to bring a sailboat here from Port Jefferson."

Turns out, a customer has a twenty-one-foot Petrel—a fiberglass version of a Herreshoff Fish Class sloop. Our little shop right here in Noank, Connecticut, built thirty-two of these between 1978 and 1992. They're lovely craft with lots of brightwork—transom, tiller, coaming and locker tops, cabin sides, toe and rub rails, cabin doors. The mast and boom and club for the jib are of gleaming Sitka spruce. A huge Marconi mainsail seizes the lightest air and drives her full keel hull while other boats luff helplessly.

The summer before last I flopped about in a four-knot breeze with *MoonWind,* wishing for steerageway, when along came a Petrel and whispered right on by me. They fitted some of these boats with ten-horse diesel inboards; the one I'm to fetch has a five-horse Honda outboard. Even with plenteous winds it's a reassuring accessory.

Hurricane Wilma presently terrorizes the Gulf. By midweek, she'll blow by here quite vitiated—if the folks at NOAA have their data correct. Hopefully, we'll receive residual wind—ten knots would prove quite pleasant. My run will total perhaps seventy statute miles and my course will lay about 090 when once I clear Port Jefferson. The shores of Long Island Sound lie but ten to fifteen miles apart. The Connecticut side has shoals and rocks and islands in profusion, but away from shore the waters run a hundred feet deep. I only need to avoid running down the heavy commercial traffic. I plan to take the ferry over on Wednesday afternoon. The owner will meet me and take me down to the harbor. I've asked that the Petrel have basic gear aboard and one extra can of fuel.

The wind will blow northwesterly and veer around to the north— I'll easily keep on a reach the entire way. The Petrel's hull speed, a bit more than five knots, will allow me to make most of my journey the first day, and I've allotted two days to return. I suppose I could continue into the night as she has running lights, but I little fancy keeping alert for fifteen hours just to save—what? The wind? The wind will blow on the morrow.

Thursday night I hope to anchor just inside the mouth of the Connecticut River. I'm not familiar with the New York shore, but the Connecticut River feels like home to me. I've just this moment checked the tide on the Internet. Ebbing all Friday morning, it will take me out of the river and urge me the final sixteen miles to Noank. If I can't make Old Saybrook—the mouth of the Connecticut—by Thursday evening, I can certainly settle for either Clinton or West-brook, but neither has much accommodation for anchoring.

They forecast moderate wind and seas, though the wind blows out of Ontario now, bringing a whiff of wood smoke and more than a hint of November. I shall keep my eyes open for flocks of errant penguins. The season requires long johns and thick wool socks; Thursday night they predict a possible frost.

Yet—two days on the water, uninterrupted by all the carking concerns of day-to-day living—what could prove more fulfilling? If this is mere escapism—so be it! Cast off that mooring pendant, mate, and let her sails fill! Me for a long swell and a breeze like a lover's ecstatic clasp and the live limb of the tiller in my fist and the cry of the tern as she skims above the heave and surge of the tide.

PORT JEFFERSON, NEW YORK

Wednesday evening the boss drove me down to Bridgeport to catch the ferry over to Port Jefferson. We stopped for Mexican food, and the understaffed kitchen provided our food at the latest possible minute: well cooked, notwithstanding. I boxed my final fajita and finished it on the observation deck. The car ferry proved just what you'd expect—a big, awkward, top-heavy excursion boat with a dining room that serves pizza, burgers, and fries, a saloon bar, and an upper deck from which to enjoy the view.

I laid aloft and went forward and watched the sun go down as we cleared the harbor. Aside from the crew, nobody else showed interest in sharing this pleasure, though I suspect there was enough to go around. Halfway across, my ears got cold—all I had on was a ball cap—and I dragged my gear below. I had filled my duffel bag to the brim. Somehow I'd managed to cram in my sleeping bag—along with a lantern, a spotlight, two books, charts, a coil of line, a tool kit, foul-weather gear, and plenty of extra clothing. My grub I kept separate in a soft-sided bag with a shoulder strap. A handheld GPS and a cell phone adorned my belt, and in my jacket pocket curled up a little brass horn, guaranteed to wake the dead—if they happened to sleep within a dozen yards.

At Port Jefferson, I dragged my worldly goods down two flights and off the boarding ramp. My host appeared and took my duffel bag. His back has had a kink in it ever since. I received the four-minute sightseeing tour on the way back to his cozy home in Setauket. His lovely wife gave me honey with green tea in it; their Airedale gave me unexpected snuggles. Then we watched the last game of the

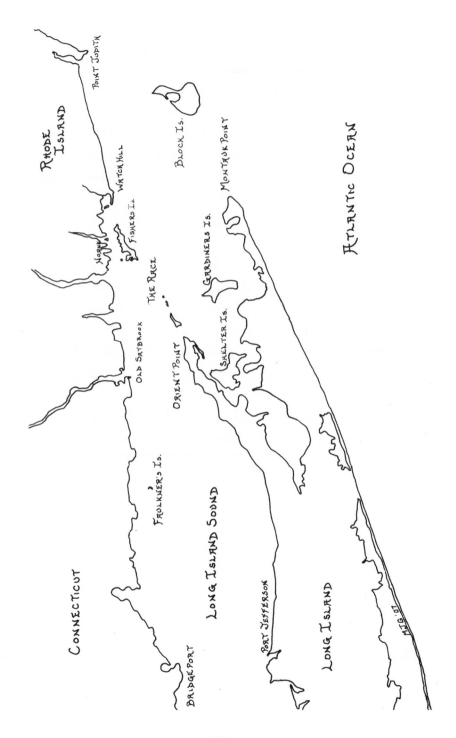

World Series and stumbled off to bed.

Daybreak ascended with more than its usual vigor. It promised to be raw and windy and bleak: quite seasonable, in fact. After a breakfast enhanced by good strong coffee, we made our way to the harbor, loaded a rowboat, and pulled out to the Petrel. Even at rest, a Herreshoff boat constitutes a veritable work of art. The small, rustic marina serves a sheltered, placid harbor appended to Port Jefferson.

But now I had little time for admiration. I must receive the guided tour, including, of course, the amenities. These consisted of a well-made cedar bucket with a cover, the center panel of which could be removed. A Dacron bail allowed one to dilute one's contributions with salt water. After the guided tour I took my leave, my host having counseled me to hug the starboard shore until I merged with the channel out to the sound. The motor performed as promised and took me out past the jetties. The tide and the wind had a lively altercation in the channel; the Petrel took little notice. Most of the day I had fifteen knots and a three-foot chop, but she didn't pound at all.

I soon discovered she had too much sail on her—I had difficulty keeping her off the wind. I headed up, set the tiller into the comb and, sailing close-hauled, took a double reef. This improved her handling. She surged along, rail-down, but my vertical mileage equaled my horizontal. I'd planned to hold a course of 090, but I had to allow for drift—the wind and sea were just abaft my beam. I settled in at 080 but struggled to keep her a point one way or the other. At that, the sea hit my flank and caused too much spray. Rather than don foul-weather gear, I chose to point a bit higher. Then the spray went over the foredeck and left me dry—for the most part. Halfway aslant the sound—about eight miles from either shore—I began to tire of going up and down. The apple I'd eaten earlier became restless, and opted to come aloft for a better view.

If the wind increased I would need to take my third reef. I opted to head to windward thirty degrees until I could shelter beneath the Connecticut shore; first I would need to clear the Thimble Islands. Having passed these, I set an easterly course by Faulkners Light. It proved a bit calmer here, but the drab and defecting day was cooling down. In twenty miles, I'd fetch the Connecticut River. Was that blue line the jetty? Then the tide turned against me and suppertime receded.

NORTH COVE, OLD SAYBROOK

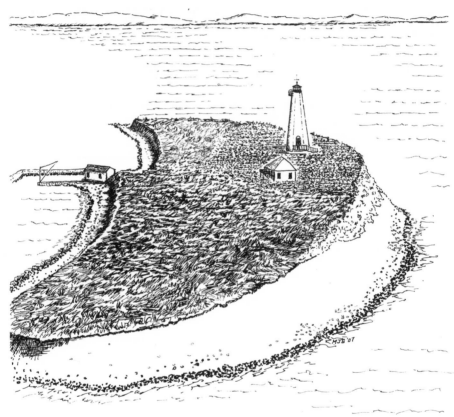

FAULKNER'S ISLAND LIGHT
LONG ISLAND SOUND
GUILFORD
CONNECTICUT

Thursday afternoon. Having crossed the sound to Connecticut east of New Haven, I saw ahead Faulkners Island. Surrounded by rocks and shoals, this island supports a lighthouse perched high on a scrubby bluff of about three acres. Built in 1802, it is the second oldest lighthouse in Connecticut. By the time I passed the island, the day waxed duller and yet more dull; the tide had commenced to change and impede my passage.

I pulled twice on the lanyard; the Honda growled. I kept the motor going at three-quarters throttle. The wind had abated some but I kept her reefed; during my twenty-five-mile passage aslant the sound, whenever I thought I might shake out my reefs, I would see the seas leaping a couple of miles ahead and stay my hand. Now I rolled by Guilford, Madison, Clinton, and Westbrook.

The shoreline ahead, which had floated, blue and indistinct, reattached itself to the water's edge. The lighthouse at the end of the jetty jutting out from the west bank of the Connecticut finally came into focus. The second lighthouse above it at Lynde Point showed stark and white against the autumnal shore. With an hour to go, the fading light spread a vermilion smear between the lowering sky and the gray horizon. I drew a deep breath and commenced to blow on the mainsail. It must have helped—I rounded the jetty just as the dim light failed.

Up the river I followed the lighted buoys. A mile upstream, the shore and the river became one shade of murk. I squinted into the gloom. Somewhere ahead lay the entrance to North Cove. Occasionally, I concede to current technology. I'd borrowed a searchlight; now I clicked the switch. A million candles danced forth through the dark and showed me the channel marker into the cove. A second green can, a third, and then I entered as protected an anchoring spot as one could desire: a half-mile basin surrounded by stately homes with private piers.

In the mooring field, half a dozen sailboats roosted snugly. I picked up one of a dozen deserted moorings and settled in for the night. As I put my little craft to rights, out of the corner of my weather eye, through the gloom and wrack, I glimpsed a falling star. I took it for a winking of the Infinite—and winked back. Then again, it may have been merely a silver hair that the breeze blew across my sight.

Meanwhile, my simple portion was chilly air, cold food, and a bottle of water that would start to gel come morning. But I had a lovely warm sleeping bag and a battery-powered lantern. I snuggled into my bag with all my clothes on, pulled my watch cap well down over my ears, and commenced to read. Letters of Albert Einstein: more humanistic than what you might imagine, and reassuring. After thirty pages I doused my light.

I don't sleep very soundly in strange lodgings. The cuddy doors had been unshipped, and the sky was at my shoulder. All night long my mind was awhirl but, came the dawn, I rose and greeted the river. Fruit and yogurt, crackers, and well-chilled water found me fed better than half this world's children. I coiled my lines, cleared my deck, and cast off.

The breeze, now veered to due north with the coming high pressure, barely stirred. I started the Honda and headed out to the river. Here I encountered more breeze. I shook out yesterday's reefs and killed the motor. The tide and current and wind were all behind me; I wafted down to the sound with sails spread wide. I met one larger sailboat coming home under power, her sails furled, her rigging pearled with mist, her skipper in oilskins. We met with a nod and a half-raised hand and left the silence unbroken.

I passed the first lighthouse, threaded the jetties, bade farewell to the jetty light, and glided out into the sound. Here the breeze blew a moderate eight knots. The little Petrel settled onto a broad reach and rode the tide along the muted shore. This is perfect, I sighed. Having passed a day both battered and bounced, I get to enjoy a serene close to my voyage.

"Ha!" said the gods.

THAMES MOUTH

HARBOR LIGHT
NEW LONDON
CONNECTICUT

Friday morning. A couple of hours east from the mouth of the calm Connecticut, a line of foam stretched straight across the sound from Connecticut to Long Island at right angles. On the farther side of this demarcation, the water turned glum and troubled. The wind picked up and the Petrel wet her rail.

I refused to reef. After all, the weather boded fair. In eight or ten miles, I should enter the homey shelter of Fishers Island. Now I encountered the influence of the North Atlantic meeting Long Island Sound. Fishers Island, six miles long, diverts the ocean through the Race—a slot five miles wide between itself and Orient Point, Long Island. Two hundred feet of water try to pass over a reef of sixty feet. I chose to keep as far from this playground as possible.

Some of the ocean chooses to pour inboard of Fishers Island. The gaping mouth of Thames River, just to the north, dumps its tide and current into the mixture. At times, this mixture of Race and river and wind and ocean tends to get a mite choppy. After what seemed like hours, I'd bounced and rolled and pitched my wet way through it.

Behind me, two Coast Guard cutters emerged from the Thames— running interference for a formidable submarine. They build these monsters just upriver; beyond spreads the naval base where some of them make their home. One Coast Guard boat swung by my stern and gave me a looking-over then swerved away. Fortunately, my rocket launcher was quite well camouflaged. The sub slid over the troubled water at ten knots, passed through the Race with no regard for a nasty five-knot rip, and plunged toward some highly secretive, needful mission.

"You're quite a quick boat," I thought, "with the wind astern, but I don't much like the cut of your forestays'l."

Now I drew close enough to home to name the rocks and ledges. Three miles ahead, between the Connecticut shore and Fishers Island, repose both North and South Dumpling. This latter stands unoccupied: a hunched-up acre of rock and writhen brush. North Dumpling has a lighthouse—privately owned and maintained—a large brick house, a wooden house, a boatshed, and a windmill. A heliport and a pier complete her survey. An amphibious craft—a "duck"—squats by the shore. A gentleman's retreat from civilization: two acres of paradise two miles offshore.

By now the sea had subsided; I leaned with the breeze and flew. I could have passed between the Dumplings—plenty of water there. I chose to amuse myself by beating to windward, and barely cleared North Dumpling's clutching pier.

Now I lay just a mile outside Mouse Island—my harbor mouth. I sailed another mile or so and tacked back into the outer harbor, just outside the breakwater. Here, in the acres of mooring field, rides another Petrel. I started the motor, dropped my sails, put my fenders over the side, and puttered into the channel, passing quite close to another pair of moored Petrels.

I'd thought about sailing into my slip to impress the cheering masses, but the wind blew dead in my face. Tacking up our narrow channel has very little appeal. I motored past row after row of finger piers. I idled around the head of A Pier and waved to a skipper taking his sails ashore. It's nearly November; tomorrow his boat gets hauled.

My boss was on the lookout; he'd seen my varnished mast as I rounded Mouse. He seized my shrouds as I drifted into the slip. My slip mate was one of his clients—another Petrel. His shop, Creative Dynamics—formerly Golden Era Boats—built thirty-two of these Petrels at this pier head. My boss shook his head empathetically as he rigged a pair of spring lines.

"I understand there wasn't much wind," he joked.

"No," I replied. "The sound was calm as a puddle." I doffed my oilskin jacket and my life vest; I began to stow gear and collect my scattered belongings.

"Belay that," my boss admonished. "Let's go to the pub and get some chowder and coffee."

Coffee! I hadn't been truly warm for hours and hours. Coffee! I followed him with the docility of a spaniel.

CAPTAIN DANIEL ELDREDGE

Day has cracked slightly, allowing light snow to wisp through. I imagined December as balmy and sixty degrees with a ten knot breeze and a sunny sky: perfect sailing weather. Apparently, I've awakened in someone else's latitude. Poor little *Moon Wind* languishes in her slip while I stoke the fires and plan my day around other people's boats.

After deliberating nearly an entire day, we decided to move. We looked at three antique Capes, chose the best and moved in: the Captain Daniel Eldredge House—1704. I haven't yet researched what sort of vessel he skippered three centuries ago. This may have been a prosperous skipper's home in colonial days but perhaps not his ultimate one. It had but four rooms downstairs and a sleeping loft around a central chimney. Three fireplaces, of course. The largest measures just over five feet broad across the back. The hearthstone could serve as a single bed. I burn the largest wood that I have but need to procure some bolt wood, else waste cords of stove wood to little avail. For the tiny woodstove heating the kettle in the kitchen, I need to saw all my present wood in two.

The spacious dining room is a late addition—a mere generation ago—but keeps with the original house insofar as it has floors of fairly wide wood, pale walls, dark trim, and multi-light sash. Two sets of French windows open upon a broad deck. There is an extra bedroom above the dining area. The kitchen was modernized and a large laundry room separated from it.

My desk fronts the fieldstone chimney up here in the loft. The wide oak boards beneath my feet, which look extremely old and scarred, are not always fastened as well as you might expect. The floor above the room with the largest fireplace has been removed, as well as some of the joists, to make the house more open and more light.

From my perch aloft, I can oversee the new dining room and, beyond, through the French windows, watch the snow accumulate on the deck. No, not the best boating weather, children. Only the men working lobster boats fare forth on days such as these. And the brightest lobsters don't come out in this sort of weather. They stay home and pen their memoirs.

The little no-name Petrel that I sailed back here from Port Jefferson comes into the shop next week. She's found a new owner—a local chap—and he means to do right by her. All she really wants is cosmetic work—minor repairing of locker tops and cabin doors, extending the motor mount, reglassing the lazarette deck, touching up the brightwork. I'll have three Petrel masts and booms and clubs to sand and varnish up in the loft—a regular mass production. As none of them needs wooding, I'll be spared removing all of the bronze hardware and standing rigging.

The skipper has plans for building a Saint Pierre dory: twenty-three feet with a cabin and small diesel inboard. A seaworthy and fuel-efficient craft for coasting about the islands and catching fish. Or chasing them, at any rate. He estimates it will keep us busy all winter. Then the spring rush will leap upon us: Customers will clamor, boats slip into the water, and the same excitement as ever roil our blood and drive us semi-terrestrials back to the ocean.

Perhaps in a million generations we shall have evolved some

flippers and tails and joined our cetaceous brethren. We shouldn't need to get hauled to have our bottoms painted. We might have a couple of barnacles but—what of it? What joy to be free to cruise the seas without distress about the occasional storm; without a cluttered cabin and lockers full of superfluous gear; without need for a binnacle or a temperamental motor. What bliss to spend every winter in tropic climes—just eating shrimp by the bushel and sporting with mermaids.

But then again, where should we step our masts?

THE INDEFATIGABLE PUSSLET

Yesterday the Petrel came into the shop—the last of her kind and truly a thing of beauty. Nathanial Herreshoff knew his stuff, all right. Most boats, nowadays, favor a balanced rig—main and headsail about the same size. The Petrel disdains such things as gennys and spinnakers. Her voluminous main can catch the merest breeze and turn it to advantage. Coming about proves no problem—if anything, you've weather helm to spare.

When the breeze freshens, the boat will let you know what time to reef: When the helm fights back, it's time to take in sail. Then you run close-hauled for a bit while you drop the main and twiddle with the pendants. No need to toss about in irons with the mainsail slapping you silly. Of course, you might need to slack your sheet in order to raise the sail once you complete your reefing. Some of these boats have a small bronze winch on top of the deckhouse just for such events.

A Petrel's small jib needs no attention whatever. Clubfooted with just one sheet and a small traveler, she comes about without the slightest fuss and never snags as most loose-footed jibs delight in doing. There's nothing less fun than balancing on a pitching fore-deck, fighting with a genoa whose sheets are fast in the tender clasp of an amorous halyard cleat. Or, on *MoonWind,* the corner of my hatch cover. I ought to rebuild that cover so it closes tight to the deck.

Having a high-cut jib has some advantages. Such as visibility. A window works fine if located in the right spot. I had a window installed in a jib one time and should have told the sailmaker exactly where I needed it. Instead, I assumed he must know his business; after all, he sailed. Wrong again, Mister Bunthorne. I couldn't see oncoming boats until my rail was underwater. My weather rail. The rest of the time, I got to admire the fish. At least his prices were reasonable.

I asked him why he hadn't a boat of his own.

"First of all, I never, ever, lack for invitations—my customers can always use more crew. But mostly I've found it bad for business," he said. "I like to race, and sailors are fierce competitors. If my boat won, my customer would think that the sails I made him weren't quite good enough. If my boat lost, they'd question whether I really knew my business."

A choice, it seems, of which foot you'd rather have snarled in the running rigging.

Friday we had snow first thing in the morning, then freezing rain, then overcast and, just after lunch, a raging snow squall accompanied by thunder. In Buzzards Bay, sixty miles to the east, they registered winds of ninety miles per hour. By two o'clock the sun shone brightly; the harbor lay still and reflective. We had a lovely sunset. This is the sort of various day that New Englanders delight to boast about. I'd rather just have the lovely sunset, thank you.

Now the world has cooled off, anticipating winter, and the wind has found the numerous leaks in our decrepit shop. I need to go up on the roof this week with half a sheet of plywood and cover the worst of the holes. Last year a raccoon took up lodgings in the loft and had a litter of cubs there. We have birds by the bushel in between the walls. When customers ask me what keeps our rickety shop together, I answer truthfully,

"Guano."

I still have hopes that our indefatigable Pusslet will prove a sailor. I gave her a fathom of quarter-inch braid, which she drags about the house in her mouth, or kicks into elegant snarls. Last week I discovered she'd tied an overpaw knot a foot from one end. Yesterday, she completed a figure-eight. If I leave my *Bluejacket's Manual* on the floor, opened to "Seamanship," I expect by summer she'll have mastered the bowline, clove hitch, and Carrick bend. It's good to have somebody handy with knots aboard. I'm thinking for Christmas, I ought to buy her a rigging knife—the type with a marlinspike.

CHRISTMAS MORNING, 2005

Christmas morning again, not yet light, and a four-foot Yule log ablaze on the hearth. Twenty-eight degrees; no snowflakes, no hurricanes, no hail, no drought, no clatter of little reindeer on the roof. Not yet, at any rate. I continue to hope Saint Nick might choose to come by boat this once—perhaps a Peapod drawn by a brace of porpoise. He certainly could find a vacant slip this time of year. Then he could leave our presents aboard our boats. I think the time has come for a new tradition.

My son Ezra and his adorable friend Melati stopped here this week. Thursday they borrowed my Whitehall pulling boat and exercised her a bit. They took advantage of the mild day to row as far as Ram Island. There they went ashore to visit the sheep.

I remained in the shop and messed about with the Petrel until the skipper took us all for Christmas lunch to the Chinese buffet. When we returned, we had our little party and exchanged all manner of semi-precious gifts. I received a soldering iron, a Dremmel tool set, and some original notecards made by our professional photographer, who has worked part time at our shop some twenty years.

I, of course, had made a last-minute foray to the marine consignment shop in Mystic the evening before. There I perused the hundreds of secondhand books on boats and boating and marine history and boatbuilding and sailing and seamanship. I nearly went aground among the strakes and shoals and stays'ls until it struck two bells and the mate commenced to dog down the doors. Despite this, I came away with an armload of books and a Wedgwood plate commemorating the *Bluenose:* that most famous and most swift Canadian schooner.

The volume on wooden boats surprised us all. The skipper turned it over. The jacket's reverse displayed a stunning color photograph of a little Herreshoff sailboat at anchor. Not a Fish Class but a Petrel: a fiberglass hull with lots of brightwork, so well crafted as to fool the compiler of the book into thinking her a wooden boat. The skipper recognized the boat—told us the location of the photo and the name of the photographer.

"There's the lazarette cover for the diesel," he exclaimed. "No wooden boats had those."

Within were three more reproductions of the same photo from slightly differing perspectives, but nowhere had they identified the boat. Four pictures of a fiberglass hull in a book of wooden boats. What an advertisement for our boat shop were only credit given.

Friday morning I drove Ezra and Melati to Hadlyme to continue their holiday sojourn. Melati came away with one of Paula's books on horticulture and a jar of our homemade elderberry jam. Perhaps when she finishes her degree we shall see her a bit more often. I certainly hope so.

I returned to Noank and worked on the Petrel. Checked on *Moon-Wind* and fired up her motor. The water pump doesn't appear to work well and I need to remove the motor to rebuild it. When I shall find the time is another matter.

A local sailor came by to discuss some repairs he needs. Then, of course, he had to regale me with a proper yarn. He used to own a sloop that had no lifelines and, as he so quaintly put it, "One day I just happened to take a walk over the side."

Fortunately, he caught hold of the jib sheet and was towed alongside for a while. The sun shone, the warm water soothed; he rather enjoyed the ride. As his only companion, ignorant of sailing, couldn't steer into the wind, it seemed he should give up amusing himself and spend his energy getting back aboard.

Good thing, too. Having struggled on deck, he discovered he bled rather profusely from a puncture wound and, having been in warm water, had never felt a thing. He found it droll to realize he very well could have died.

I presume that one of these less-than-halcyon days, I shall ascend the companionway to discover Old Mortality at the helm—he of the frigid whiskers and icy smile. Then he shall cry an ultimate "hard alee!," put the tiller over a final time, trim her smartly, and set a course for a farthest shore beyond some unimaginable horizon.

LEARNING THE ROPES

The trouble with being poor is, you have to learn so much. You can't just buy a beautiful boat and sail off into the sunset. First, you need to repair it. By the time you complete what needs to be done, half the summer is spent. Following this procedure with several boats nearly qualified me to work in our boat shop. That's where I learned how I should have effected all of those repairs. And, gaining more competence every year, I naturally take on more involved projects, which take more time and money. Being the timid, conservative type, I know my limitations. A twenty-six-foot boat suffices for now. I can't keep up with all her repairs, even though she's docked behind our shop.

What is it with sailboats, anyway? Why do they drag us away from our homes and force us to take them sailing? Is it wanderlust or a sense of adventure or merely dissatisfaction with our residing on dry land? The answer is "yes."

But I find that, in addition to these, something runs deeper. That same emotion that moves you when you watch the endless surf drag back the shingle or watch the endless stream divide the coppice, moves you while reaching over the rollers, mile after mile. A feeling of the infinite; a feeling that life goes on, no matter what; a feeling of being a part of this world's pulse.

Then the wind picks up and the sea gets snotty and you literally have to hang on for your life. And that is grandiose, too, without pretension. For if you must die—and Lord only knows, you must— why sit around your living room and watch the Green Bay Packers? You need a green bay? I know just where to go. You need to float your trusty canoe down a placid stream through the forest? I know just where to go. You need a pond to watch a miracle—a dragonfly's metamorphosis? I can take you there.

There's nothing to keep you from being immersed; there's nothing to keep you from soothing your troubled soul. Nothing except your forty hours; nothing except the roof to mend; nothing except that cocktail party with people who bore you silly. I get caught up in all those things myself—I ought to know.

You need to make the most of your every hour. Life is awhirl—let yourself get caught up in the maelstrom. What do you mean: You have a boat in a slip but no time to sail? There's really no time to do much of anything else. If your spouse doesn't feel the call, go by yourself. If your marriage can't stand for each of you to have a separate vocation, you haven't a marriage but merely inhuman bondage. The stronger your love, the more you can be apart. A part of something larger than yourself.

Take your children, take your cat, but go. If all you can spare is an afternoon on the millpond, spare it—go. Teach your kids to flip the canoe; teach your cat to cut bait. Something will come of it, be assured—if nothing save perspective.

Water teaches respect. Forces beyond our control, beyond all reason, teach us humility. Fog and gale and ice will always challenge us. We needn't change this Earth; only learn to accept her ways. A sail is not for taming the wind but for taking advantage of it. A paddle is not for moving rocks but for steering your boat around them. With GPS and running lights and radar, one can still be humbled by the sea. With carbon-fiber paddle and Kevlar hull, one can still be rolled by the river, dragged beneath a clutching snag, and drowned. Smugness has no place upon the water.

Long ago, I gave up the urge to race in boats—to compete with other people. The course I sail has no beginning, no end. I need to lose and find myself, to journey and sojourn. I used to resist mortality. Now I keep my weather eye on the voyage, not the harbor. Now I steer my frail craft by a light I must believe in. Now I rise on the massive swell that provides a view of eternal continuity. Science and logic provide us charts, the world provides the water; Heaven above provides the wind, but Spirit demands the helm.

A Word from the Waterfront

HADLYME AND THEREABOUTS

THE HADLYME–CHESTER FERRY

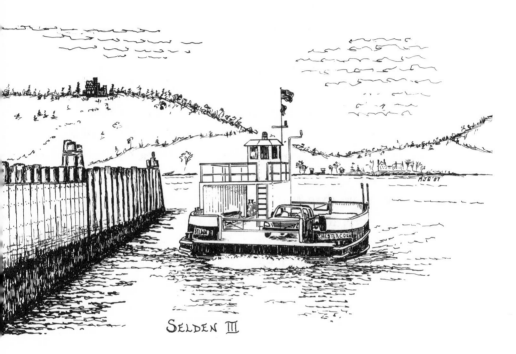

SELDEN III

The Hadlyme–Chester ferry crosses the Connecticut River where I grew up. The current vessel—in use nearly sixty years—is a small steel ship with a black hull and white sides and superstructure: a squat, inelegant creature, but so a part of our lives as to prejudice us in her favor, regardless of appearances. To cross the river otherwise, one must either go down to its mouth and take the highway bridge, or go up to East Haddam at Goodspeed's Landing and use the old steel swing bridge. Either choice adds several miles to your trip. The ferry proves much more scenic and, off season at least, saves time.

Unless the ferrymen stop to talk to someone.

During tourist season, of course, taking the ferry is not to be even considered, except early in the morning. The *Selden III* carries only nine cars. In the summertime there are often twice that many lined up and waiting. The round trip, including loading and off-loading, takes at least twenty minutes. You expect to see cars drive down nearly to the river, assess the situation, then turn around and head for one of the bridges.

The ferry's season runs April through November. In April the freshet often delays the ferry's operation. Not because of the strength of the current—it would take more than that to overcome her great engines. At either shore extends a steel ramp that pivots in a sturdy housing built into the bank. Powered by an electric winch and driven by cables, this ramp lowers to latch onto the ferry's deck. When the river rises more than two or three feet, the ramp cannot elevate enough to meet the deck of the ferry. Everyone local knows better than to rely upon opening day.

Waiting in line on the Chester side gives you a view of the castle. This belonged to William Gillette, the well-known actor who, from 1889 through 1932, portrayed Sherlock Holmes on stage with enormous success. He purchased a hill, the Seventh Sister, overlooking Hadlyme Landing, and built a small fieldstone castle. Now a state park, Gillette's Castle is a "has to be seen" attraction. The ferry, whose landing abuts the park, runs a close second as a fair-weather tourist attraction. For those of us growing up in Hadlyme, it simply served as means of crossing the river.

Being chummy with the skipper and crew was only taken for granted. The deckhand operates the ramp, directs traffic, helps people park ("C'mon, c'mon. You got another four inches."), collects your fare, punches your receipt, declares the weather to be no worse than usual, and inquires after your aunt.

But the pilothouse remains the skipper's awful domain on the second deck—"the bridge." A perfectly vertical steel ladder provides the only access. The bridge supports an open deck with a steel railing, large enough for a dozen people to lounge. But this is strictly forbidden. You should never, ever, consider ascending that ladder. Unless you're local and the only one taking the ferry that trip. Then you may—if you qualify as one of the cognoscenti—go aloft and hobnob with the skipper in his wheelhouse.

This is a cozy structure barely large enough for two people, though most of the time the door remains secured open, and the visitor merely leans on the doorjamb to jaw. The pilothouse boasts a binnacle having a large brass wheel on either side. The ferry, you understand, does not turn around. The skipper merely changes sides and runs the ship in reverse. You have, perhaps, three minutes under way to make the quarter-mile crossing. But it takes several minutes to off-load and reload cars. During this time the skipper can take his ease. Not that you could distract him much when he's actually at the wheel.

Making a landing—getting into the cuneiform slip and nuzzling up to the ramp—proves fairly routine unless the wind is howling. The two to three feet of tide and minimal current present no problem. Those who don't understand that you need to head up against the elements in order to make a safe landing are usually dismayed to see the ferry make a broad arc crossing the river and approach the slip at an angle. They fear she has been swept aside by the wind and current.

When traffic slacks, the ferry may idle long enough for the skipper to descend and replenish his cup of coffee. On the Chester side, the ferrymen have a hut where they keep their arcane gear. Other than this, the west bank hasn't much in the way of attractions—scarcely a house can be seen. In a small field filled with wildflowers, mowed but once a year, you can pick a small bouquet while awaiting the ferry. Or, if you recognize a neighbor's car ahead, you can always walk up and lean on his window to discuss last night's referendum on the budget.

"The way those people spend money is virtually criminal . . ."

On the east bank—Hadlyme Landing—the old piers have gone. So have the remains of a boatbuilding industry that flourished a century past. A handful of colonial homes adorn the approaching road. The stateliest fronts the river, overlooking the few remaining stumps of the former landing. This once provided a place to dock for the small steamship connecting Hartford to New York, which ran until the advent of World War II. A small, two-story studio, having its second-story deck built around a large ash tree, used to be the chandlery shop.

Upstream from the ferry slip once stood the remains of William Gillette's pier. He kept a little houseboat here—a hundred and ten feet long—until it mysteriously burned down to the waterline one day and disappeared into the river. The channel comes close to shore at the foot of the castle; a few yards out run thirty feet of water. For the Connecticut, a slow and shallow river, this constitutes one of the deeper stretches. The piers stood in eight feet of water. When I grew up, a part of that pier—a quarter of it, perhaps—remained in good enough repair to provide seasonal use for a pair of twenty-foot shad skiffs.

From these piers to the foot of the rather precipitous hill supporting the Castle spreads a little grassy, alluvial plain a hundred feet deep, home to numerous huge sycamore and ash. This little park beside the river has a caretaker's cottage—a small, shingled house with red trim, nestled against the cliff. Gillette had been dead ten years when I was born, but an old couple still occupied this cottage and oversaw the premises during the time I grew up. My father managed to convince them that they should allow me to keep my dinghy, *Petite Chose,* at the pier. I imagine a few representatives of the Treasury overcame any resistance he may have encountered.

Between Gillette's landing and the ferry slip lies a quarter-acre dirt parking lot. From here people launch small boats at the tiny gravelly beach, or fish from the shore. Now that the old couple no longer guard the park, people stroll or picnic beneath the antique trees.

A few hundred yards below the ferry, Whalebone Cove joins the river. This tidal estuary and marshy cove extend perhaps a mile, and abound with birds and fish and various other creatures including small boys. It is fed primarily by Whalebone Creek, which runs beneath the road that goes up the little hill to Hadlyme four corners. At this point the creek is substantial enough to justify a rugged concrete bridge.

Closer to the river, a mere finger of this estuary passes beneath that same road; here exists no proper bridge but only a conduit running under a causeway. Beside the road spreads an acre of rice and cattails filled with red-winged blackbirds. This stream, despite being narrow, has four or five feet of water in it at high tide, and teems with rather small but ravenous fish. After walking only a mile, I could sit on the headwall above that large conduit, dangle my legs, and fish and fish and fish. No one thought I would ever outgrow this wasteful, pernicious habit.

But when I turned twelve, I acquired my very first boat, *Petite Chose,* which I kept at Gillette's old landing. And boats have forever spoiled me, and prevented my doing anything useful, ever again, for all the rest of my life.

THE ROCKY HILL–
SOUTH GLASTONBURY FERRY

I was returning home from Hartford one day in my old VW Bug. The summertime traffic oppressed me and, when I came to Rocky Hill, I turned off the main road with its sprawl and fast food and endless promise of promiscuous consumption, and headed down toward the river. The Connecticut River.

You need to understand, the Connecticut River is my home; has been my home ever since I fell into it as a child and drowned and transmogrified into a muskrat. I've spent more hours in and over and around that river than anyone, except maybe the old carp who lives in Whalebone Cove. I've scarcely seen my river these past ten years, though I live less than an hour's drive to the east. Last I knew, my hole in the riverbank had snapping turtles in it. And you know the kind of housekeepers snapping turtles are. It irks me just to think about it.

I drove my VW Bug down to the river where a ferry crosses from Rocky Hill to South Glastonbury. Fortunately, not too many people employ it, for it doesn't go much of anywhere. Besides which, it carries only three cars every trip. They don't employ a sophisticated craft such as the *Selden III* downriver at Hadlyme. This ferry involves two vessels: a barge and a tugboat. A tugboat so small that it most resembles the sort of boat an indulgent father might build for his pre-teen kids.

Every trip across the river, the deckhand on the barge casts off the line attaching the two vessels, the tugboat skipper turns his boat to face the opposite way, and the deckhand makes her fast to the barge again. It takes but a couple of minutes, and the two men seem so nonchalant that I wonder why the boats can't do it without them. The tug remains on the downstream side, the better to shove the barge against the current.

They haven't a slip or even a piling to moor to at either shore. The paved road simply slopes down into the water. The barge has a steel ramp that the deckhand flops down to meet the pavement, and the tugboat shoulders the barge against the shore while you drive your car onboard. Up comes the ramp, the skipper turns his tug around, the deckhand makes her fast again, and they shove off.

There's little to see excepting the river itself. On the Rocky Hill side stands a little abandoned redbrick mill; a bit farther on, a couple of modest houses. On the Glastonbury side there are woods interspersed with fields. Except for a small marina downstream, both banks of the river remain seriously underdeveloped. I find this extremely cheerful. You can pick wildflowers or watch the ferry or count the leaves on the trees while you wait your turn. During the passage, you can sketch the skipper in his pilothouse, about six feet away. I generally lean on the opposite rail and look upstream, where the river flows from out of the woods, and dream.

This trip I remember best. They ferried my Volkswagen Bug across and I started toward South Glastonbury. I wondered if perhaps a shortcut headed south toward Hadlyme. I turned off the pavement onto a dirt road leading between two fields. I often took my VW into the rough. I'd removed her extra seats and used her to bring in my firewood. Her low first gear enabled her to climb trees, albeit slowly. I never worried much about getting stuck, although I admit, the lack of clearance beneath the chassis often claimed my attention.

I left the fields and came to a sort of open wood undoubtedly used as pasture. A yard-wide stream in a gully ran athwart it. A small bridge spanned the gully. Two loose planks formed its deck. I got out and moved them until they matched my wheels.

I continued on. They kept this shortcut a well-kept secret: the weeds between the ruts grew rather tall. The track became fainter and fainter. Soon I simply navigated in between the trees. One odd thing: I never met anyone coming the other way. If not for that high stone wall that someone thoughtlessly left out there across the road, I might have continued that shortcut home and had something to tell you about.

HADLYME

My earliest memory of Chapman Pond dates from 1952. My
father and I walked down the woods road from the farm where we
had gotten permission to dig a Christmas tree. We had a hundred
acres of our own but it grew only cedars and hemlocks. This farm had
Norway spruce. We dug two trees: one a well-shaped tree for our
living room; the other a tiny tree that I planted, myself, in a corner of
our yard, too close to the stone wall and in the shade of large maples.

It still grows there, half a century later, but stunted—no more than
twenty feet tall. The Christmas tree, after a brief sojourn in front of
our library window between the two tall bookcases, we planted in
the yard, nearer the house than the barn, where it throve quite well.
Today a magnificent tree in its prime, it stands fifty feet tall:
producer of countless cones that delight the squirrels.

Oh, yes. I meant to tell you about the pond. It connects to the
river and has a couple of feet of tide and marshes filled with yellow
flag and mallows. After the holidays, we returned to the farm and
wandered downhill through the woods for half a mile. You could also
follow the old cart track leading down to the water. In those days it
hadn't grown over. You could even drive it if you weren't in a hurry.
I find it deplorable how much most people hurry, nowadays. I've

managed to overcome my early freneticness for the most part.

People used to ask me why I didn't strap an outboard on my canoe to ferry goods out to the island when I built my cabin. It would save time, they explained.

"Time for what?" I always asked. After working, running machines all day, why would I want to listen to a noisy, two-stroke engine? And how could I listen to the summer wind soughing through the cottonwoods? Or hear the cry of the heron? Bad enough to hear traffic crossing the swing bridge at Goodspeed's Landing. I enjoy my world unpolluted by motors, thank you, kindly.

Besides—paddling is a yoga: stroke and exhale, stroke and exhale; feel your shoulder muscles tense and relax, tense and relax. And listening to the whisper of my smooth hull cleaving the water delights me, no matter how many years I may have paddled. As I said, you could navigate the cart track if you weren't in a hurry.

When we came to the pond, we discovered two men ice fishing. In those days the glacier had receded only as far as Massachusetts, so we still had lovely winters. The ice on Chapman Pond looked about a foot thick where the fishermen had cut holes, and they had driven their pickup truck onto it. Brockway Island, opposite Hamburg Cove, has a full-sized house on it, and someone drove the lumber out there many years ago. We had ice in them days, children.

I can remember Coast Guard icebreakers coming upriver because the small tankers couldn't deliver their heating oil to Hartford. When the Coast Guard finished, huge shards remained, jammed to either side of the frigid channel. They gave the tide something worthwhile to wrestle with. Our neighbor across the brook back home, an elderly woman, recounted skating the fifteen miles to Middletown as a girl. That would have been about the turn of the century. No, children—not 2000.

For various reasons, things were more laid-back before my time. The riverboat even stopped at Hadlyme—population two hundred seventy-four (What's that? Oh, she *had* the baby. A girl? Good for her.), two hundred seventy-five—until the late nineteen thirties. It carried freight and passengers between New York and Hartford.

There still remain vestiges of old pilings out front of the Hamilton house below the ferry slip where the landing used to stand. I kept my canoe at the Hamilton house when I built my cabin on the island known as the Old Haying Grounds, because they would cut salt hay there, out beside Chapman Pond. At high tide I needed to watch for the rotten stumps of those pilings beneath the surface.

The Hamilton house, a stately colonial shaded by huge trees, had an addition that someone fished out of the river a lifetime ago. Dr. Alice Hamilton, the first woman ever to obtain a medical degree from Harvard, lived there until her death at a hundred and one. I was just a boy, then. My father once met her. Her sister, Edith, the popular Greek scholar, wrote those books on mythology we still have in the study.

Did I tell you about those fellows who were ice fishing on the pond?

IN NEED OF A BOAT

I grew up on an old farm in Connecticut. A hundred yards behind the house spread what we called "the cow pasture"—a boggy area beyond which were the fields and the orchards. One little stream and numerous springs fed it. Alders and brush provided a haunt for birds and bugs and frogs and one small boy.

When I turned six, my father had a portion of the cow pasture dredged, creating a pond a hundred feet long, half that in width, and deep enough to hide a hippopotamus. We used it as a swimming hole all summer long, as a skating rink all winter. As long as we were willing to clear the snow.

My father went to the state extension center and procured two milk cans (antiques now, no doubt) alive with fingerling fish: one of largemouth bass, the other with bluegill sunfish. In a couple of years, the pond teemed with fish; with frogs and turtles and muskrats. Heaven on Earth for a little boy, but dirtier.

I fished, I swam, I chased whatever moved with a fine-mesh net. I learned to eat bass and frogs' legs; I studied dragonfly larvae; I watched the wood ducks teaching their young to swim. Life was complete.

Except—I needed a boat. A couple of steel drums and a wooden deck and—behold! I had a raft. The deck remained awash and was rather tippy—every time I shoved with my pole, one corner went underwater. My very first boat! I even tried a mast and a sail but without much real success.

When I turned twelve, my father bought me a pram. I painted it royal blue—inside and out. I had a miniature navy anchor, a life jacket, and oars. What more could I want?

A lot. My father helped me build a trailer to pull behind our car. The pram and I discovered the Connecticut River, a mile down the road. We set a mooring and rigged a clothesline arrangement to an old pier. Two twenty-foot shad boats kept me company.

I knew enough now—and had permission—to venture off alone. Not very far—there were plenty of places to fish within a mile. I rowed and rowed and saved my lawn mowing money. The following summer, I went to Montgomery Ward and bought a motor: three entire horsepower. Now I was Lord of the River!

About this time, I started sailing lessons downriver in Essex: a ten-mile drive but only a four-mile boat ride—not including the mile walk to the boat. With tide and current and wind to contend with, it took me over an hour to go each way. An hour buzzing along in my little boat—what utter bliss!

In those days, the boat traffic on the river was negligible. A couple of tankers a day brought oil to Hartford. A few motorboats and small sloops, or occasionally a canoe, plied the mile-long reaches. Weekends in the summer became rather busy but still without the freneticness of today. I never saw a cigarette boat until I was in my twenties. The craze for plastic kayaks remained thirty years off.

Knowing enough to avoid the channel, a child of fourteen could laze down the river any afternoon and stay out of trouble. And I learned the channel and had a chart almost immediately—my father had been a navigator in the navy. And I learned to sail. Three summers

I attended sailing school, where we raced little Bluejays around and around the marks.

One consuming desire overwhelmed me—to have a real sailboat of my own. With just enough money to purchase a sail, only one viable remedy prescribed itself: convert my eight-foot pram to a sailing dinghy. Then take a liberal dose every day of my life.

So I did. Life was complete. With three-horse motor, five-foot oars, and a sail, what could stop me from circumnavigating this little world?

MAROONED!

HADLYME PUBLIC HALL

The four of us could just fit in the dinghy. All of us were twelve—
a good age to be; grown up enough to be trusted, we thought, with
a boat on a good-sized river. I had the helm, of course. Jack sat in
the bow. He lived down the hill, just across the brook. Out in the
country, you hadn't many neighbors within a short walk. Fortunately,

Jack and I got along well. We played ball together, had both joined Scouts, and come fall would hunt together.

This past Christmas, I had been given a 20-gauge shotgun by my dad. Jack had received a .410. In those days, our dads taught us gun safety as soon as we had the strength to pull a trigger. We often had target practice, well supervised, out back of the house. The hillside across the pond absorbed our bullets. The next house sheltered safely over the hill. I shared my sister's .22: the one with the stock and barrel cut down to fit her when she was little.

In the center of the pram sat Jack's cousin, Glenn, whom I'd met the summer before. You can't expect to like everyone. Next to him sat Arnold. Arnold's granny lived in the old saltbox by the overgrown meadow that used to be a millpond. She'd lived there forever, I guess, or maybe longer. Her grandfather, or perhaps her great-grandfather, had built the old water-powered gristmill that shows on my map of the village from 1860.

I always enjoyed visiting Arnold's granny. Her house was filled with old magazines and clippings concerning the village, for she had intended, these past thirty years or so, to compile its history. She had been creative all her life; many of her oil paintings adorned the walls. Now she was more than elderly and rambled a bit, and what had been once artistic disorder and mild eccentricity had devolved into clutter and a mild, genteel senility. She lived upon tea and crackers and a tiny pension.

The cedar roof on her old saltbox grew moldy; some shingles fell out. Her long gray hair turned white; some hairpins fell out. She drove her shabby car to the store very slowly; her left front wheel clutched the centerline for support as she herself clutched the banister coming downstairs. She parked in the unpaved circular drive between her old white house and the small gray barn. The barn leaned toward the house for consolation.

The yard was rank and lovely with wildflowers. Forsythia and roses tangled together. Lilacs grew up to the second-story eaves. The crab-apple in the island of the circular drive burst into glorious blossom every May. A monstrous maple dominated the front yard. An even taller butternut tree shaded much of the back.

An army of daylilies camped along the little stream that wrinkled behind the house. When the stream overflowed its tiny banks every spring, the excess water was allowed to divert through the basement. It entered via a short terra-cotta pipe, swept around the old furnace through a semi-circular trough, and exited via another ceramic pipe. The pipes had screens across them to keep out the mice.

Arnold used to visit her for part of every summer and occasional weekends. We slept over at my folks' or at his granny's, and went everywhere together. "Everywhere" meant we could walk to the corner store and buy penny candy or, on hot days, dig in the cooler, searching for birch beer.

In those days, our store had a big red freezer chest filled with loose ice and bottles. There was no such thing as soda in cans. After a while, the ice melted some, and you'd have to plunge your arm into icy water to find the kind of soda you wanted: grape or orange or root beer or cream or cola. Or, if you lucked out, birch beer. The white haired woman who owned the business made change from a cigar box. Her store was distinguished by having the hundred-box post office in the back. Her son was postmaster. I'd collect our mail, then we would sit on the shady porch and make our sodas last.

Our "corner store" was situated at the "new" four corners, where the recent state road made its turning. The old four corners, half a mile toward the river, where the former main road crossed, were nearly abandoned. The original store and post office stood empty. The little Hadlyme Public Hall remained.

But another store prospered, just a few doors up the road from the closed one. The owner's children, younger than us, played bare-foot on the wide board floors and waited on folks and made change from an antique, nickel scrollwork register. The family, as was common then, lived above the store.

The owner worked in her garden as often as possible. She sold what little surplus she had: rhubarb, corn, and raspberries. Her little flock produced dozens of eggs. People brought back their used egg cartons over and over. The half-empty shelves in the store held mainly staples. She kept her sodas in a Frigidaire along with the cheese and the carrots. If we cut down Stonehouse Hill behind our barn, it wasn't any farther to this store. We hadn't bikes; we walked the mile each way.

That describes our village: two stores, the PO, the garage, the church, and the old Public Hall, where the village held its Halloween parties and potluck suppers and square dances. My mother organized us kids and we put on a play one summer. Across from the church stood the one-room schoolhouse, last used for education during the thirties, where we met for Pilgrim Fellowship. We didn't have our own firehouse until later.

By the time we boys outgrew our interest in trick-or-treating, we were looking forward, instead, to hunting season. In the winter we would play hockey on the millponds. In the summertime we fished.

I had an eight-foot pram my dad had given me, and I saved my lawn mowing money to buy a motor. It had only three horsepower but it sure beat rowing. Jack and I used to go out and fish in the cove or mess about on the river.

Today the four of us headed up to the island. There was nothing up there to do; it was nothing but woods. The island lay less than two miles above the landing. The landing had been important once, a long time ago, when steamboats stopped to take on freight and passengers. They had built boats there and a ferry still traversed the river endlessly, three seasons out of the year.

At some broken-down piers, a couple of local shad fisherman docked their twenty-foot boats. I'd rigged a line and two pulleys between the end of the pier and an unattached piling for my pram. Today we all piled into my boat and headed up the river. With four of us in her, the gunwale stood only the width of your hand from the water. If it hadn't been calm, she would have swamped in a minute. As I had only one life vest, I chose to sit on it. I would have felt stupid wearing it when no one else had one. As it turned out, none of us drowned or even fell in the water.

We made it to the island and stalked about, Fenimore Cooper style, in the woods. The island stretches half a mile, close to the riverbank. After a while, we separated. Arnold and I explored the sandbar. We found some boards protruding from the sand—perhaps the remains of a wreck. We furiously delved with broken boards in the hope of buried treasure.

Suddenly I heard the sound of the motor. We tore down the shore and there went my boat, on her way back to the landing, with Glenn at the helm and Jack, my buddy Jack, merrily waving.

"We're marooned!" I hollered.

There remained but the two of us, now, to share the treasure.

"Don't worry about it," said Arnold. "They'll come back."

We tromped about all afternoon, dug for another hour, then built a fire on the sandbar. My pack contained the hot dogs and a canteen. Arnold cut green sticks with his knife, peeled the ends, and slipped them lengthwise into the hot dogs. We grilled them till they blistered and ate two each. Then we waited.

"Does your dad know where you've gone?" Arnold asked.

My rules were explicit: Never go off without informing someone where I was going and what time to expect me.

"No," I answered.

"How about swimming to shore," he suggested. "It isn't far."

I thought about that awhile. How could we explain coming home all wet? What would happen if Jack and Glenn came back and we had gone? I visualized each panic situation and its plausible consequences.

My father had always admonished me: "If you get lost, stay where you are. Someone will come and find you."

Did this qualify as lost? I had departed without permission and left no note. I had taken too many for safety in my pram. Lost might have been an improvement.

"They ought to be back anytime now," I said, peering hopefully down the river. "We'd better stay where we are. At least we have a fire so they can find us."

The sun had departed. We gathered a pile of wood to last the night and started to build a lean-to. It sounded easy the way the Boy Scouts explained it. But we hadn't proper materials—no evergreens boughs, no vines or cedar bark to bind it together. Nothing but huge old silver maples, some cottonwoods, and an overabundance of ferns. We built a rickety frame of dead sticks and covered it with ferns. With any luck, it might exclude a mild inundation of falling leaves and deter every second moonbeam. The chance of our suffering greatly from either suffocation or privacy while inside of it was slight.

We squatted by our burning sticks, cooked the remaining hot dogs, and watched the flames. The dark settled in around the dwindling fire and filled in the empty spaces. It crept around our lean-to. It blanketed the river. It insinuated its goblin voices into our boyish ears.

A huge cottonwood tree leaned out from the bank; its long dark limbs descended toward the sandbar. The more wood we heaped on the fire, the more shadows we created. We burned our whole night's supply of wood in an hour. Nothing could have tempted us to forage after more fuel. Arnold had wrestled the last few sticks away from me when I heard the motor.

Here came my dad in my little boat, alone. He had a shielded kerosene lantern perched on the forward thwart. He held a powerful flashlight in his fist. We fought to be first in line to take the blame.

Jack and Glenn had tied up the boat and walked home, pleased with their joke. Jack's father, who didn't hear it till after supper, did not find it funny. He called my dad, and the two of them set out. Jack's father went up the riverbank, through the woods, with a heavy flashlight. Mobile telephones had not even been dreamed of, and the two men were too far apart to signal with lights. It took quite awhile before everyone got home.

Jack got a tongue lashing from his father, who then sent him up the hill to talk to my dad. Our fathers did not subscribe to corporal punishment but, when they roared, we stood up straight and listened. They made it extremely clear how stupid we'd been: going off without life vests, without permission, without any common sense. I lost my boating privileges for a month.

The fish in the river considerately waited until my sentence expired. Arnold's vacation dwindled. He mowed his granny's yard; we compared the two stores. His mother came, ten days later, and took him home. I wouldn't see him again till after Christmas. When my month of expiation came to a close, Jack and I took the boat and went fishing together. We made it a point to practice common sense, and always wore our life jackets walking home.

SELDENS ISLAND

A mile or so below the ferry landing lies Seldens Island. The Seldens settled in Hadlyme when waterfront property was readily available. They still own sizable chunks of it today; mostly off Selden Road. The island huddles against the shore with an estuary behind it. Steep and wooded, about five hundred acres, it fronts the channel running up the east bank of the river. This estuary, six or eight feet deep, opens into a cove near its northern end. One of the Selden homes overlooks this lovely landscape from a distant prospect. Half-wild meadows run downhill to the cove, over which an osprey often hovers in the hope of breakfast.

This estuary, Seldens Creek, meanders south a mile or more before rejoining the river. Well back of the island, the meadows on the mainland turn to salt marsh; a minor estuary wends through this marsh until it meets the creek. A couple of feet of tide run in and out. The sun turns much of the salt marsh into flowers; the river turns the estuary to fish. Bream and crappie, perch and bullheads, pickerel and bass have taken up housekeeping here.

The Selden family, having regard for generations of watermen yet to come, donated their island to the state to become a park. Aside from a very small camping area on a level spot at the north end, the entirety of the island remains pristine. Somewhere amid the hemlocks hides a spring. No one in my day thought to profane the woods with directions to it. Go and find it yourself. If you miss it but gain the summit, you'll be rewarded with a glimpse of shimmering river.

Of course, you'll want to go there during the week—preferably during that time of year when tourists hide in front of their televisions. Today would probably do. It's presently coming down Coastal Blend—a mixture of freezing rain and icy snow—ideal canoeing weather. Sometimes, I used to force myself to endure more pleasant weather in my efforts to amuse the local fish—when the mallows bloomed and the red-winged blackbirds called from the cattail brakes.

If you paddle up the little estuary leading off the creek, you meander through the marsh a few hundred yards back to the mainland. Around the last bend, you suddenly emerge from the reeds that blocked your view of the woody shore. There, on a tiny knoll, once perched a tiny trailer. Even in my day, no one had camped in this plywood wreck for years. Sun and rain had conspired to return it to the Powers of the Earth. Just north of the knoll, a little stream comes chirruping out of the woods to meet the marsh.

Here, where the water runs freshest, one can find an abundance of yellow perch—the prettiest fish to be found in local waters. Now, yellow perch have an affinity, a craving, a less-than-discerning appetite for worms. In forty minutes, just after the tide has turned, one can catch more perch with a dozen worms than any two people can savor at one sitting. But be forewarned. A yellow perch has more small bones per acre than any fish its size. This delicacy is best eaten with your fingers, hot from the skillet. Sitting upwind of the campfire greatly enhances the flavor.

You can't help liking the yellow perch. Truly a voracious creature, he goes for a worm with an admirable abandon. Then he fights like the dickens and, invariably, tries to stab you in the hand with his dorsal fin when you kindly offer to extract the hook. His dorsal spines are especially designed with the soft wet hands of the fisherman in mind—they resemble sail needles. If you don't stroke back that dorsal fin until it is well tucked down, you'll wear the smarting reminders of it stitched across your palm. If ever you plan an incarnation as a stately great blue heron who spends her time at the back of Seldens Creek stalking gay young perchlets, remember: Always, always, swallow them headfirst.

THE WILY FLOUNDER

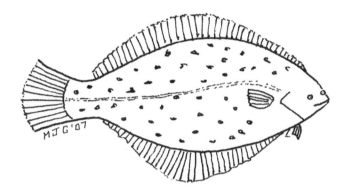

In the next village over, in a cedar-shingled cottage, resided an older couple. Being country folk and local, they'd been here since the Flood. But they had few pretensions and, for some reason, seemed to like me. Across the road from their house sprouted a little barn. Inside slept an old blue truck—a '49 Ford. But underneath the barn, around the back by the half-acre vegetable garden, dwelled the boat. Just a planked skiff, about sixteen feet, she patiently reclined on her trailer, awaiting the old man's fancy.

He invited me to accompany him one day. I was twelve that summer and fishing had overcome me. Every spare moment I spent with a rod in my fist, coercing small piscine creatures to play with me. This would be different. Our quarry: the wily flounder. This old man had catching fish down to a science. Rods and reels did not

257

prove expeditious. Fishing was a way of filling his freezer—one of his freezers. The half-acre garden produced an abundance of vegetables but little in the way of protein. Whence the boat. This would prove a lesson for me in how one might survive in a world without a grocery store.

The old blue truck carried us down to a tidal flat connected to Long Island Sound. It seemed that we parked in the middle of nowhere: a woodsy, remote dirt road. The old man got out.

"First things first," he told me. "Just reach in the glove box and hand me that roll of paper. I gotta take me a dump."

This was just an amazing revelation. My father would never, ever, go into the woods expressly to "take a dump." My mother would not go into the woods at all. When the old man returned, we set about catching bait.

We each held a pole supporting a net about three by twelve feet. Then we walked through the shallows, surrounded a school of mummichogs, and treated them to a boat ride in the bait bucket. We launched the skiff and proceeded to feed the little flounders their lunch.

The boat—flat-bottomed—drew about next to nothing. The minimal outboard hadn't much appetite. Considering gas cost twenty-five cents per gallon, I doubt that our boating venture cost more than a dime.

We traversed a stretch of shallow water between a grassy island and the shore. Here the old man set what he called "tip-ups." These consisted of the disc-shaped corks used for floating gill nets, each transfixed by a batten, painted bright red. A baited hook secured to eight feet of line depended from the shorter end of this batten. We set these contraptions in the water on their sides. When a fish took the bait, the batten would tip upright.

We set about ten of these several yards apart, let the tide take them, and followed them in the boat. The old man ran the motor;

I tended the tip-ups. At a certain point, we retrieved them and took them back to the start of the course. "Le sport" was not in the least a consideration.

Around and around we puttered and watched for strikes. We might have filled the boat with fish had the flounder cooperated. Only a pair of them came aboard to visit. We gave them the guest room suite and informed them that supper was served at six.

After the tide had changed, we gave it up.

"Gol durned flipping fish," the old man mumbled. Except he pronounced the first three words a bit differently. He gave me both the fish when we returned. "Cook 'em as soon as you can," he urged. "They won't get any better."

His grandson recently sold the cottage after his mother died. The shakes on the house—the third or fourth set—had crumbled and turned green. The sills of the barn came away by the handful; birds flew in through the roof. The boat, blown full of leaves and seeds and rain these forty years, had rotted away. Twenty-foot maples grew in the vegetable garden.

"I can remember," he said to me, "when I was little, Grampy took me flounder fishing one day. He'd just retired and he'd bought this new, blue pickup truck. You'll never guess what he use to keep in the glove box."

A BOATWRIGHT

When you traverse the river road connecting Deep River and Essex, you'll notice that most of the houses seem rather imposing. Where the road and the river diverge a few hundred yards, you can see only occasional stately drives—generally introduced by a pair of gateposts —and sometimes gates.

One house, however, small by comparison, tucks against a slope overlooking the river: a sturdy white house, at least a century old, with a long lawn leading down to the water's edge. There, half supported by pilings, stands a workshop—a boatbuilder's shop. Alongside of it, a pair of iron rails runs into the river. Art Finkeldey, the boatwright—a spare man in his sixties when first I knew him— had keen and kindly eyes and grizzled hair. His shop, light and cheerful, had ample workbenches built against the walls. Neat without being fastidious, he took his time, yet wasted little of it; enjoyed conversation, yet never sought it out.

I moored my Rhodes 18 at his place a couple of summers forty years ago. He set out only three moorings; one of them for his lobster boat—a twenty-four-footer he'd built for himself and his wife to enjoy on the river: a pretty thing but seaworthy, painted white and yellow. I was young, then—just out of high school—and ignorant of maintaining a wooden vessel. My sloop, old and carvel-built, remained unsure of whether the water belonged inside of her or out. Much of my time I spent remanding the river.

Art was a man of skillful hands; an artisan; a waterman. Prodigal of his energy and knowledge, he inspected my overturned hull the following spring. "You need to reeve out that caulking and replace it," he said and, tucking his old, companionable pipe in his pocket, proceeded to demonstrate how to do just that. Eventually I caught on.

Fiberglass had gained in popularity in the sixties, but plenty of shops continued building with wood. By this time Art, semi-retired, spent most of his time repairing boats rather than lofting them. On the walls of his shop hung photos and drawings of those he had built in the past: the largest and most impressive a ketch-rigged H-28.

His workspace stood on a mezzanine surrounding the boat bay on two sides. On pleasant days, the double doors of this bay stood open, allowing sunshine and swallows alike to regale him. There was just enough room on this mezzanine to work on a skiff or a dinghy. A potbellied stove consumed the mill ends and shavings. Art Finkeldey's workshop smelled of oak and cedar—not of resin and solvent. He faired hulls with a whispering plane instead of a howling grinder.

Wooden boats—direct descendants of trees—always seem so alive. Wood refers not only to desiccated planks but also to living groves. A dugout canoe, adzed hollow to within an inch of the water, is nothing less than a tree with a sense of adventure. A boat with ribs is a tree that would be a creature: a woods creature gone aquatic, as has the whale. We say that a wooden boat must breathe; we give her a mother's name. Her offspring gambol amid the uplifting waters.

Last season I kept *Moon Wind* in a slip behind the bait shop. Across the pier lay an open launch belonging to the ferryman—his private pleasure craft. A lovely, older, wooden boat, she's painted white and yellow. She has some tumblehome and a pleasing shear, and steep, bluff bows to counter a heavy chop.

"She'll handle just about anything," said the ferryman. "A good old boat—built in the nineteen fifties. Cedar over white oak—she'll last forever. Got her over in Essex for next to nothing. Been neglected for years but, when I sanded her down, I couldn't find anything wrong. Didn't replace a single fastener. Built by a guy who's been dead these twenty years—someone you've never heard of—Arthur Finkeldey."

THE FLOOD

Past the foot of the hill, back of our barn, Hungerford Brook makes its way toward the river. It passes behind the houses of our neighbors for half a mile before merging with Roaring Brook, which, eventually, becomes Whalebone Creek and flows into Whalebone Cove below the ferry landing.

Hungerford Brook hasn't water enough to canoe. Roaring Brook has—after a good rainstorm. I used to put in below the post office, just beneath the bridge on Route 82.

That's the bridge the flood swept away in 1982. A low-pressure system parked at the mouth of the Connecticut River and redistributed Long Island Sound over six or eight towns. A foot of rain had fallen the first five days; eight more inches fell that final night.

That bridge stood nine feet above the bed of the stream. When the dam at Urbans Pond caved in, acres and acres of water came hurtling downstream. Surprisingly, the dam on Clark Hill Road didn't break or even scour significantly. But all of that water wanted to join with the river quick like a bunny—to use one of my father's pet expressions. When it came to the bridge at the main road, it tore the concrete abutments out of the bank. The deck of the bridge

263

collapsed and washed away.

That evening, a woman from our village, a much-loved teacher, returning from a meeting in Lyme, couldn't start her car. One of the fellows at the meeting offered to drive her home in his six-wheel dump truck. They came to where the bridge had been and saw a foot of water above the road. Just up to the hubs. The driver slowed a bit but didn't anticipate trouble.

His truck disappeared in the torrent. It tumbled a couple of hundred yards, then hung up at the bend. The driver heroically tried to dislodge his passenger. He barely saved himself. He spent the rest of that terrible night clinging to a tree amid the flood.

Late the next morning, I walked to where the bridge had been. The water had receded to waist-deep. The sun shone brightly. The cable railings spanned a twenty-foot gap in the road. The steel guard posts dangled ludicrously from the cables. Great slabs of concrete littered the bed of the brook. Downstream, exposed, the truck lay on its side.

The rescued driver revived in intensive care. They buried our teacher from the larger church uptown. Even so, people stood in the back.

Hungerford Brook demolished the old bridge back of our barn. The bridge upstream remained, but the bank on either side had scoured until no car could pass. Other towns had suffered similar damage. The local papers showed a car jammed in the crotch of a tree, six feet off the ground.

The piano factory in Ivoryton had half a million board feet of rough-cut lumber—select-grade maple and sugar pine—sticked and stacked in their yard. When the dam on Falls River failed, all of that lumber fetched up in a field a mile below the factory. The insurance company declared the lumber a loss: free for the taking. I made three trips with a friend and we salvaged perhaps four thousand board feet. That little field had a tangled crop of upended planks ten feet deep in places. Falls River, forty feet wide, tinkled merrily in its bed.

So cataclysm has its way with our world. All about are the ruins of bygone building. War and storm, eruption and rot, all have their way at last. Those of you who would live forever would need to mourn both friends and civilization. Evolution would pass you by, nations would disappear in strife, continents return to the ocean bottom. All this, and more, is in your head already. See to it that it has a place in your heart.

MYSTIC AND NOANK

THE GENIUS OF J. S. BACH

Well, the blizzard missed us, here by the shore. Hartford revels in nearly two feet of fresh powder; we received six inches. About chin high on our half-grown Pusslet, who wants back into the house after a brief surveillance of the bird feeder. The omniscient gods of meteorology threaten warm weather later this week. Work has slowed and I'd welcome a row up the Mystic River with my eager young Whitehall pulling boat. I'll need to purchase a little folding anchor for her, eventually, and some roding, and procure a bucket in which to coil it down. I may need to move my bow eye lower to facilitate towing. My seven-and-a-half-foot Shaw and Tenney spruce oars whimper plaintively for more varnish.

At present, three boats await their turn to play in our small shop: a century-old, hard-chined wooden catboat, a neglected Ensign, and another local Petrel. Just now her gleaming mast, and those of two other Petrels, plus booms and clubs, rest in the loft, waiting to be addressed with sandpaper and determination. The former, at least, is seldom in short supply. I've decided to hang the three thirty-foot masts from the trusses and varnish them all at once. All of the standing rigging has eyes spliced round the mast—beneath the track, of course—and looped over special bronze fittings. Working around these splices and their hardware provides constant amusement. There are eight per mast: three pairs of shrouds, a headstay, and a forestay for the small jib.

It's difficult to comprehend the hours expended maintaining wooden yachts. A twenty-one-foot Petrel has a lot of brightwork by today's standards. The usual seasonal maintenance, including minor repairs, involves at least forty hours. To wood the boat may require three times that. A fifty-foot wooden boat could keep someone busy year-round. Having owned an all-wood sloop, I can empathize. I caulked, refastened, scraped, and painted more than I ever sailed. When we call a brightly varnished boat a work of incredible beauty, we mustn't forget to emphasize the word *work*.

John Keats asserted timelessly: "A thing of beauty is a joy forever." Certainly is, lad. Just roll up your sleeves, Johnny, take a hold of this little badger, dip his tail in the varnish, squat beside this stretch o' coamin', and show us how to keep it bright forever.

I must confess: Having both worked on boats and written about working on boats, I prefer the latter. But given the choice between wetting the rail of a beautiful boat or simply writing about her, I'll take the former option every time. I don my dust mask.

Our spar loft has a decent view of West Cove—once you fight your way to the eastward windows. The floor bristles with plywood patterns, gear from boats, defunct woodworking equipment, and buckets of hardware. A crowded bench runs the entire length of the north wall. Above it, a deep shelf, also running the length of the loft, overflows with twenty types of marine hose; with rub rail guard, with sail bags, with Neptune knows what else. Above and below the bench are tiers of Petrel masts. On the opposite wall, racks supporting booms and oars and spinnaker poles run nearly floor to ceiling. The cross ties of the gambrel roof threaten to dump their load of cedar boards, outriggers, spars, and a mold for a pulling boat. Another long mold and three more masts depend beneath the beams. As I work, the fluorescent fixtures overhead illuminate a million motes of exalted sanding dust.

I've tuned in the classical station. During the warmer months, the starlings squabble ceaselessly within the well-seasoned wallboards. This winter's day without wind sounds sagely quiet. Now, late afternoon, everyone else has gone home; the shop below is still. No sound remains save the genius of J. S. Bach. Some days I listen to Billie Holiday, some days to Jimi Hendrix. Today there is only the genius of J. S. Bach. And the swish of two-twenty sandpaper—to and fro.

A VIEW FROM THE MASTHEAD

Today they hauled me up the mast. Slightly more humane than keelhauling and fewer fish to contend with. Merely a short ride in a bosun's chair to replace the topping lift on the mainmast of an old Alden Challenger.

They strap me into a canvas harness and haul me aloft by means of the main halyard—my grinning mates tailing said halyard from a winch while regaling me with a description of the last fellow they sent aloft and how they dropped him and how long it took them to scrub the deck clean, afterward. Witty lads, these.

Halfway up, I encounter the spreaders and have to holler down to slow up a bit as my knees are just a bit jammed. They ease me over the spreaders and I catch hold of the shrouds to keep myself from spinning about. There, that wasn't too bad. Now I'm nearly there and my ears begin to get tangled in the rigging. Now I'm two-blocked: the swivel of the bosun's chair is tight against the halyard sheave. End of the line. Top floor. Gents' haberdashery to your left, toiletries to your right. Watch your step, please.

Someone hollers from below. What are they doing away down

there when it's so balmy and relaxing up here? What a magnificent view of the harbor. Look at all those pretty little boats. Look—there's mine—over there. Yes, yes, I *am* working. Oh. Lower the line in my sack so they can affix the new topping lift. They must think I've actually escaped from the gravitational field of the earth only in order to amuse *them*. Oh, well.

Down goes my lanyard. I remove pliers from my built-in kit bag and try to straighten the cotter pin securing the clevis pin that in turn secures the sheave around which the new topping lift will be passed. Someone, in his infinite wisdom, has already swaged a stainless-steel eye at each end of the new topping lift that will not pass through the block. Therefore, the sheave must be removed.

The clevis pin revolves gaily and the block swivels away as I fight to straighten out the legs of the cotter pin. It seems I must employ two pair of pliers. I clamp my legs around the mast and hope not to drop any tools. It's a long reach to retrieve them. The crew below has wisely retreated out of harm's way.

Two pair of pliers prove more trouble than one. The backstay, just behind me, hampers shoulder movement considerably, and all four slings of the bosun's chair are directly in my way. I'm working above my head and the reach is tiring. The cotter pin giggles as it spins out of my grip for the forty-second time. Got you, you little . . .

Replace the pliers, remove the clevis pin, remove the sheave, stow all in my kit bag and haul up the new topping lift, hold it in my teeth while I untie the lanyard, which I then proceed to coil, secure and stow in my sack. Do you guys think you could refrain from rocking the boat *quite* so much? Thanks. What? Yes—it *was* lots of fun.

Now wrap the topping lift around the sheave, insert the sheave in the clevis and hold it perfectly aligned while replacing the clevis pin (this requires merely three hands and some choice nautical expletives) and then insert a new cotter pin. Again employ two pair of pliers to spread and double back the legs.

Simple. Only half an hour to accomplish three minutes' work. I can't understand people's reluctance to use rings instead of cotter pins.

Okay, guys, I'm ready to descend. Do what? Straighten the wind indicator. No problem. Except that I can't quite reach it. What? No—it *wouldn't* help if I stood up. But maybe with this long adjustable wrench . . . There. Nearly perfect.

I'm ready to come down. Say again? Okay. "Please?" What? Yes, I'm quite comfortable. Where you going? Wuddaya mean you're shovin' off? It's only three o'clock. Hey! Hey, guys . . .

FEBRUARY THAW

The ice has departed the harbor. Not that salt water freezes much here in Connecticut, but I prefer open water. A few inches of snow linger on the piers and boats but by afternoon some scuppers will run. Patches of old snow alternate with patches of busy robins.

In just a few weeks the boatyard will awake from its torpor and the yard crew rouse the travel lift, which now hunkers, cold and somnolent, over the lift slip. The tractor and pay loader have worked all winter rebuilding the banks with concrete beams and boulders. By early April the plumber will reintroduce fresh water to the piers, and the second head, bath, and laundry rooms will once again open for business.

Covers will come off boats ashore—those that the wind hasn't helpfully removed—and weekends will discover boat owners looking up at their hulls with thoughtful expressions.

Were my sloop in the water, I'd be tempted to sail today. The air feels crisp and new and the water shines from reflecting the low-slung sun. Fishers Island, a mere two miles offshore, stands out against the blueness in minute detail—the penciled trees, the rocks, the stately houses.

Our local ferry, a forty-foot steel workboat, chugs over and back several times a day. She runs all winter except during gale conditions. Fog and snow prove no deterrent, and the steep heavy chop when wind and tide collide in the sound comes in the benefit package.

Scarved and mittened islanders stand on her open deck in every weather. They come to the mainland to retrieve their cars to work or shop or visit. In the summertime, duffers jam the skipper's boat— off to the island to play a round of golf. Sometimes nearly twenty people crowd between her rails.

I have to remember to ask her skipper if he's seen the seals this winter. Our seals come down the coast from Maine and Nova Scotia and spend a couple of months disporting themselves on the rocks outside our harbor. As I recollect, the ocean in Maine stays none too warm about this time of year and I can imagine elitist seals bragging to friends, "We thought we'd go south for the winter—perhaps Connecticut."

They tell of one seal who used to climb on the piers—probably pricing a slip for winter storage. Then someone informed her how many mackerel it cost.

Next winter I plan to leave *Moon Wind* in the water. This spring she gets her through-hull fittings renewed and several coats of ablative bottom paint. Aside from zincs, her bottom should remain labor free for three seasons. I also need to replace the standing rigging, rewire the mast, affix a new VHF antenna, reeve new halyards, rerig the lazy jacks. Let's see—what else? Oh, yes—scrub the mast and check the track for nicks, replace the bulbs in all the lamps, and put new boots on the spreaders. And paint the topsides.

I hope to get all done by the first of May. Easy, you say—I work right here in the yard. Yep—come April I'll begin working here at least seven days a week—some of it even for pay. My boss can empathize—he has three boats of his own. Not counting his kayak. Or his Sailfish.

Another month of lassitude before the pressure builds. Now I scuff through the snow as I walk out the pier with wood and tools and notebook. After a dusting of powder this morning everything glistens pristinely. What an astonishing world we inhabit!

The ferry takes a couple out to the island—their arms filled with groceries. They hand aboard their old springer spaniel, her stumpy tail aquiver: old Abigail, who sports a brand-new blue-and-white bandanna. A seasoned sailor, she eagerly anticipates the crossing.

Bon voyage, Abigail!

With any luck she'll be home in fifteen minutes . . .

THE PEAPOD

A young man came into our shop one day last year. He'd practiced being young for several decades and had the process refined.

"I have a project for you," he said with a chuckle. "Are you game?"

When he showed us the boat, we shook our heads in dismay. It can be fixed, we told him, but would cost him more than if we built him a new one. That wasn't a problem, he told us.

The boat was an ancient wooden Peapod fourteen feet in length: a double-ended, round-chined pulling boat with high, fine ends and hardly any rocker. Carvel-planked of cedar over numerous oak frames, she weighed but a hundred pounds. Her keel was rotten but her garboards were good, her stems not bad, but unattached, her breast hooks decayed, her planking sprung loose at both ends, her butt blocks splitting apart. Most of her twenty-five frames were broken—her hull had no shape whatsoever.

We bound her together with a length of line and trailed her back to the shop.

"I found her in a field," her owner said. "She needs a bit of work."

Some seams gaped so wide you could drop a pencil through them. Not a fat, round carpenters' pencil; just an ordinary, yellow, hexagonal pencil.

First, I made a new keel. I bolted the stems to it, then temporarily clamped the strakes to the stems. I fabricated stations of heavy plywood, using for contours those portions of frames still intact. After installing a few such stations, fastening them to the keel, I removed every copper clinch nail securing the planking, grinding off each clinch. I removed the broken frames and surrounded the hull with wide nylon straps with ratcheting load binders. I put wooden spreaders between the inwales to prevent the boat's collapsing and cinched all the webbing—click by click by click.

The planking conformed to the stations and drew together. Success!

We then installed new frames: white oak, green from the mill—planed and ripped to half an inch thick and seven-eighths wide and popped in a steam box twenty to thirty minutes. Left too long, they grew brittle. Springing them into place and clamping them before they lost their limberness—a matter of minutes—took two of us.

Then I refastened her—near twelve hundred screws. I made and installed new butt blocks, new breast hooks, a few feet of outwale, a portion of inwale, four short sections of planking, new brackets for the thwarts, and, voilà—a boat! Resurrected from a meadow, no less. I reaved the old cotton and oakum from her seams.

We put her in a slip to swell for a week. She floated just awash. We stood a sign on her seat: PLEASE DON'T EMPTY ME—I'M SWELLING. Then we hauled her; let her dry out a couple of days, flipped her over, and I caulked her. Now her widest seams would only pass the lead from that yellow pencil. The caulking came from a tube but proved more than adequate.

Then I spread faring compound—nearly a gallon—and wore out several dozen sanding discs. Eventually, her hull grew smooth as smooth. Then I applied primer. Then just a bit more fairing compound—there and there and there.

Finally, I painted her topsides white, lavished green anti-fouling paint on her bottom, and screwed a bronze half-oval the length of her keel and all the way up both stems. We flipped her again and I sanded and primed and painted the inside—a lovely creamy yellow. Then I affixed a canvas-covered bumper all the way round her outwale and gave her new bronze oarlocks and sockets. Then she went back in the harbor to swell some more. By the end of the week she bobbed in her slip, begging for someone to row her.

We had a launching party with champagne and cake. And each of us took the old girl for a row. With seven-foot sculls she skimmed above the tide as a pelican skims—wings just touching the water.

Her owner was ecstatic—his face one huge smile. "I wasn't so sure you could do it," he exclaimed.

His wife—a lovely lady—plucked at my sleeve. "I hadn't a doubt you could pull it off," she whispered.

ROOM TO MOVE

Though the frost nipped at the flowers this morning, the air quickly warmed to fifty degrees and deceived us all into thinking it another lovely spring day. The little crocuses, grateful for every sunbeam, basked by the wall. By noon it dropped back into the forties; on the waterfront, the breeze and humidity made it downright chilly. Midafternoon, the rain set in. I suppose we should be thankful it wasn't snow. It began to snow Wednesday—even by the water—till I looked up at the sky and rehearsed my scowl.

Last Friday, I began work on a Dyer 29—a lithe, attractive power-boat built in the nineteen eighties. She stood blocked up in the yard, due to come into our shop this past Monday. I removed the radar and its mast, then measured the height from the bottom of her keel to the top of her bow pulpit: just over ten feet. Just a bit too tall to fit through our doors. Off came the pulpit. Now they could take her away. On Monday, the yard crew came by.

"How soon before you bring her into our shop?" I asked.

"We supposed to bring her into your shop? First we heard about it."

"But how soon can you move her?"

"Just let us know when you're ready."

"I'll let you know," I said.

To quote Robert Burns: "The best-laid schemes o' boats an' men gang aft a-gley."

My boss reconsidered: I should remove the windscreen, bring it into the vacant shop, and refinish it before bringing in the vessel. When I returned to the Dyer Tuesday morning, the yard crew had her upon the adjustable trailer, hitched to the old blue tractor.

"I said we'd let you know when we were ready," I expostulated.

"Don't try to impress *us* with your five-syllable words," the crew replied.

"Put her down," I said. "There's been a change of plans."

"No sense putting her down, here. We'll set her outside your shop."

It makes life easier, having the boat so handy to all our tools. With a stepladder secured to the swim platform I can access her easily. Tip-toeing around the cabin sides on the narrow deck proves vastly more amusing, but not what I'd enjoy with any sea running. Fortunately, the sea remains calm in the parking lot most days.

I removed the windshield wipers, the running lights, disconnected the cables for the radar and navigation, unzipped the dodger panels and rolled them up, disconnected the frame, and backed out the forty-two screws securing the windscreen. Sixteen screws had bungs; the rest had slots jammed full of layers of paint.

Then I started a slim wood wedge into the joint between the windscreen and cabin top, and worked a razor knife through the joint just ahead of the wedge to sever the adhesive. Advance a wedge, slit a few inches, advance a wedge. I could have used the heat gun, but it might have bubbled the paint on the cabin top, which didn't need refinishing. To write about all this has provided me most of the fun.

When I finally had the windscreen free, I braced it with furring strips to prevent any distortion that might crack the glass. The whole thing weighs but a hundred pounds, but I had doubts whether it would bounce if I dropped it the ten feet. I rigged a sling through the windshield wiper openings. Then we called the boom truck man. Hook it, lift it, set it down. Yes, you're very welcome. Nearly as easy as tossing it off the boat.

I should explain that a twenty-nine-foot boat nearly fills our facility. When the Dyer comes into the shop, we'll scarcely have accommodation to work around her. But we boating people get so used to tight quarters that we wouldn't feel right, having an excess of space. If you bring a waterman into your fairly large house, he'll seek out the smallest room and curl up there on your cable-length coil of five-eighths double braid.

I knew one sailor who locked himself into a bathroom (not a head) one winter with fifty years worth of *Yachting,* and wouldn't come out until it turned warm enough to paint his bottom.

A DAY TO REFRAIN

The chilly rain slants down this April evening, pours from the eaves, drenches the prodigal flower beds, drives the Pusslet indoors. Not a Sunday to mess about in boats. A day to refrain; to plan, to dream, to scribble. My outboard motor lies in the crushed-stone drive beside the woodpile: six cord of seasoned wood against next winter. If I weren't so lazy, I'd have built a fire today; my thermometer seems stuck at forty-seven.

Yesterday, I spent the afternoon with my boss, working on his sloop, a Gulf 27. Installing new cockpit drains; climbing about in a bilge with scarcely room to use a wrench. But we got it done and removed the previous system. We help each other ready our boats for the year.

I've removed *MoonWind*'s outboard motor in order to trim the cutout in her transom. Nine pieces of teak to fabricate and sand, install and finish: a mere ten minutes' work. Then grease my motor, replace the zinc and pop it back into place. I've just installed a deck pipe, chain stopper, and larger cleat on the foredeck. I need to retune my rigging, scrub my bilge, resecure my water tank, varnish all my brightwork. Only routine maintenance. Although my forward hatch needs total restoration. What would we do if we hadn't repairs and refinishing? Merely sail about and enjoy ourselves? How boring.

Some days I think wistfully of how my life would change had I only my kayak. After each trip, I'd hose it off and throw it behind the garage. Five minutes of maintenance in exchange for a day of boating. With *MoonWind,* five minutes gets me as far as removing her sail cover. The cost of a mooring would buy a quality kayak every year. Triple that cost—the price of a season's slip—would take me around the world.

But nothing compares to sailing upon the ocean. Merely having a boat provides potential for a vacation. Imagine having a cottage on the beach—and changing beaches anytime you care to. If you prefer some solitude, a mooring answers that need. If you care for society, rent a slip and share your summer with four hundred other boaters.

Laundry and shower lie just beyond the head of the pier. Restaurant and tavern in the parking lot. Ship's store and bait shop right around the corner. Grocery and bottle shop, bakery and luncheonette a five-minute walk away. But all of these prove merely a prelude to sailing.

When you cast off, there's nothing but the boat beneath your feet. Anything you need you carry with you, or learn to live without. One savors the immense quiet; the feral independence; the wide, unbridled sea. Leave your dull ambition in your dock, but keep your keen decisiveness with you, always. Learn to respect yourself, your mates, the water. Especially the water. The ocean demands the deference due the most fickle world leader: some days the tempestuous dictator; some days the pacific advocate of peace.

Voting for placid weather is not an option. When the sea becomes tumultuous, double up your dock lines and put the kettle on. When the day grows cold and rainy, I much prefer to stay in my slip, curled up with a book and a cup of coffee. I don't care to hazard myself against inclement weather. If I cared to do that, I'd sign up today for an Arctic expedition.

Today the chilly rain sheets off the roof. The Pusslet stands at the opened door, looks at the rain, looks up at me, and shakes one furry forepaw. Wet paws have no appeal, she says. Unless, of course, she chooses to play in the sink. Drinking from the faucet and batting the water provide ongoing amusement. Hanging over the toilet bowl to watch the water swirl never stales. Venturing out on a soft day of drizzle and mist hardly damps her ardor.

This battering rain confines us all to harbor. Today she appears content to drape herself over an old smoke-blackened beam above the living room, and enjoy a well-deserved rest. After all, she spent a productive afternoon climbing the open pantry shelves and rearranging spice jars about the floor.

MYSTIC AQUARIUM

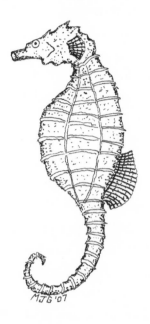

A few years back, they erected this funny-looking building just north of Mystic Seaport. Looked like a newfangled missile silo or a stubby grain elevator. They filled it with fish and squid and penguins and whales and called it the Aquarium. The purpose appears to enable you to watch aquatic creatures without getting your feet wet.

Quite a novel idea. You no longer need to fall off your boat to observe how the other two-thirds live. Don't know why I didn't think of it myself. I used to have guppies in a tank when I was a kid. If I'd only had the foresight to put a couple of whales in with them, I could have charged admission. Guess that's why I remain a poor man. Every time I caught a whale, I always threw him back.

The folks that run the Aquarium never throw anything back. They have a most eclectic assortment of bony fishes, cartilaginous fishes, cephalopods, and echinoderms. There: I've used up my quota of polysyllabic words for this installment. I never indulge in taxonomy much, but I can tell you a bit about the critters in some of the tanks using everyday, household names.

As you enter the darkened aquarium, a vertical, cylindrical tank containing jellyfish commands immediate attention. Live, pulsing jellyfish have no equal for beauty. They come in a variety of mellow hues and sensuous shapes. The original shape shifters, they fascinate the impressionable—as attested to by the numerous small nose prints left on the glass. The Windex people should demonstrate their appreciation and sponsor at least this tank.

Another large tank contains sharks. Their modus operandi demands they swim endless circuits of their world, glaring forbiddingly and baring their impressive arrays of fangs. Numerous small boys frantically dance and gesticulate about the huge enclosure.

The other cartilaginous fishes, the rays, also have their own tank. The stingrays, surprisingly graceful in their element, glide beneath the large manta: an aloof and stately presence. The Aquarium has recently added a petting tank: an open pool where cownose rays come by to have their ears scratched. My sister-in-law had one attempt to kiss her as she leaned over the water. Having attempted this myself, I applaud the creature's daring.

The largest tank inside the building contains dozens of fishes from the Atlantic. The small tanks they reserve for the more exotic species. I happened to find the seahorses quite droll. Their notion of a derby consists in their bouncing very slowly along the bottom, clutching at every passing weed with their tails. I went to the window and put two dollars on the tiny chestnut mare.

Suddenly you come to a large glass window and see a streamlined sea lion hurtle by. How little effort this creature expends to propel himself so swiftly. Up he goes to shove his snout into the air; down he comes and, with merely a wag of his tail flippers, makes an entire circuit of his world. When you go outside, you can look down at him making his endless rounds, deterred by neither snow nor rain nor heat nor gloom of night. Other sea lions cavort and swim and bark and snarfle and wrestle on the rocks.

The beluga whales have a sizable enclosure: about an acre. The inside window to this is layered with spectators. Outside, feeding hour attracts the most attention: The trainers encourage the whales to jump and frolic and speak to receive each tasty mullet. Small children stand on the railings in total awe of these gentle, magnificent beasts.

Two of the indoor exhibits concern not aquatic creatures but vessels. A large glass case contains a ten-foot-long detailed replica of the monstrous *Titanic*. Around the walls hang photos and illustrations of her magnificent interiors and an historical perspective on her building and demise. An audio clip relives the final transmissions of the ill-fated liner after her fatal collision with the iceberg.

The other ship is PT 109—the small naval vessel skippered by John F. Kennedy. Inadvertently struck and sunk by a Japanese destroyer in the dark, she proved the mettle of the future president. He swam to the nearest Pacific island, a disabled crew member in tow. He then swam to another island whence he contacted the fleet to effect a rescue. His courts-marshal exonerated him, and his heroism brought him national recognition.

A short documentary, composed of clips, covers the salient points of patrol torpedo boats and aspiring candidates. Children of six, reliving their grandparents' war, consistently man a mock-up of the bridge of a PT boat.

The sea lion show proves the culmination of any visit. Between the acts, you can easily find a concession to fill your needs, whether you crave a Mystic Aquarium T-shirt or merely lunch. Political correctness frowns on any requests for fish-and-chips.

The pool provides the focus of the little amphitheater. As in Greek theater, both an actor and chorus participate throughout. The latter devote themselves to the narrator, whose claim to attention resides in a pungent bucket. The way that young woman throws fish about reminds me of our food fights in the school cafeteria.

The cast radiates exuberance. They jump about and shout as they wait to perform: to dive, to leap, to plunge, to roll over. The show climaxes in each sea lion's dive deep into the pool, followed by a prodigious, vertical, water-clearing leap. If a big black Lab could balance a ball on his nose while clapping his paws, he might just get an audition for one of the parts. Any scuba shop would carry flippers his size.

I enjoyed the Aquarium almost as much as did my three-year-old grandson. But when I got home, I must confess that I felt so guilty that I poured some seawater into my boating shoes.

THE DIFFERENCE BETWEEN
A HALIBUT AND A HALYARD

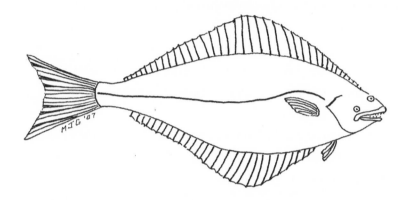

Rain and rain and, then again, more rain. Day after day. At times it lets up just enough to begin some outdoor project for a couple of hours, but humidity precludes painting or varnishing. This being two-thirds of our business at this time of year, wet weather sets us aback. Fortunately, another Petrel has wandered into our shop, begging to come in out of the rain and have her brightwork sanded.

So I've clambered about and shared some energy with her. I know John Ruskin would never have approved of my treating her as a sentient being but then, to my knowledge, he never owned a boat. A brilliant man and contentious, but he never felt the sea beneath his feet—at least not on a craft small enough to inspire intimacy. Nor had he ever a live-limbed tiller in his grasp on a fine reach on a lovely morn with a fresh breeze and all the involutions of this mad and oppressive world left behind.

My forward hatch has arrived at last. Should the weather relent, I'll motor *MoonWind* into a slip and install the hatch this weekend. Just now, they forecast ten feet of rain per hour for the next ten days. Simply owning a boat may make all the difference, as Grampy Noah found to his great relief. Following this deluge, I shall sail over the housetops in downtown Mystic en route to the Rocky Mountains. Tracking the seagulls should eventually bring me to the tidal flats around Denver.

Perhaps I can open a chandlery there or teach folks how to eat lobster. How many generations before Denveronians learn the subtle difference between port and starboard? How long before the sight of mariners garbed in rubber boots and oilskins doesn't send them into paroxysms of mirth? Even in the Ocean State—Rhode Island— not everyone knows a halibut from a halyard. Odd, that, in a state comprised of salt water.

Still the rain continues. Every couple of days I bail my Whitehall, lest there be more water within than without. If only the temperature would edge up farther past fifty, it wouldn't oppress so much. May notwithstanding, I could delight in sitting by a cheery log fire with a nourishing book and the Pusslet curled beside me. This isn't Pusslet weather. She should appreciate not having responsibilities or needing to go anywhere. Would I could claim as much. Or, perhaps, as little. One of these days—the lattermost—I shan't have any responsibilities, ever. Nor wind in my sails, nor bearings to take, nor weather to contend with.

For now, at least, this sodden day offers objectives. The most pleasing, so far, to settle in and communicate a bit of myself—though never all—to this most commiserative page. Every year, I find myself drawn irresistibly to the water. Every spring, the allure of gardening wanes. Every summer, travel via anything save a boat appears absurd. Every autumn, the leaves are welcome to pile against my house. And one of these winters, I'll simply refuse to settle in by the fire.

Sailing and writing are what I most enjoy. The years flit by, and my gray hair grows ever whiter. The time to procrastinate has expired. I need to control the remains of my life. I need to relinquish my dilettante proclivities and commit myself to living. This year I mean to do some serious sailing. This year I mean to publish my very first book. In less than a year I'll have my sixtieth birthday. I've run out of reasons for doing and not doing. The weeks, the months, go by with alarming rapidity. People I know my age have been dead for years. This mundane world has no claims at all . . . What's that? . . . Now?

The Pusslet has come to tell me it's time to make supper.

FARTHER SHORES

A PROPOSITION

NESSIE

When I was twenty-five years old, I worked for an engineer in private practice. He had his shop and office in southern Connecticut—close to Long Island Sound. He had designed and built a one-man diving bell; had tried it, successfully, and wanted to market it. He needed sponsoring—someone to make the maritime world sit up and take some notice. He knew a couple of gentlemen at Harvard who had a plan to do some exploration. They only lacked funding, a crew, and a boat.

I had an eighteen-foot sloop—not nearly sufficient to hoist a diving bell. They would require at least a forty-footer: something with a crane and accommodations for four.

"Something like a steel fishing boat?" I asked.

"Not at all," answered my boss. "Just wait and see."

So off we went to Harvard University. We had an appointment to meet with two men: a financier and a scientist.

"But where do I come in?" I wanted to know. "Do they want me to learn to man your diving bell?"

"Not at all," answered my boss. "Just wait and see."

I pictured myself in my old machine shop, fabricating parts for diving bells. But the gentlemen at Harvard had far more grandiose plans for my career. They didn't require much convincing of the efficacy of the diving bell—that had proved itself. But they needed personnel.

"Have you much experience sailing a boat?" they inquired.

I tried not to sound as diffident as I felt as I answered in the affirmative.

"Would living aboard a big wooden sailboat for six months be a hardship?" they asked.

Doing what? I wondered.

"Why, nothing more than being her skipper," they responded.

My mouth began to water. I thought I could manage that.

"Good," they replied, and conferred between themselves.

"What's going on?" I asked my boss. "Where do they want me to go?" He looked at me and grinned from ear to ear.

"Just wait and see," he told me.

Salvage work, I thought to myself. Maybe sunken treasure? Why would they need a wooden sailboat? Something quiet; something that doesn't . . . oh, my gosh. They want to salvage and decommission old mines—that must be it. And they want a boat that won't detonate mines triggered by a metal hull or engine noise.

I swallowed some bile and felt the sweat beading on various covert parts of my anatomy. Six months walking tiptoe about the deck? Six months scarcely daring to crank a winch? My oily old machine shop sounded suddenly secure and rather comforting.

Now the three of them had their heads together. Well, I thought, you've put your big foot in a clove hitch this time, mate. I hope they pay well. I suppose I need to designate a beneficiary: someone willing to adopt my little boat.

"Come over here and sit down," they said, "and listen to our tentative proposition."

I wiped my hands on my trousers. My feet seemed reluctant to approach the conference table.

"I'm afraid we can't pay you for more than your food and travel," they began.

I forced a crooked smile; six months risking my precious life, and they couldn't bother to pay me for my time.

"We want you to skipper our boat and fit her out—we'll need your expertise to help us with that. We hope to get a government grant," they confided.

Lovely, I thought—my taxes at work: funding to blow my poor young self to bits. I hope a coffin's included.

"What we'd like you to do is spend a summer in Scotland," they continued.

Oh, well, I thought—I'd just as soon die in Scotland as anywhere else.

"You see," they concluded, "we're putting together an expedition to find the Loch Ness Monster, and we need to have a sailboat in order not to scare her."

HOLIDAY FUN

I spent Labor Day weekend at a slip in Massachusetts and got to observe—and participate in—a bit of the goin's-on.

Upwind a piece, a powerboat and a sailboat, both about thirty-six feet, shared a slip between two finger piers. The wind ripped through the harbor at fifteen knots. There's nothing like a little breeze to bring out latent talent.

Anyway, the skipper of the powerboat enlisted the aid of a couple of fellows—I wouldn't dare call them sailors—to give him a hand to "turn this rig around." It seems he wanted to scrub that side of his boat away from the pier. Because of the breeze, he thought he needed some help to turn around. Boy, did he ever. The two clowns on the finger pier each cast off a mooring line, and the skipper gave her plenty of throttle to overcome the headwind. But the clowns neglected to cast off the farther stern line made fast to the walkway.

You guessed it. The powerboat, still tethered on the inboard quarter, pivoted on that line and slewed around, crashing into the sailboat alongside. The skipper slammed her into reverse, but their rails caught together. The sailboat got a good shaking before she came loose. The skipper then proceeded to try again. Take two: the skipper gave her plenty of throttle to overcome the headwind . . .

After abusing the sailboat a second time, it dawned on the skipper there might just be a problem. I forbore to listen to what he called the two fellows on the pier. Some of those words I hadn't heard since I served in the navy. For some reason, the powerboat skipper scuttled his plan to turn himself around. With a bit more effort he might have scuttled the sailboat as well.

That proved just the beginning. That afternoon another seaman, running a forty-foot cabin cruiser, came waltzing into the water between the piers and aimed for his slip, upwind. At the last moment, halfway into his berth, he had the revelation to back her in. Except he had cranky engines. He backed her down, spun the wheel, and . . . lost his starboard engine. Next thing he knew, he had also lost control. The wind obligingly slammed him into our pier across the way. Amazing the amount of sail area on some of these powerboats. Had I been aboard, I'd have taken at least one reef.

His poor wife scurried about the deck without a line, a boat hook, or even Knight's *Modern Seamanship*. She probably wouldn't have had quite enough time to read the relevant chapters. The wind pinned their boat, amidships, against a piling at the end of a finger pier. The bow and stern took it in turn to bounce off innocent sailboats in adjoining slips. At one point, the powerboat's bow came within a foot of *Moon Wind*'s transom. I recollect telling myself, "I don't need this."

Four of us leapt aboard moored sailboats and struggled to fend her off. Another fellow jumped into his dinghy and started the motor.

"Quick," I said to the woman, "find a long line to pass him." A minute later she came on deck with a mooring line; it may have been twelve feet long.

The fellow with the dinghy took their roding, anchor and all, and zipped to the opposite pier where three stout fellows waited to take a strain on it. The skipper put his one engine in gear and scraped his inglorious way along the piling, as the impromptu crew hauled him about and warped him into his slip. His swim platform suffered numerable indignities.

Finally, a fifty-foot ketch came stumbling into the harbor. Through a gaping hole, I could count her vee-berth cushions. I spoke with her skipper later on the beach.

"I can't understand it," he said to me. "All I did was put on her on autopilot and lay below for thirty seconds."

Amazing how quickly some rocks can move when nobody keeps an eye on 'em.

COD FISHING

POINT JUDITH LIGHT
POINT JUDITH
RHODE ISLAND

For a modest fee, one can join in a charter boat party and spend the day fishing for cod off southern New England.

We left home about daybreak and drove an hour and a half until we fetched up at Point Judith in Narragansett. Harbor of Refuge they call it and for good reason. Two arms of breakwater nearly meet in a loving embrace of the harbor. Within lies sanctuary from rips and wind.

We found our boat, an eighty-foot steel vessel, and strode aboard. The weather promised no worse than usual, the fish awaited us anxiously; we were healthy and hungry and wanted a second breakfast. By eight o'clock, the diesels commenced to churn and, ten minutes later, we backed away from the pier.

A pot of coffee simmered in the deckhouse where twenty people, mostly men, crowded about and fumbled with the sugar. Once outside the breakwater, we felt the effect of contrary tides and a stiff breeze. The seas ran only four or five feet but the chop would rattle your dentures.

Every vessel handles the sea in its own particular way. Our vessel responded in a delightful screwing motion that reminded me of trying to land a sizable eel using very light tackle. The stern lifted ever so gently then pirouetted—and I found I had poured my coffee inside my shirt. Perhaps these doughnuts would be easier to manage. And they were. At least until my stomach began to lurch. I've been aboard numerous small boats; been to the Caribbean twice on large ships, crossed the Atlantic through fifteen-foot seas on a steamer, and never felt more than a passing queasiness.

This topped them all. Just for garnish, the diesel fumes followed me everywhere and gagged me. I asked around but no one had any Dramamine. Ten miles offshore, our little ship auditioned for an Archimedes screw—and got the part. I'd never known that a boat could pitch and roll and yaw and shudder simultaneously.

The doughnuts grew disgruntled. They told me the lodgings were less than suitable and gave me notice they were moving out— *immediately*. I made it to the lee rail and granted their request. My companion shook his head.

"It's no use chumming for cod," he said. "They *never* come to the surface."

I gave him a twisted smile and wiped my mouth. We finally arrived at our destination. The skipper backed her down and headed her not quite into the wind and angled only slightly into the chop. The shuddering stopped. Only the pitching, rolling, and yawing remained.

All about, people baited up and claimed positions to fish along the rail. The leeward rail maintained the most popularity: You don't get spray—or other fluids—blown back onto your face. I needed the leeward rail for my penance, but no one seemed desirous of my company. The waist of the ship was the easiest place to fish—close to the water and least affected by pitching. I found myself ostracized to the bows where the pitching magnified.

Up, up, up and then—ohhh, not again—down. I decorated the bow of that boat and never charged for my service. The doughnuts were gone. The eggs and toast from six AM were gone. Last night's supper was gone. Last *week's* supper was gone. Nothing remained save lovely, lovely bile. There seemed no shortage of that.

I staggered to the fantail. That proved considerably calmer, but even more diesel exhaust collected there. If you ever need an antidote for a good digestion, I recommend diesel fumes.

I finally lay down on a bench in the deckhouse and tried my best not to fall off it. I succeeded at this—ninety percent of the time. The scarcity of cooperative cod consoled me. After what seemed like weeks, we headed for port.

I stumbled ashore and avidly gulped some fresh water. An hour later, I tried solid food. Success! That night I slept like the dead.

In the morning my lover brought me coffee—and doughnuts.

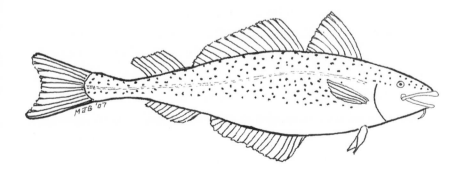

SAN JUAN

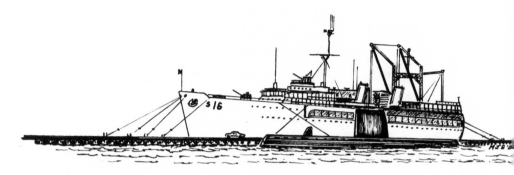

USS HOWARD W. GILMORE AS 16

We arrived in San Juan sometime in January. The sunshine proved very welcome. Our five-hundred-foot submarine tender, USS *Howard W. Gilmore,* AS 16, sent her hawsers ashore. Braided half of nylon, half of steel, they would keep Puerto Rico from drifting off during the night.

We warped in and made fast and settled in for a fortnight. Of course this was nothing more than a paid vacation—one during which we put in forty hours, plus four section duty. Every fourth night, a fourth of the crew remained aboard and repaired any submarines that came to call. Of the three squadrons in our care, only a couple of subs came to visit; the other twenty cruised abroad or lazed at home in Charleston, South Carolina.

San Juan Harbor abounded with naval vessels—mostly American. Our division officer cautioned us not to get into trouble ashore (Who? Us, sir?) and to keep away from Old Town, where the Shore

Patrol with their .45s would not even dare to venture. We should always remember that we represented the greatest navy known between Mars and Venus.

San Juan didn't lack entertainment. Moro Castle, her ancient cannons trained at long-dead foes, perched on the promontory guarding the harbor. The markets and shops displayed colorful clothing and jewelry to purchase for our sweethearts. The rum distillery offered guided tours.

(Is it true they gave you free samples, Jack? Hey, Jack.)

(Don't shake him like that—he'll be all right by tomorrow.)

At night the city throbbed with Latin music. Latin beauties and treacherous drinks concocted of local rum tempted the incautious. Quaint cafés and elegant restaurants lined the narrow streets.

The waterfront attracted me. It would have been grand to tell you how I went island-hopping, sailing a native outrigger; how I was captured by mermaids and forced to . . . but nothing so picturesque happened. San Juan was too twentieth century; a bit too Americanized. I wandered through the seafood markets down by the piers and tried out my high school Spanish.

I made the acquaintance of the fish we know as the dolphin: the dorado—from the Spanish for "gilded." This blunt-browed fish shimmers with vibrant colors that gradually fade and dull as the creature dies. Pompano and octopus and brightly colored, unfamiliar fishes adorned the stalls and, finally, at a crooked pier, lay a couple of fish with sails—little Sunfish.

Two of us hired one for the afternoon, and we scooted about the harbor, forgetting, at least for a while, about repairing pumps and valves for submariners. Fortunately, we forgot about sharks as well. How vulnerable one is—hiking one's tender buns way out over the low, low rail.

On our journey home, cleaving the crystalline water of the bay, I looked down from the boat deck, thirty feet up—whence one could see the bright, bright bottom clearly at fifteen fathoms—and spied a twelve-foot shark alongside our ship. Would that have changed my lurid mind about dangling body parts in the warm Caribbean? Bet your bowline, Skipper!

From the height of three feet, the sea is not transparent. Who knows what hungrily lurked beneath our Sunfish? Who knows what ravening carnivore craved imported morsels? We never gave it a thought.

However, the porpoises did come by for a visit that afternoon. Closer and closer they leapt about our little boat until I began to wonder: How many eight-foot porpoises would fit in our tiny cockpit? They chased us around the harbor—we romped together all tropic afternoon.

I enjoyed my visit with these graceful beasts, though they never came close enough to pet. For that you must visit the Dingle Dolphin in Dingle Bay, County Kerry. And who knows if that docile creature still sports about, or beyond? For my visit to Dingle was numerous years ago. As most things I remember seem to be . . .

SANIBEL ISLAND

SANIBEL ISLAND LIGHT
FLORIDA

My sister used to own a condo on Sanibel Island, off the Gulf Coast of Florida. Three miles of causeway and bridges connect it to Fort Myers. A sizable island, it caters mostly to tourists, but, having a four-story building limit, it hasn't the feel of high-rise Fort Myers Beach across the bay. The broad sandy shores abound in shells. You can find conches, sand dollars, and sea urchins; murex, whelks, augurs, donax, and sundials. But you mustn't take the shells of living creatures.

People who fish can surf cast or charter boats. The lighthouse at the southeast end of the island—an old steel structure built in the eighteen eighties—marks shoaling beaches. I watched some fellows in waist-deep water casting and casting and casting.

"What is it you're after," I asked one.

"Stripers," he said. "They come in here all the time."

"You mean—like these?" I queried.

Four fat stripers swirled about him as he frantically cranked his reel. One of them passed between his legs. Each was as long as my arm. They disappeared before he had finished swearing. What had he planned to do, I wondered. Maybe dangle the lure between his legs? I left him muttering inane imprecations: Did he really think that fish's mother could bark?

Farther along, more accomplished fishermen read the water. Egrets and curlews and flocks of squeaking turnstones stalked little fish and crustaceans along the foreshore. Terns and pelicans plunged in the sea incessantly, and cormorants and their cousins, the anhingas, surface-dove and swam after scaly prey.

My sister's condominium edged the canal. Her deck—on which I enjoyed my early coffee—overhung the water. This canal provided a home for several small alligators—most less than seven feet long. A gallinule, or moorhen, stalked the muddy banks in search of breakfast, clucking her chronic discontent with the world. A stately anhinga swam and dived, then perched in a bush and spread her wings to dry. Each morning an osprey groomed herself on the same limb of a huge willow overhanging the water.

Occasionally, a 'gator would slowly swim to the deck in the hope that I might trail my toes in the water. Fortunately, my toes are too well disciplined to swim without my permission. A variety of wildlife abounded, except for the larger mammals. I never saw any more formidable than a corpulent New Yorker in yellow shorts.

One day I sauntered down to the beach for a swim. Little geckos scuttled out of my shady path beneath the shady willows. Beyond, the bountiful May sun kept busy, burning the brilliant sands. As I waded out beyond the bar, a number of fish bumped against my legs, but I couldn't see what they looked like for the glare. I swam for a while and encountered still more fish. When I waded ashore, an elderly lady in a white linen suit and a broad straw hat awaited me anxiously.

"You really shouldn't wade out there with all of those stingrays," she said to me.

"All of those *what*!?" I exclaimed.

"They've begun to breed," she informed me. "They've come inshore."

And so they had. I shaded my eyes against the glare. Hundreds and hundreds of little rays schooled in the lucid water.

"We sent one chap to the hospital just last year," she continued. "If he'd been as skinny as you, he might have made it."

I shivered a bit; it wasn't as warm as I'd thought.

"They won't bother you when you swim," she explained. "Only when you wade."

I thought of the hundred yards I'd just been slogging across the shoals.

"You need to shuffle your feet," she said. "That way you nudge them out of your way when they stop to rest on the bottom. It's only when you plant your foot on their backs that they whip their tails about and sting your leg."

Peering both ways, I saw the shallow water roil as far as I could see. I thanked her for her advice and spent the rest of my morning collecting shells. Look at this huge helmet shell. It was propping open a door on Middle Gulf Drive.

SWIMMING AT GLENDALOUGH

HOWTH HEAD LIGHT, HOWTH, COUNTY DUBLIN

The southernmost suburb of Dublin, on Dublin Bay, is known as Dalkey. The Dublin Area Rapid Transit whisks you from Dalkey, describes an arc around the bay, and, after numerous summary stops, deposits you at the end of its line in the fishing village of Howth. If you find the unmarked public way, you can climb the unpeopled headland via sheep paths that part the yellow gorse. From the breezy summit, you will look down at the lighthouse on its rock and, to your south, see most of Dublin and across the bay to Dalkey.

They say that, on a clear day, you can even see Holyhead, in Wales, across the Irish Sea. But they also say that, from Dingle, on a clear day, you can see Boston. Especially after nightfall from inside the pub.

I used to fly over to visit my sister, at Dalkey, in early autumn. By then, the tourists had all departed and Dublin had resumed its unhurried ways. The large pink hotel in Dalkey stood nearly vacant. The public houses catered, again, to mostly local folk.

When I say that my sister's home overlooked the water, I mean you walked down her broad front steps to the flagstone terrace, took four steps to the waist-high wall, and startled at a breathtaking drop of eighty feet to the shingle straight below. Visitors bet on the time remaining till a storm undercut her precipice and tumbled her house to the sea.

You could swim from my sister's beach—once you waded among the slippery stones. A winding and irregular set of steps ascended the hill nearby where it wasn't so steep.

Dalkey has a public swimming place: a huge outcropping that runs down into the ocean. The only way out of the water consists of a steel ladder anchored to the ledge. Going in, of course, one can dive—the rock shelves off within a few feet of the sea. Only men used to frequent this swimming spot; nobody wore bathing suits. That has recently changed, albeit slowly: Naked women are taking over the rock.

You can swim in the sea in October, without your extremities turning three shades of purple, due to the Gulf Stream. This tropical influence keeps the seashore moderate all winter. Dublin, seven hundred miles north of New York, rarely experiences frost. My sister had palmetto trees that flourished in her yard. The sea stayed so warm, we used to boil our eggs for breakfast by lowering them in a colander over the cliff at high tide; although it took them nearly ten minutes to cook rather than four.

One day we visited nearby Glendalough: the site of Saint Kevin's monastery, dating from the sixth century. What remains, including a magnificent round tower, stands stark and stunning amid a wood, artistically set off by ascending pastures. The lough—limpid, placid, and rural—invited us. The sandy bottom sparkled. We shucked our clothes and went in. It felt a bit colder than the Irish Sea: bracing and delightful.

Later, we climbed the hill beyond, and followed the narrow stream that feeds the lough. The hill becomes rather abrupt; the stream becomes, in places, a vertical torrent. A vigorous waterfall has scoured a hemispherical basin from the solid rock to several feet in depth. What could prove more entertaining, on a bright October day, than a quickening dip in a sunny hillside pool? Again we stripped off our wrinkling clothes. The smoothed rock basin, pale in hue, reflected the sun back through the swirling water. Nothing obstructed the bottom. You waded knee-deep among the surrounding rocks, then flung yourself in. By the time I had waded in knee-deep, I could no longer feel my toes. I dove in and surfaced beneath the waterfall.

I understood, then, how a lamb chop feels when you take it from the frying pan and thrust it into the freezer. The Gulf Stream, somehow, hadn't made it quite as far as this pool. My hands and feet no longer responded to repeated, frantic messages from my brain. I turned and floundered back to the bank. My fingers and toes would not obey; I hauled myself out with my teeth.

GUNNERY PRACTICE

On our way to Guantanamo Bay, the crew took gunnery practice. Our repair ship was nearly thirty years old—a relic of World War II. We sported a couple of five-inch guns, mostly for use against aircraft, or perhaps as paperweights. Compared with the rapid-fire cannons now in use, we might just as well have had a pair of muzzle-loading twenty-four-pounders aboard.

The crew limbered up the foredeck gun, fiddled with the little elevator that brought shells up from the magazine until it worked smoothly, then stationed a couple of powder monkeys down in the hold for passing ammunition. Fifteen men form the gunnery crew for a five inch/38: a Pointer and a Trainer, each seated on the turret; the gun captain and his second-in-command, the Rammerman; also one Gunnersmate, Sight Setter, Sight Checker, Fuse Setter, and Hoist-man. Before the advent of cartridges, two Powdermen and four Projectilemen would have completed the complement. I doubt we had more than ten men on our gun.

Then they sent out a boat crew to set the target adrift: a fifty-five-gallon drum. The ship hove to a mile away and the lads had a fine time, banging away and giving a dozen rounds a sniff of fresh air. Fortunately, they didn't harm the drum any. It would have been a shame to waste the taxpayers' money. In those days, a drum like that cost four bucks. Fortunately, Uncle Fidel didn't send a squadron against us.

When we arrived in Cuba, we tied up at a long pier at the US Navy base. Between ourselves and the shore were a couple of hundred yards of pier undergoing repair. A chunk of the steel-and-masonry deck, six feet thick and three or four feet wide, had been shorn away for maybe a tenth of a mile. It didn't look pretty.

"What happened?" we asked.

"Oh," they said. "Some bright young commander brought in a 'tin can'—a destroyer. One a them big Forrest Sherman Class boats: four hundred feet, three thousand tons. Nearly backed her down in time ta make a respectable landing. You think the pier looks bad, you shudda seen the 'tin can.'"

"Where's the commander, now?" we inquired.

"Oh, they shipped his butt out," they told us. "Sent him ta Alaska and issued him a broom. While he's waitin' ta get his twenty in, his job is ta clear the snow from the Arctic Circle."

Across the pier from us lay a missile cruiser—over five hundred feet of potent menace. One morning I climbed the ladder to our boat deck and looked down at them having their target practice. But they didn't loose any projectiles. They couldn't even be bothered to set out a target. Maybe they couldn't afford to waste four dollars.

This was my first exposure to modern warfare. They hadn't a crew in sight. Somewhere, snug below, someone sat at a computerized console with the inevitable cup of coffee and pushed buttons. On their main deck stood a raised hatch secured with a pair of doors. In less time than it takes to read this sentence, the doors flew open and a twin rocket launcher thrust up out of the hold, whirled and elevated till it homed in on its theoretical target, and then . . . stopped. The following instant, two Terrier missiles could have been deployed.

The anachronism of a sailor, holding an eighty-pound five-inch shell while he waited for the breech to open and another man to catch the ejected casing, should have been laughable. Had not the nation's security been involved.

Of course, our ship would never go off to war. Modern vessels with modern weapons had long since joined the fleet. In two years aboard, I never saw that gun fired but the once. But it made us, the crew, feel infinitely better.

If a dragon came flying over our ship, we knew there was someone willing to risk the uttermost embarrassment for the sake of our defense. I'm talking about our bosun's mate with the crossbow.

CAPE ANN

Thacher's Island Lights
Cape Ann
Rockport
Massachusetts

Rockport has always been special to me—even though I've never sailed by it. As children, my elder sister and I would visit our favorite aunt, who vacationed there. Our father's sister, Deborah, had become heir to the family summerhouse: turn of the century, weathered shingles, ten rooms and a wide veranda. The house sat in two acres of hay field off an unpaved road. From the second floor, one could see the twin lights on Thachers Island. They seemed far off; they were scarcely a mile distant.

I returned to Rockport recently—perhaps ten years ago. The house looked the same except for the tasteful addition of a three-bay carriage house. But Deborah has been gone these twenty-five years. A vigorous woman of eighty-five, she dropped down dead in the snow one day while putting out food for the birds.

Rockport has improved as a tourist trap. Bearskin Neck, overrun with gift shops and boutiques, vies with Motif #1: the small red fish house out on the pier, which appears as pristine as ever. Most of the budding landscape artists determined to portray it would scarcely know a codfish from a catboat. Fifty years ago, you could have taken a nap in the middle of Main Street and not more than four or five cars an hour would have run you over.

Deborah would take us into town for provisions and library books. Never having learned to drive, or seen much use for a car, our aunt would stride the mile into the village, rain or shine. Returning, laden with parcels, she'd take the bus. Occasionally, we'd visit the pound at the head of the pier and treat three little lobsters to a bus ride.

My greatest thrill was to visit the North Atlantic. A short walk from the house brought us to an immense outcropping of granite, sloping from the road down into the sea. To watch the tide roar in and crash against the bearded rocks, to stand just yards away from all that power, gave me my introduction to the sea. Long Island Sound, back home in Connecticut, seemed a millpond by comparison. This was the North Shore's version of that "stern and rockbound coast" of the Pilgrim Fathers.

Close enough to the ocean for constant renewal spread a large tidal pool. A shallow depression in the ledge, perhaps ten by thirty feet, it sufficed to support a habitat of its own. Little fish and crabs resided permanently in this pool—except when a perigee tide would inundate it, ousting some of the tenantry but introducing others. Best of all, it had room enough to sail my brand-new boat.

I received, I think my eighth birthday, a twenty-inch wooden sloop with a deep fin keel. One could secure the tiller, cast off her pendant, and off she would go. Eventually, she would round up, come about, and return to her home port. Give or take a few miles. It didn't much strain my vivid imagination to be aboard her. Taking the helm, I shoved off for parts unknown. Many have I discovered. Some folks aver I never really returned.

One evening, Deborah took us down to the rocks. A gale-force wind assailed the shore, although no rain had fallen. For the very first time, I saw what wind and water together might do. We stood at least a hundred feet from the tide. Twelve-footers roared in and dashed themselves on the ledge. Barrels of spray flew high in the air, descending with a slap. The retreating sea growled and sucked and heaved upright as the next wave met it. Together they fell and wrestled among the rocks. The din increased—the ravenous heavens howled. The tearing wrack disrobed a cowering moon as the glowering sky descended on the sea. Eventually came the torrent and we fled. The banshee wind shrieked havoc behind us up the black lanes of horrid, clutching hedges.

How fortunate to return to Deborah's sturdy home and sit in the flickering inglenook to dry and drink hot chocolate. On the hearth, the dry logs roared; the windows sheeted rain. The rising wind shrieked ruin to ships at sea. Many a boat has perished on Rockport's reefs. My aunt gazed into the fire with distant eyes.

"Why won't she answer me?" I asked my sister.

A MURMUR FROM THE BROOK

HUNGERFORD BROOK

Long ago, there flourished an old, old farm in southern Connecticut. By the time I arrived, aged four days, the henhouses had been torn down, the twenty cows disposed of. The barn stood empty save for furtive wisps of hay sticking beneath the rafters. The hay tongs had gone. The wheeled hoist rusted quietly on its track beneath the ridge board. The truck and the tractor had gone to one farm, the Clydesdales to another.

However, two decrepit hay wagons remained intact: one behind the barn, the other beside the farm road a few hundred yards out back. I grew up playing on these. But one could drive imaginary teams only so far. After they'd run and run and run some more, they had to be fed and watered and groomed and put up for the night.

The brook down the hill was better. It never stopped running. Well, maybe in August if it hadn't rained for a month. By then the trout had all retreated upstream to the reservoir—except for the ones I'd managed to catch and fry in the cast-iron skillet. These brook trout grew small and extremely wild, and never has any fish since tasted half so good. I spent my every spare minute learning to catch them. Those fat, complacent creatures they call trout and raise in concrete pools haven't the spunk or character or troutful *je ne sais quoi* to develop flavor.

A few small frogs and water striders and minnows and, once in a while, an anadromous little eel, complemented the trout. It was damp and cool and shady by the brook. Huge sycamores and maples towered above, and dappled the valley with shady greens and browns and blacks and patches of light that glinted from the bits of quartz beneath the sparkling water. The brook devoted its energy to churn and gurgle and frolic along the edge of our property until it joined with Roaring Brook and spilled to the river beyond.

The two abandoned dams below our house no longer held back water. One spanned the stream, but the central stones had tumbled from their places. The lower dam consisted of a jutting wall that stopped where it met the brook. The rock had been used to build the bridge abutments. Flumes and mill foundations could not be found.

The road beside our farmhouse received paving in the forties. Beyond the barn—down Stonehouse Hill and crossing Hungerford Brook—it remained unimproved. The road and bridge were still passable as I grew up: Some days three cars used it. A local lad, perhaps fourteen, driving a tractor made from a Model A Ford, went down the hill with a load of hay behind him, dropped into a gluttonous rut, heaved on the jerking wheel, and hopped the bank. Fortunately, his tractor fetched up against a tree; shaken, he stumbled away. The town eventually closed off Stonehouse Hill.

After that, nothing more could interrupt my idyll. The road grew over, the plank deck on the little bridge rotted away. Between the sturdy dry wall piers flowed a shady pool nearly waist-deep at center: a deliciously cool refuge from the summer. Except during freshets, one could squat on the water-smoothed rock in the stream above the pool, mesmerized by the age-old song of water over stone.

The wooden railings on the bridge fell down. You discovered, quickly, which of the mossy planks would bear your weight. In '82, after a week of torrential rains, we had a terrific flood. Farther up the swollen stream, dams burst. Logs and boulders crashed through the valley all night. Eight feet of water scoured its way to the river. Beside the barn, a hundred precipitous feet above the torrent, the steep bank trembled. The bridge disintegrated. The dry wall abutments vanished in the night. The steel beams lodged among the trees downstream. The pool clogged. The wary trout departed.

But by then I had outgrown that world. As I am slowly, assuredly, outgrowing this one.

Some colonial lad once played about this millpond as his father worked the mill. Some Pequot lass, a mere five hundred springs ago, collected trout lilies here on this bank where the standing half of our hugest maple rots. A different trout, a different frog, disported themselves in this new brook shaped by the glacier—a mere fifteen millennia gone by. And someway I shall wade this brook in ages yet to come, still trying to ignore the strident cries of my father up the hill—calling me home to supper and my bed.

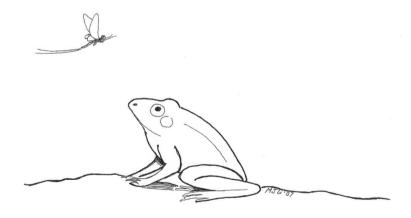

GLOSSARY

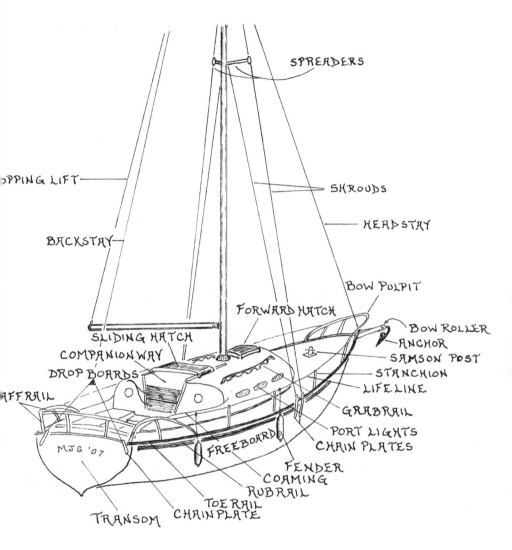

Welcome aboard. For those of you who don't carry a rigging knife, I'm appending a brief glossary so you can keep your roding spliced and not go adrift.

ABACK—having the wind in front of the sails instead of behind them. This stalls the forward progress of the vessel.

ABAFT—behind; AFT of.

ABEAM—in the vicinity, or direction of, the BEAM (the width of the vessel)—at a right angle.

ABOARD, ON BOARD—on a vessel.

ADRIFT—afloat; unattached. Said of vessels, things lost overboard, and those who can't find their way home from the pub.

AFT—toward the back of the vessel.

AGROUND—stuck on the bottom of a body of water.

AID TO NAVIGATION—any of various devices or constructions serving to guide mariners to safe waters. Some of these are:
> LIGHTHOUSES
> BUOYS
> BEACONS
> CHANNEL MARKERS
> DAY MARKERS

ALEE—toward the LEE, or LEEWARD; downwind.

ALL-A-TAUT-O—secured, put to rights, squared away.

ALOFT—above, overhead.

ALONGSIDE—beside a vessel or pier.

AMIDSHIPS—in the middle of the vessel.

ASTERN—in the vicinity, or direction of, the STERN.

ATHWART—across; from PORT to STARBOARD. See THWART.

AWASH—with the water just breaking over it; as a vessel or reef.

BACKWIND—*vt*—to purposely expose the front of the sail to the wind in order to back, turn, or stall the vessel.

BACK—*vi*—the changing of wind direction in a counterclockwise direction; opposed to VEER.

BALLAST—weight added to a vessel, either internally or externally, to make her more stable by offsetting the pressure of the wind against the sails.

BATTEN—*noun*—a flexible strap inserted into a long pocket in a sail to help maintain its shape.

BATTEN DOWN—*vi, vt*—to secure a hatch, door, or cover. Derivatively, to prepare for rough weather.

BEACON—an AID TO NAVIGATION: a small tower or structure on the shore, usually having a light or reflector, or emitting a radio signal.

BEAM—the greatest width of a vessel.

BEARING—direction, expressed in degrees, between a vessel's heading and any point. The intersection of two or more such lines determines the vessel's position at that given time. Such position is generally referred to as a FIX. A bearing can be in a vertical plane, measured from the horizon, or on the Earth's surface, where it can be either: compass bearing—using magnetic north as zero; or relative bearing—using the heading of the vessel as zero.

BEAUFORT SCALE—a scale of wind strength ranging from force zero (calm) to force twelve (hurricane).

BELOW—down; under, beneath.

BERTH—a designated or appropriated place to moor, anchor, or dock a vessel; a place to sleep on a vessel: a bunk or bed.

BILGE—the bottom-most (wettest and dirtiest) inside area of a vessel.

BILGE PUMP—a pump, usually permanently installed, to empty the bilge of water.

BITTS—a pair of juxtaposed stubby posts used to secure a line by wrapping or hitching.

BLOCK—a pulley.

BOAT HOOK—a light pole with a terminal hook used to seize pendants, lines, cleats, or rails during docking or anchoring. Also used to FEND OFF, or to discipline other boat owners by pulling them overboard.

BOW—the front of a vessel.

BOW PULPIT—see PULPIT.

BOW ROLLER—a sheave, or spool, at the end of a BOWSPRIT over which the anchor chain and RODE are led.

BOWSPRIT—an extension of the bow, generally a spar or beam, used to support rigging, sails, or anchors.

BREAKER or ROLLER—a wave whose top rolls over: normally, a wave passing over SHOAL water.

BREASTHOOK—a horizontal structural member connecting the GUNWALES to the STEM.

BROAD REACH—a course during which the wind approaches over the quarter, or flank, of the vessel.

BULKHEAD—a wall running ATHWART the vessel.

BUOY—an AID TO NAVIGATION: a moored, floating device whose function is to designate safe water or mark an obstruction. They are differentiated either by color, shape, assigned numeral, or by containing a light, bell, whistle, or gong, by emitting a radio signal, or by any combination of the above.

BY THE LEE—sailing before the wind, but allowing the wind to get ahead of the sail, resulting in the possibility of an accidental JIBE.

CABIN—the enclosed portion(s) of a vessel, generally lower than the cockpit in a small vessel and accessed via the COMPANIONWAY. In a small boat, one cabin contains facilities for cooking, eating, sleeping, storage, etc.

CAN—a green (formerly black) cylindrical BUOY having a flat top and an odd number, that marks the left-hand side of a channel when entering.

CAST OFF—to let go a line.

CATBOAT—a boat having a single mast and no jib.

CHAFING GEAR—any piece of soft material utilized to prevent chafing or abrading of a line or sail. Commonly, a sheath surrounding a mooring or anchor line or enclosing the SHROUDS or the ends of SPREADERS.

CHAIN PLATE—a metal strap secured to the hull to which STANDING RIGGING is affixed.

CHANNEL—a narrow, or restricted, navigable passageway whose safe limits are designated by CHANNEL MARKERS: sets or series of BUOYS, BEACONS, DAY MARKERS, etc.

CHAOS—a condition resulting from spending too much time ashore.

CHART—a map of a body of water or a portion thereof, including adjacent land, showing SOUNDINGS, AIDS TO NAVIGATION, CHANNELS, OBSTRUCTIONS, COORDINATES, COMPASS ROSE, etc.

CHOCK—a piece of hardware, normally mounted on a rail, used to guide a line or cable.

CLEAT—*noun*—any of various designs of hardware on a vessel or pier used to secure a line.

CLEAT—*vt*—to secure a line to a CLEAT.

CLEW—the after, lower corner of a sail.

CLOSE-HAULED—sailing toward the wind, at which time the sails are hauled close to the vessel.

CLOSE REACH, BEAM REACH—a course having the wind ABEAM.

COAMING—a wall or solid rail around a vessel's COCKPIT to divert water.

COCKPIT—a semi-enclosed area, generally aft, from which the vessel is steered, and having seats for passengers.

COME ABOUT—to change course so that the bow of the vessel crosses the source of the wind.

COMPANIONWAY—the passageway, generally a doorway, or a doorway and connected hatch, from cockpit to cabin, commonly via a short stairway or ladder. The doorway can be secured with either doors or DROP BOARDS.

COMPASS ROSE—two representations of a compass, true and magnetic, superimposed with a common center and printed on a CHART.

CONSTANT WATERMAN—someone who delights in the greater portion of our Earth. A harmless monomaniac with habitually wet feet.

COORDINATES—position on the globe as determined by a gridwork of LATITUDE and LONGITUDE and expressed in degrees.

COURSE—a planned direction, or series of directions, by which a vessel is steered to a destination, taking into consideration the wind direction, weather, AIDS TO NAVIGATION, traffic, obstructions, currents, shallows, points of interest, and sobriety.

CUTTER—a vessel having one mast, a JIB, and one or more FORESAILS attached to FORESTAYS between the mast and HEADSTAY.

DAY JOB—therapy for people suffering boat deprivation.

DAY MARKER—a small tower or pole supporting a reflector or target, used to mark a CHANNEL or OBSTRUCTION.

DEGREE—one of 360 equal divisions of a circle.

DOCK—*vi, vt*—to bring a vessel alongside a pier.

DOCK—*noun*—the space between or alongside piers used to secure a vessel.

DOCK LINE—a short line for securing a vessel in a dock.

DOWSE—to lower a sail quickly.

DRAFT—*noun*—the depth of a vessel in the water.

DRAW—*vi*—designating the amount of DRAFT.

DRIFT—*noun*—lateral movement of a vessel through the water due to wind.

DRIFT—*vi*—to float either in or out of control.

DROP BOARD(S)—a board, or series of boards, fitted into grooves to secure a COMPANIONWAY.

EBB—outgoing tide.

EYES—the deck of the boat far up in the bow.

FAIRLEAD—a fixed loop for guiding a line or wire rope.

FAIRWAY—the center of a channel; an arbitrary passageway through a mooring field or anchorage.

FALL OFF—to cause a vessel to head away from the wind.

FENDER—a pliable device placed between a vessel and anything liable to cause her damage or be damaged—usually, another vessel or a pier.

FEND OFF—*vi, vt*—to push (the vessel) off anything liable to cause damage or be damaged.

FINGER PIERS—short, parallel piers at right angles to a longer pier.

FIRST MATE—your first spouse: the one who mysteriously disappeared from your vessel on that trip to the islands. See SECOND MATE.

FIX—position, either determined or requested, and expressed as COORDINATES.

FLOOD—incoming tide.

FLUKE—the blade of an anchor; the portion that digs in.

FOREDECK—the front, and exposed, portion of the vessel's deck.

FORESTAY—a strand of RUNNING RIGGING running from the FOREDECK to a point well up the mast. Its purpose is to support a FORESTAYSAIL—similar to a jib.

FORWARD—toward the front of the vessel.

FREEBOARD—height of the TOPSIDES.

FRESHEN—the increasing of wind speed.

FURL—to roll up a sail on a SPAR or STAY.

GALLEY—the kitchen area of a vessel.

GENOA JIB—a jib large enough to overlap the mast.

GPS—global positioning system: an electronic device that uses signals from man-made satellites to PLOT position.

GRAB RAIL—a rail running along the cabin top, inside or out, for holding on to.

GREAT CIRCLE—any circumference of the Earth whose center coincides with the center of the Earth; e.g. the equator and all lines of LONGITUDE.

GUNKHOLE—a small, shallow, insignificant harbor or waterway.

GUNWALE—the joint or structural member where the deck and hull meet. In an open boat, the reinforcing member around the top of the hull.

HALYARD (sometimes HALLIARD)—a line or wire rope used to raise or lower a sail.

HANK—*noun*—a clip for securing the lead edge or LUFF of a jib to the HEADSTAY or FORESTAY.

HANK—*vt*—to secure by HANKS.

HATCH—an opening in a deck or cabin top secured by a HATCH COVER, either hinged or on slides.

HEAD—*noun*—(a) the upper corner of a sail. (b) a toilet.

HEAD—*vi, vt*—to direct the vessel.

HEAD UP—to direct the vessel toward the wind. See POINT and PINCH.

HEAD OFF—to direct the vessel away from the wind. See FALL OFF.

HEADING—*noun*—the direction of the vessel, usually expressed in degrees.

HEAD STAY—a strand of STANDING RIGGING running from the foremost mast to the STEM.

HEAVE TO—to stop the progress of a sailing vessel by steering abruptly dead into the wind.

HEEL—*vi, vt*—the tipping of a vessel due to the pressure of the wind.

HEEL—*noun*—the amount of such tipping, usually expressed in degrees from vertical. See also WETTING THE RAIL, RAIL DOWN.

HELM—the place or means of steering. Also used attributively.

HULL SPEED—the theoretical maximum speed of a sailing vessel relative to the water.

INBOARD—*adj*—toward the centerline (of the vessel).

JIB—a sail rigged all the way forward and attached to the HEADSTAY.

JIBE—*vt, vi*—to change course so that the stern of the vessel crosses the source of the wind.

JIBE—*noun*—such a change in course.

KEDGE—to move a stationary or drifting vessel by setting an anchor at a distance, then hauling the vessel to it.

KETCH—a two-masted vessel having the aftermost, smaller, MIZZENmast normally forward of the HELM.

KNOT—*noun*—(a) one NAUTICAL MILE per hour. (b) an arcane method of fouling a line to prevent its running freely.

LAND BREEZE—a breeze originating over the land and blowing toward the water.

LANDFALL—the first sighting of land from a vessel on the water.

LATITUDE—position on the Earth's surface, measured in degrees, north or south of the equator.

LAUNCH—*vt*—to dispose of troublesome passengers overboard.

LAZY JACKS—pairs of slack lines run on a diagonal between the mast and boom, between which the sail is set. Their function is to contain the sail when it is lowered and prevent its billowing out of control.

LEE or LEEWARD—the downwind side; the sheltered portion.

LEE HELM—the tendency of a vessel to sail away from the wind. Opposed to WEATHER HELM.

LEEWARD—away from the wind; downwind.

LEEWAY—a vessel's lateral movement off course to LEEWARD: combination of SET and DRIFT.

LIFELINE—a taut line or wire rope running about the perimeter of the deck high enough to hold on to or lean against. Generally attached to the PULPIT and TAFFRAIL and supported by STANCHIONS.

LIFT SLIP—a narrow area of accessible water, enclosed on three sides, often straddled by a gantry crane—used for launching or hauling vessels.

LIGHTHOUSE—a large tower or building on a shore or reef displaying a light, often accompanied by a whistle or radio signal.

LOBSTER POT—a boudoir for modest lobsters.

LONGITUDE—position, on the Earth's surface, measured in degrees east or west of Greenwich, England.

LUFF—*noun*—the forward edge of a sail.

LUFF—*vi, vt*—the shaking of the LUFF due to insufficient wind, usually caused by the sail being too close to the wind.

MAIN HATCH—the opening in the cabin top to permit access, usually connected to the COMPANIONWAY and generally secured by a sliding cover.

MAINSAIL—a sail attached to the principal, or main, mast.

MERMAID—a fond recollection of one's beautiful wife at home.

MINUTE—one sixtieth of a degree of circumference.

MIZZEN—a sail attached to the aftermost, or mizzen, mast.

MOORING—a weight or anchor permanently placed on the bottom of a body of water, to which is attached a mooring BUOY, to provide permanent, seasonal, or temporary quarters for a vessel or float.

MOORING FIELD—a designated area of shallow water having such permanent anchors attached to floats. Each float has a mooring PENDANT by which to secure a vessel.

NARROWS—a narrow body of water between two landmasses. The navigable portion is the CHANNEL.

NAUTICAL MILE—one minute of arc (one sixtieth of a degree] on a GREAT CIRCLE or line of longitude; 6076 feet.

NOAA—National Oceanic and Atmospheric Administration.

NUN—an AID TO NAVIGATION. A red, cylindrical BUOY having a conical top and bearing an even numeral, that marks the STARBOARD side of a channel when entering.

OBSTRUCTION—anything localized that might interfere with the passage of a vessel: usually a rock or a wreck.

OFFSHORE—away from shore.

ONSHORE—toward the shore.

OUTBOARD—*adj*—away from the centerline (of the vessel); outside of.

OVERBOARD—off the vessel and into the water. A favored destination of necessary tools.

PENDANT—a short length of line connecting a float to a mooring or anchor. A short length of line or wire rope having a block or eye or hook at one end.

PINCH—to sail so close to the wind as to be inefficient.

PITCH—alternating elevation and depression of a vessel from fore to aft due to wave action.

PLOT—to plot a COURSE is to consider all the determinates and then commit the course to a notebook, CHART, or electronic navigational device. To plot position is to utilize a minimum of two BEARINGS whose intersection determines the position of the vessel.

POINT—to sail close to the wind; to be CLOSE-HAULED.

POINT UP—to sail closer to the wind. See HEAD UP.

PORT—facing forward, the left-hand side of the vessel.

POT BUOY—a small BUOY attached to lobster or crab pot (trap) and assumed by the inexperienced to be an AID TO NAVIGATION or a MOORING.

POUND—action of a vessel slamming its bow against the water as it PITCHES.

PULLING BOAT—a rowboat.

PULPIT—a rail, high enough to hold on to, running around the FORE-DECK. Often called BOW PULPIT.

QUARTER—that portion, or quadrant, of the vessel between ABEAM and ASTERN.

QUARTER BERTH—a bunk or bed in a back corner of the cabin, often confined by the sides or floor of the cockpit or by the central engine compartment.

RAIL—a structural, decorative, or auxiliary length of material. See LIFELINE, STANCHION, PULPIT, TAFFRAIL, TOE RAIL, RUB RAIL, GUN-WALE, GRAB RAIL.

RAIL DOWN—sailing with the vessel tipped over (HEELED) until the lower, or LEE, rail is at, or below, water level.

REACH—*vi, vt*—to sail with the wind ABEAM (BEAM REACH or CLOSE REACH), or on the QUARTER (BROAD REACH) of the vessel.

REACH—*noun*—such a course. More specifically, a beam reach or broad reach.

REEF—*vt, vi*—to fold a portion of a sail against, or roll it up around, a SPAR, and then secure it, in order to reduce its exposed area.

REEF—*noun*—such a tuck or fold in a sail.

REEF—*noun*—a series, or line, or area of barely submerged, or partially submerged, rocks or coral.

RELATIVE BEARING—a horizontal direction, expressed in degrees, relative to the bow of the vessel.

RIG—*vt*—to set up SPARS or RIGGING or sails on a vessel.

RIG—*noun*—any of a variety of ways to rig vessels, considerations being the number and placement of masts, the shape and placement of sails, the amount and placement of STANDING RIGGING. Common rigs are CAT, SLOOP, CUTTER, KETCH, YAWL, and SCHOONER. There are further variations that can only be appreciated by having a friend hold your head underwater for a minimum of half an hour or until your gills work properly.

RIGGING—lines or wire ropes used to support or control SPARS or sails. See RUNNING RIGGING and STANDING RIGGING.

RODE—the line attached to an anchor.

ROLL—alternating swaying of a vessel from side to side due to wave action.

ROLLER or BREAKER—a wave whose top rolls over; a wave passing over SHOAL water.

RUB RAIL—an exterior rail near the top of the hull used to protect the hull from collision or rubbing.

RUN—to sail with the wind behind the vessel.

RUNNING LIGHTS—lights used under way on a vessel designating PORT (a red light), STARBOARD (a green light), plus a minimum of one white light.

RUNNING RIGGING—movable lines, often running through FAIRLEADS or BLOCKS, used to control the lateral position or tension of sails. See SHEET, HALYARD.

SAMSON POST—a stubby, vertical post on the FOREDECK for securing a line.

SCHOONER—a two-masted vessel, the foremast being smaller than the main-mast.

SCOPE—the ratio between the length of a mooring or anchor line being employed and the vertical distance from the bow to the bottom of the water.

SEA BREEZE—a breeze originating over the water and blowing toward the shore.

SEA SERPENT—an inglorious beast of deep waters who feeds primarily on carping spouses.

SEASICK—a malady attributable to spending too long ashore.

SECOND MATE—your second spouse. The one to whom you confide the fate of the FIRST MATE in the hope of future cooperation.

SET—lateral movement of a vessel through the water due to current.

SHACKLE—a piece of hardware used to connect lengths of line, wire rope, or chain to a sail, anchor, other hardware, or one another.

SHEET—*noun*—a line to control the lateral position of a sail.

SHEET—*vt, vi*—to tauten a sail by hauling on a SHEET.

SHOAL—*noun*—an area of water shallow enough to endanger a vessel.

SHOAL, SHOAL OFF—*vi*—to become shallow.

SHROUDS—see STANDING RIGGING.

SLACK—*vt*—to loosen, ease, or let out.

SLACK TIDE—that period between the ebbing and flooding of the tide when there is little or no current.

SLOOP—a boat having a single mast, a MAINSAIL, and a JIB.

SOUND—to measure the depth of water near or beneath the vessel.

SPAR—a pole that supports a sail: a mast, boom, gaff, etc.

SPILL—*vt*—action of the wind escaping the sail without effectively driving the vessel forward. This can be the result of too much HEEL or of the sail being too slack (LUFFING) and can be unintentional or intentional, either to prevent heeling or capsizing, or to slow the vessel's progress.

SPREADERS—struts on the mast usually projecting at right angles to PORT and STARBOARD that serve to distribute the load of the SHROUDS.

SPRING LINE—a DOCK LINE that prevents the vessel from shifting forward or backward.

SQUARE AWAY—put to rights, straighten up, neaten, organize.

STANCHION—a post that supports a LIFELINE or railing.

STANDING RIGGING—lines, rods, or wire ropes supporting the mast, the lower ends of which are secured to CHAIN PLATES attached to the hull. Some designations of standing rigging are:

> HEADSTAY (running forward to the stem)
>
> FORESTAY (running forward)
>
> BACKSTAY (running aft)
>
> SHROUDS (running to either side)

STARBOARD—facing forward, the right hand side of the vessel.

STEER 310, etc.—a compass course, arrived at by rotating clockwise from north the designated degrees and following the projection of that radian.

STEERAGEWAY—sufficient forward progress for effective steering.

STEM—the structural member running up the BOW; the lead edge of the vessel.

STERN—the back of the vessel.

STOWAGE—the placement of things on a vessel. This affects her TRIM—how low and how symmetrically she rides in the water, which greatly affects her performance, and often her stability and safety.

SWELL—a long wave.

TACK—*vi, vt*—to change the course of a sailing vessel so that the wind approaches from the other side of the vessel's centerline.

TACK—*noun*—(a) a specific, or nonspecific, course. (b) the lower, forward corner of a sail.

TAFFRAIL—a rail, high enough to hold on to, running around the STERN of the vessel.

TELLTALE—a wisp of yarn or ribbon attached to a sail or to the STANDING RIGGING to show wind direction.

TENDER—a small boat used to ferry passengers and goods to and from a vessel.

THWART—a seat or cross brace in a small boat. Derivatively: THWARTSHIP, THWARTWAYS, ATHWART: across.

TILLER—a long handle connected to the rudder, used as a lever to steer the boat.

TOE RAIL—a low rail running around the edge of the deck to prevent one's feet from slipping overboard.

TOPSIDES—that portion of the outside of the hull between the deck and the WATERLINE.

TRACK—a rail on a mast or boom to which a sail is attached by means of slides or cars.

TRANSOM—the aftermost, THWARTSHIP, vertical portion of a vessel.

TRAVELER—a TRACK, rail, or bar ATHWART the vessel, having a slide to which a SHEET is secured—used to help TRIM a sail.

TRIM—*noun*—how a vessel sits in the water. See STOWAGE.

TRIM—*vt*—(a) to shift ballast, freight, or crew on a vessel to achieve desired TRIM. (b) to adjust the tension of a sail for efficiency.

UNDER WAY—a progressing of a vessel through the water.

UPWIND—toward the source of the wind.

VARIATION—the amount of difference between true and magnetic north.

VEE BERTH—a V-shaped bunk in the bow of a boat.

VEER—clockwise change in wind direction. Opposite to BACK.

VESSEL—any waterborne craft: a boat, a ship, a wreck, a raft.

VHF—very high frequency. A multi-channel radio for sending and receiving.

WARP—*noun*—(a) a length of line connecting a lobster pot to its POT BUOY. (b) a line used to tow or haul a vessel.

WARP—*vt, vi*—to haul a vessel to another float or vessel.

WATERLINE—a line composed of the points on the hull that contact the water when the vessel is at rest in still water.

WAY—progress of a vessel through the water.

WEATHER, WINDWARD—the side, or direction, from which the wind is blowing.

WEATHER HELM—the tendency of a vessel to sail into the wind. See LEE HELM.

WEIGH ANCHOR—to raise the anchor clear of the bottom.

WETTING THE RAIL—in this case, the rail referred to is a structural member running the length of the boat at the point where the deck and hull join, or the TOE RAIL. This rail doesn't usually get wet (submerged) until the sea and wind are severe enough to HEEL (tip) the vessel significantly.

WINCH—a mechanical contrivance having, normally, a ratcheted drum, or spool, used to tension or wind up a line, wire rope, cable, or chain.

WINCH HANDLE—a lever fit to a WINCH to impart mechanical advantage.

WINDWARD or WEATHER—the side, or direction, from which the wind is blowing.

WING-AND-WING also WUNG OUT—sailing directly before the wind (RUNNING) with sails spread to either side of the vessel.

WORKING JIB—a jib small enough not to overlap the mast.

YAW—*vi*—the slewing of a vessel due to inappropriate steering or the overwhelming of her steering due to wind or seas.

YAWL—a two-masted vessel having the aftermost, smaller, MIZZENmast, aft of the HELM.